A World Apart
My Life Among the Eskimos of Alaska

by
Wilford Corbin

Publication of Wizard Works

ISBN: 1-890692-03-4

Wizard Works, P.O. Box 1125, Homer, AK 99603

Acknowledgements

For their patience and encouragement, I thank the members of the creative writing group in Sylva, N.C. I need to say thank you, too, to Nina Anderson. Every suggestion she made was right on. To Cathy and my son, Tommy, who re-typed the entire manuscript from a rough draft after I lost everything on my computer, I acknowledge more than debt and gratitude. You saved me in more ways than you know. I also need to thank my brother Tom, and my son-in-law, Robbie, first-class computer teachers. To my wife, Virginia, who always stopped whatever she was doing to listen to me read stories, then offered suggestions, I thank you for every one of our forty-seven years together. A special thanks to Mamie Moses, 93, my first -grade teacher. She's the one who started this whole thing. Many thanks to former student and fellow Alaskan, Dr. Betty Wallace, for pointing the way. Thanks also to Jan O'Meara, who helped turn my manuscript into a book. Her expertise and the suggestions she made were invaluable. She made the process easy for me.

Contents

Dedicated
To Toby and Lars
Eskimo mentors, engineers, sociologists, teacher-aides
and my best friends in the world of ice, snow and cold winds

Alaska

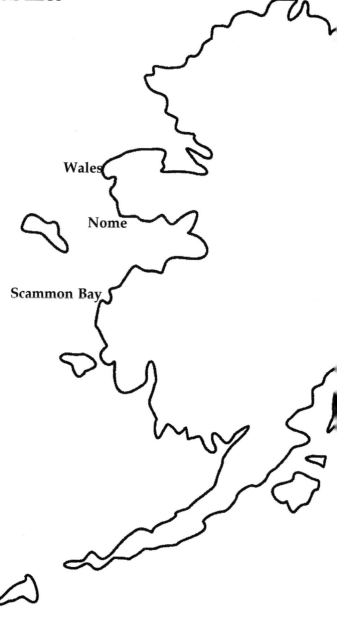

Wales

Nome

Scammon Bay

rbanks

Juneau

Winds in Eskimoland

The plane landed near the base of towering snow-capped mountains, then taxied alongside a grove of tall Sitka spruce to the tiny terminal. "So this is Juneau, the capital of Alaska!" I mused in August of 1955.

After the plane came to a stop and the props stopped spinning, the pilot walked into the passenger section and asked, "Where are you folks going?"

"First I'm going through orientation for a few days here in Juneau. Then I'm going out to teach at Wales. It's a little Eskimo village on the Bering Strait," I replied.

"Several new teachers have been coming up here lately to teach in the Indian Service schools," he said, "But some don't stay long. Just last week I brought a teacher up here that was going out to some little village in the Aleutians. He had on a suit and fancy shoes. He stepped off the plane and walked around, took one look at the mountains, then got right back on. He sat down and asked, 'Where's this plane going?' I told him, 'It's going straight back to Seattle as soon as it gets refueled.' And he said, 'That's where I want to go.' He went into the terminal, got his ticket and went back to the Lower Forty-eight."

"Is teaching up here really that bad?"

"I'm not trying to discourage you," he said, "but we had one couple come up here a few years back. They were from some big city. They went out to teach on an isolated island where there's no landing strip and where the supply ship only comes once a year. They didn't get their coal up off the beach soon enough. So winter set in. And snow covered it over. And they didn't hire anyone to go get it. They pitched a tent in their living room and lived in it all winter. They didn't hold a day of school. They left the village on the first boat in the spring." The pilot chuckled.

I began to wonder whether I might be putting myself—and my family—at risk, but if we turned back now, there would be no job waiting for me at home. And what would our friends there think? Also, how could I pay for the return trip and reimburse the government for the trip this far? And why was the pilot telling me this stuff? Was he trying to drum up more business for his airline?

As I walked toward the terminal, I saw four or five small planes parked nearby. I gazed upward and was awed by the height of the mountains. They rose from sea level to some eight thousand feet—all were capped by ice and snow. Never before had I seen such an impressive sight! The mountains in my hometown, which I enjoyed climbing, rose to only around three thousand feet above the valley floors. I wondered what it would be like to climb one of these. During our three days in Juneau, I looked up at the mountains repeatedly, saw the steepness and the rocks, and wondered if rocks ever loosened and tumbled into town. An old-timer later told me that sometimes rocks actually did roll down and damage the back of some buildings.

The job offer was exciting. The Bureau of Indian Affairs, usually called the BIA, had hired me to provide health services and education at Wales, Alaska. a tiny Eskimo village just fifty miles across the Bering Strait from Russia. In July of 1955, Russia and the United States were racing to see who could make the most atomic bombs. Evacuation drills were routine in schools throughout America. Distant Early Warning radar sites, known as the DEW line, were being built, including one on top of Cape Prince of Wales Mountain. A forty-man US Army detachment was living in Quonset huts on the beach one mile north of the village, and ten Eskimo National Guardsmen were recruited, trained and equipped with M-1 rifles. But Wales would be a sitting duck if Russia decided to attack. Folks at home in North Carolina had advised against going. They said, "It's too close to Russia." The head of the department of education at Western Carolina Teacher's College put it bluntly. He said, "Don't go!"

My wife, Virginia, and I decided after our first child was born that we would not hire baby-sitters. We preferred that she stay home with our children and that I be the breadwinner. But my monthly salary as a beginning school teacher in the 1950s was not enough to pay house rent, put food on the table and make payments on a car that would be worn out on the curvy, dirt mountain roads before I could clear the title. Dining out, going to the movies or vacation trips in summer were never options.

Virginia's older sister, Hazel, and her husband, Dennis Stamey, were teaching in the Territory of Alaska at Aniak on the Kuskokwim River. Dennis said teaching salaries were much higher in Alaska. He told me, "BIA salaries are higher than those of the Territory. They have a high turnover rate and are always in need of teachers in the remote areas. But they prefer husband-and-wife teams in the isolated villages, even in one-teacher schools, and since Virginia doesn't teach, you are fully qualified for a one-teacher school. If you apply, you should do so by telegram, because school administrators in the BIA office in Juneau hardly look at letter mail. Most communication in Alaska is by radio and telegram."

Without discussing it with Virginia, I wired my resume to the BIA in Juneau. The cost was sixteen dollars, which I feared Virginia would consider a waste! The next day I received an answer by telegram offering the one-teacher school at Wales, at the western tip of the Seward Peninsula. Several days later an airmail "special delivery" letter arrived with details.

"The village is located in a tundra climate. It has an average daily wind of twenty-one miles an hour. The population consists of 128 full-blooded Eskimos. They speak their native tongue, although some speak English. Travel is paid by the BIA. If you stay two years, the BIA will pay round-trip airfare to your hometown for summer vacations. If you only stay one year, you pay for travel home. If you stay less than one year, you reimburse the government for the trip up. You should take only your clothing and what few personal items you need. Living quarters and household items, such as bedding and kitchen utensils, are furnished. You are required to purchase a year's supply of groceries, which will be delivered to the village in September by the BIA ship, *North Star*. The cost is deducted from your bi-weekly checks. If you accept the position, tickets for your travel will follow."

We agonized about the offer. We liked the salary. We saw the location on a map. It was pretty far north, but we reasoned that "people live there and we are *people*," so we should be able to live there as well. I signed the contract. We were heading into the farthest west point of the North American continent!

Preparing to go was not difficult, since we had few possessions to leave behind and even fewer to take with us. I would have no use for our car, cow, or refrigerator. I needed only cash, so I sold the car and refrigerator cheap. I sold my half interest in a Jersey milk cow to Virginia's brother, Harry, for fifteen dollars. We then had sufficient money for the trip and enough to get us settled in our new location. I stored all our papers and books in our neighbor's hayloft.

When our tickets arrived, we traveled across the Great Smoky Mountains to Knoxville by car, across the country to Seattle by train, then flew to Juneau.

In Juneau we checked into the Baranof Hotel, one of the two hotels in town and the one recommended by our taxi driver. The facilities at the Baranof were primitive at best. The iron bedsteads were probably brought there during the Gold Rush days, before the turn of the century. The floors creaked. The washroom and toilet were down the hall and had antique fixtures. The "hot" water was cold. Someone said, "you rough it at the Baranof." Our experience there was no exception.

Main Street in Juneau, 1955. The Baranof Hotel is beyond the Gastineau

Virginia, pregnant when we arrived, miscarried at 2:00 a.m. Fortunately, we were able to get a doctor to come to our room to help her. She lay in bed the next day, while, in a daze from lack of sleep, I went alone to the BIA office for orientation. The first person I met at the office was the head of education for the Indian

Service Schools in Alaska, Eunice Logan. Because Virginia made me promise not to mention she had miscarried, I told Eunice that Virginia wasn't feeling well, that she must have caught a virus but would try to come for orientation the next day.

Eunice said, "I understand the stress of travel. I'm also from North Carolina." She told me where in North Carolina she was from, but I had never heard of the place, so it really didn't have any meaning to me at the time. Forty-one years later I saw her obituary in *The Asheville Citizen-Times*, my hometown paper. Only then did I learn she grew up nearby. I wondered then whether this fact had any bearing on her choosing me for the teaching position at Wales.

Eunice poured some coffee. We discussed aspects of education as it pertained to Alaska Natives in general and Eskimos specifically.

My previous teaching experience had been in a self-contained classroom with only one class of sixth graders. Here, Eunice told me, I was to teach grades one through eight, all in one room, a situation I never remembered hearing discussed in education classes at the teacher's college. When teaching one grade in one room, I prepared five or six lessons each day. Now, I realized I would be required to teach forty or fifty different lessons a day. How was that possible? How could I do that? I felt the onset of panic. Eunice showed me some familiar textbooks I would be using. I had taught from some of those and I relaxed a bit.

The following morning, the BIA sent a baby-sitter to stay with Tommy, as Virginia was feeling better. She walked with me to the BIA office. We met with the director of health and safety for the BIA schools. He poured coffee for us, then sat down to tell us about living conditions in the Arctic. He said, "The building was built in 1903, and the teacher's quarters are in one end."

"You mean we will be living in the school?" I asked.

"Yes," he replied, grinning. "Your quarters are in the school building. That means you won't have far to walk, and you won't have to walk in the cold."

"Not bad."

"I agree. Cape Prince of Wales is always windy. Chill factors often approach minus 100 in winter. You should get the same type of clothing worn by the Eskimos. You should have a seamstress outfit you and your family with fur from head to toe."

"Why?" I asked.

"Because what's best for the animals to wear is also best for people." I later heard the same statement from the Eskimos.

Next we met with the director of village sanitation. After an offer of more coffee and a few introductory exchanges, he picked up a folder from his desk and said, "I have some information here about Wales." He paused as he looked at the folder then turned pages and began reading or paraphrasing, "Your new home and homes of the Eskimos in the village are without septic systems because the ground in the Bering Strait area is frozen to great depths. The school has outdoor toilets for both boys and girls. You will not have flush toilets and you'll have to learn to use honey buckets instead."

"What's honey buckets?" I asked.

He smiled. "A honey bucket is usually a five-gallon bucket with a little water and some pine oil in the bottom. It is placed in all toilets, underneath a commode seat, such as anyone can buy at a hardware store. Emptying the honey buckets at the school and your quarters is the janitor's job. You won't have to do that. I'm just telling you so you will know."

He continued, "During the summer, the contents of the honey buckets throughout the village are poured into the surf and will drift out to sea. In winter the honey buckets in the outside toilets at the school will freeze, so the janitor will probably want to bring the buckets inside the building and put them next to a stove to thaw. You'll have to put up with that. When the buckets are thawed, he'll simply empty the contents on the shore ice at the village dump. Each village along the coast usually designates a spot on the shore ice each winter to be the village dump. Then when the spring thaw arrives, the shore ice will drift out to sea and carry the village dump with it." He laughed. "I suppose that's good riddance."

He also read to us the different ways we'd have to get water. "In the summer, rainwater may be collected off the roof in a barrel or water may be carried in buckets from a stream that flows off the mountain, about a hundred yards south of the school. In winter, ice is chopped from a lake out back or blocks of snow are cut from wind-packed drifts near the building. Whether frozen or liquid, the water is carried upstairs to a 200-gallon tank, where gravity feeds it through pipes downstairs to the kitchen sink and to a shower stall in a corner of the pantry." He then looked up. "I advise you folks to boil all your drinking water because sled dogs and other animals contaminate most available sources of water near all the outlying villages. But you won't have to carry water in for the school and your quarters. That's a part of the janitor's job description."

Just as I was beginning to think the janitor had all the tough chores, the health department folks told me the teacher also served as village health official, helping in first aid chores and dispensing medicines. I would be able to consult with the Indian Service doctor in Kotzebue by short-wave radio concerning any health problem that might arise with my family as well as people in the village, however. The doctor would have a regular radio schedule each morning and each night to answer questions and give advice to people in native villages in and around the Seward Peninsula. I would have a first-aid room in the school with a medicine cabinet, stocked with medical supplies, and equipment available for use under the doctor's advice in any health situation or emergency.

Another of the teacher's duties was to hold a regular radio schedule with the BIA area field representative in Nome concerning matters relating to school operations, as well as all village relationships with the Territory of Alaska and the Alaska Native Service. I would be required to receive and send messages for the village by telegram through the Alaska Communications System (ACS). I would copy the messages with pencil and paper as they were read by an ACS radioman in Nome. To send a message to ACS would be as simple as reading phonetically; that is, spelling each word after pronouncing it. I would also be required to inform pilots and sea-going vessels about weather conditions in the strait.

Next, I learned how to complete each form in the myriad of reports required by Nome, Juneau and Washington. After three days of orientation, I was beginning to think the teacher who got back on the plane to Seattle might have known something I didn't. What was my life going to be like for the next two years? I took comfort in the fact that I wasn't in charge of the school lunch program or girls' sewing classes—those jobs were Virginia's.

Our stay in Juneau wasn't all business. Before returning to the hotel, and while the baby-sitter kept Tommy, we took time to tour a bit. A taxi drove us out to Mendenhall Glacier. As we rode up the valley toward the glacier, I noticed the spruce trees grew smaller and smaller the closer we got to the glacier, until, finally, we saw only rocks, sand and water next to the glacier. The driver said the glacier was receding.

Back in town, we strolled down Main Street to the famous Red Dog Saloon with its sawdust floor. A piano in the corner of the stage made me think what the saloon was like during the Gold Rush days at the turn of the century.

To Anchorage

After Juneau, we were sent to Anchorage where I was to learn short-wave radio communication. We checked into the Mt. McKinley Hotel, aptly named because it was ten floors tall, the tallest building in Alaska. Anchorage, with a population of 25,000, was larger than Juneau. It had two main streets, Fourth and Fifth Avenues, that were paved for about a mile each.

My appointment with the BIA radioman was at 2:00 P.M, so I had time to walk down the streets of Anchorage. Fourth Avenue had several craft stores, but what was most impressive to me was the sight of one bar and liquor store after another, each one already doing a brisk business in the middle of the day.

I walked into a craft store and saw six or eight showcases with bracelets, watch bands, gold nuggets, ivory and baleen trinkets. I had no intention to buy anything--couldn't afford it. I just wanted to talk to someone and learn more about the town. A clean-cut, middle-aged man met me near the front of the store. He asked, "May I help you?"

"I'm just looking around the town," I said. "This is my first trip here. I noticed there sure are a lot of bars in town."

"Yes, there are 105, but only three grocery stores." He laughed.

"The bars are really busy for this time of day."

"Yes, most of the men on the street and in the bars are job seekers. They come up here in droves each summer. They're looking to make a fast buck. But most of them end up losing, or drink up, what little money they brought with them. They wind up destitute or worse. Nearly every day someone gets shot. The police can't keep up with solving shootings. They list most of them as suicide. No gun, no wallet, no suicide note--nothing--but nevertheless 'suicide'."

That afternoon I met with the radioman in charge of BIA short-wave radio transmitters and receivers in the outlying villages. The building where we met was originally a two-bedroom house. Inside was a mixture of wires, glass tubes and radio equipment on tables, shelves and workbenches. I wondered, "What am I doing here?" But the radioman was most patient and understanding. He gave me a two-hour crash course on the basic techniques of sending and receiving messages. He demonstrated how to operate the type of receivers and transmitters in the school at Wales. He said that the radio equipment at Wales was old and undependable, but he would fly out to Wales soon to set up a new antenna and a new fifty-watt Northern combination transmitter and receiver. My call sign would be "KWP Two-Four Wales."

The following morning, we boarded a small two-engine, ten-passenger plane for our flight to Nome, where we were to receive our final instructions before going on out to the village.

To Nome

We flew over the Alaska Range, Kuskokwim and Yukon rivers and, finally, Norton Sound, before landing at the tiny airport on the treeless tundra at Nome. I felt a chilly breeze as I walked off the plane. John Jenkins, the area field representative for the Alaska Native Service, met us. He was a pleasant, heavy-set man, about five-ten, in his late thirties. John drove us in a government station wagon to the Polaris Hotel. He enjoyed talking and seemed eager to tell us about Nome, Wales and the Eskimos. He invited us to come to his house for dinner and more conversation that night.

After settling into a cozy room with two small beds over-spread with thick layers of blankets, I donned a light jacket and told Virginia, "I'm going for a walk down the street." The side-walks of Front Street were made of boards and the streets were unpaved and dusty. I walked east on the seaward side to the end of town, about a quarter of a mile. I passed a liquor store, a couple of bars and a combination grocery and hardware store, then crossed the street and walked back up the other side. I stepped inside a craft and fur clothing store. It smelled like a fur tannery, with its racks of hand-made fur parkas of varying colors. Gold and ivory craft items crowded the display cases. I saw no other customers inside. A small, sharp-featured, white haired gentle-man, who looked to be in his late seventies, greeted me. "Hi! I'm Tony Polet, the owner. Can I help you?"

"Hi! I'm just looking around town. I'm from North Carolina and going to teach at the Eskimo village of Wales."

"I know about Wales. Some of my seamstresses are from Wales."

"Do many Eskimos live here in Nome?"

"Half the population of Nome are Eskimos, about 1,000," he

said. "They come from villages all around. Some have moved here from Wales. But Nome has never been an Eskimo village per se. There was nothing here until the gold rush of 1898, when gold was discovered on the beach. Then people came here by the thousands. At one time the population of Nome was 20,000. I came here in 1900--been here ever since."

"Did you pan for gold?" I asked.

"Yes, nearly everybody panned for gold back then. That's why they came to Nome in the first place. It was for the gold. The beach was crowded every day in summer with people panning. Ships came here loaded with supplies--and people. Some men sold everything they owned for passage to come here. I will never forget one person who walked off a ship. He wore a wide-brimmed hat, fancy shoes and clothes. He had a new shovel and pan. He came down on the beach and asked someone how to pan for gold and was told to 'just shovel some sand into the pan and swish it around till everything is sloshed out of the pan, except the gold'. I watched as he put one shovelful of sand in his pan and swished it around several times with water until the sand was sloshed out. He looked in his pan. Didn't see anything. He took out a gun from his hip pocket and shot himself. Committed suicide right there!" .

Mr. Polet followed as I walked down an aisle of his large shop, where I passed rows of racks with different types of hand-sewn fur clothing. He said, "You'll want to wear this type of clothing in Wales, where it gets real windy." I looked at some price tags. They were sky high. I wouldn't be making a purchase here today. In another aisle were a half dozen showcases of hand-carved ivory. As I bent to look in one of the showcases, he stepped beside me and said, "Some of this ivory was carved by Wales people."

That evening,. we walked to Mr. Jenkins' house, where we were served drinks and a delicious meal of fresh salmon. Mr. Jenkins gave us a thorough overview of life on the Seward Penin-sula. I learned he was in charge of all Indian Service activities within 300 miles of Nome. That included about twenty schools in small Eskimo villages. He had oversight of federal loans to native stores and loans to individual Eskimos to start herds of reindeer. He said, "Tomorrow morning, I need to check on a herd about forty miles up the coast. The government loaned this Eskimo money to start a herd, and I need to check how he is doing. A bush pilot told me he saw the herd down on the beach this morning. You could go with me if you like."

I quickly said yes.

"OK, meet me at the office at 9:30. I've chartered an Eskimo to take me in his wooden boat. We'll go north along the beach and be gone for several hours. It'll get pretty chilly out there over the water, where you're just sitting in the boat and can't get up and run around to get warm. So I suggest you wear something warm on your head, hands and feet. Wear loose clothing on your body. Perhaps two or three layers will do."

We talked late into the night. He told about the problems people had trying to operate cars in Nome. He said, "I keep my car idling all winter, even in the garage. I only shut it off to change oil."

While I was talking with Mr. Jenkins, Virginia had been talking with Mrs. Jenkins. Then Virginia turned to me and said, "We had better go back to the hotel." I looked outside; it was still broad daylight but the sun had stopped shining. Then I glanced at my watch. The time was a quarter past one in the morning!

As we walked back to the hotel, a nippy breeze from the north fanned the grass between the small houses and along the edge of the street. When we arrived at our room, I noticed the sun had peeked over the horizon in the northeast and was shining in our window. Virginia pulled the curtains together. That shut out some of the light. She then draped a blanket over the curtain rods. She said, "This should help keep out more of the light so we can get some sleep."

The next morning at ten, I was with Mr. Jenkins and the Eskimo in his boat. They were wearing heavy pants, summer parkas and baseball caps. I wore two pairs of jeans and a light jacket, but no hat. I turned up the collar of my jacket to protect my neck from the cold wind. The water was choppy as we motored northwest about 100 yards from shore. Mr. Jenkins pointed and said, "You see that golden-colored streak along the beach? It extends for miles along the beach at Nome. That's gold. Gold is everywhere here. It's on the land. It's under the water. But it's more concentrated in that streak. That's what attracted people to Nome--that streak."

After traveling about ten miles north along the beach, I saw piles of driftwood logs in random fashion above the high-water mark that were obviously deposited by intense ocean action. I was reminded of logging operations back home in North Carolina. "Someone could start a sawmill here," I commented.

"Yes," Mr. Jenkins said. "Those logs extend for miles along

the beach. They were carried here by the ocean current and washed up on the beach in summer storms. They came from rivers south of here in Alaska and Siberia. The reason you don't see logs on the beach near Nome is because they've all been used up for fuel or sawed into lumber for building purposes."

After another mile we found the reindeer herd, of perhaps a hundred, congregated on the beach. Some looked at us, but most seemed to pay us no attention. Some swished their tails, perhaps from habit, as I noticed no insects. A few were standing in the surf. Mr. Jenkins said, "They come to the beach sometimes to cool off and get away from mosquitoes. Inland the mosquitoes are thick. Out to Wales, where you are going, you'll never see mosquitoes. The average wind out there on the cape is twice as strong as it is here. Out there it blows all the time. It's either blowing from the north or from the south, and if mosquitoes get airborne they get blown away. That's good. But if you go out in the interior where it's not windy, the mosquitoes will eat you up."

The author, with reindeer on the beach near Nome.

I was glad I wasn't going to the interior. I was also glad that the boat stopped so I could walk around on the shore to get my blood circulating. Mr. Jenkins took pictures of the herd while I walked along the dunes observing haphazard piles of battered and broken trunks and limbs of spruce and fir.

The following morning was crisp and clear as we loaded our baggage into Mr. Jenkins' van. On our way to the airport he said, "This is a good day to fly out to Wales but you'll notice the wind at Wales when you step off the plane there." Again he mentioned the wind, but the wind sock on top of the hangar here was limp.

Mr. Jenkins introduced us to the Alaska Airlines bush pilot, Bob Jacobs, who was concentrating on loading a few bags of mail and boxes of freight into an older, single-engine, gull-winged Stinson plane. He was soft-spoken, fair-skinned, slightly balding, about thirty years old, of medium build and height, and he wore dark sunglasses. He said, "You folks can get in."

I noticed the inside of the plane was well battered, probably the result of years of hauling freight, such as mining equipment and drums of gas and oil. The latch was gone off the door. Bob tied it shut with a rope, then stepped toward the cockpit. He stopped and turned to Virginia. "Would you like to sit in the seat up front beside me?"

"No, thank you," she said. "I would rather sit on the bench here in the back."

Bob then helped her fasten her seat belt. "How about the boy? Should we fasten him in?"

"No, I can hold Tommy."

I took the seat beside Bob. The plane vibrated and the door rattled as we took off, heading northwest. We lifted over the beach and soon flew smoothly over the thousands of logs I had seen the day before. Bob said, "So you are going to be the new teachers at Wales?"

"Yes."

"The teachers there now are leaving today. They're going back with me. They only stayed one year."

"We signed a two-year contract. I wonder why *they* are leaving?"

"I think they had some kind of trouble with some of the people." That was news I wished I hadn't heard.

We stopped briefly at the small village of Teller. Bob handed the postmaster a bag of mail and a couple boxes of freight. They exchanged pleasantries, including something about reindeer. After we were airborne again Bob said, "The postmaster said Johnny Kakayruk is going to start butchering some of his herd. You'll want to buy some reindeer meat because it's the best meat in the world. You can buy it by the carcass or half-carcass. Anytime you want reindeer meat just tell the teacher here at Teller by radio. He'll give the order to Johnny and I'll pick it up on my way up to Wales with the mail. Also, anytime you want fresh groceries, such as lettuce or tomatoes, just let me know on mail days when you give me the Wales weather and I'll pick it up at Northern Commercial Company in Nome."

"How will I pay for it?" I asked.

"Northern Commercial will just charge it to your account. They give credit to all the teachers up here. There's no charge for the freight. We like to be as helpful as we can to all the BIA teachers in the area."

We proceeded up the coast of the Seward Peninsula, named for William H. Seward, secretary of state under Abraham Lincoln. He was primarily responsible for the purchase of Alaska in 1867, when the United States bought it from the Soviet Union for 7.2 million dollars--considered extravagant by many at the time. The purchase was nicknamed "Seward's Folly."

We flew at some 500 feet altitude as we came alongside higher mountains with steep sides and patches of snow. The rocky and rugged coastline rose sharply above whitecaps along the shore. When we were about forty miles from the cape, we were buffeted by strong head winds. I tightened my seat belt. I looked at Virginia. Her arms were firmly around Tommy. Bob said, "I think I'll go up Lost Canyon and approach the cape from the north. It's too windy here on the lee side of these mountains." He gained altitude, then banked the plane and headed into Lost Canyon, a gap in the mountains. Encountering fierce turbulence in a headwind, the plane bobbed up and down and the wings dipped right and left.

Although my seat belt was fastened, I gripped my seat with both hands. I looked outside the plane. The right wing tip appeared too close to the rocks. It wasn't much different to our left. I turned and looked back at Virginia. She was clutching Tommy tightly. She faced down. Her eyes were closed. I saw the rope on the door had loosened and the door was banging. I looked at Bob. He smiled and said, "It'll be calmer on the other side of these mountains."

We flew through the pass and, sure enough, the plane again flew smoothly. I began to enjoy the scenery once more. We flew low over a winding river and some hills with snowdrifts from the previous winter. Bob turned the plane southwest along the edge of the Chukchi Sea. He looked to his right and pointed in that direction," You can see way out there. That's ice. It's probably part of the Arctic ice pack."

The water along the beach had large swells and three lines of breakers. We flew out over the sandy beach, then turned south over the water of the Bering Strait, named for Vitus Bering, who was first here in 1728. In the middle of the strait, the Diomede Islands came into view. Farther still, I could make out the mountains of East Cape in Siberia. Then we turned east.

"There's the village," Bob announced, pointing straight ahead. I looked in the direction he pointed and saw a line of small unpainted structures stretching three quarters of a mile along the beach. It was the most frontier-like sight I could imagine. One large, white-painted structure was near the middle. That, I assumed, was the school. I had no idea what adventures we were about to experience. But now there was no turning back!

We landed a couple of miles farther to the north and a half mile inland, on a strip of iron matting beside a small lake. A stiff wind fanned the tundra grass and made ripples on the lake. Bob said, "There's a small army detachment here that operates a camouflaged radar site up there in the rocks." He pointed toward the side of the mountain. "They have a couple of 'weasels' that run on metal tracks like bulldozers. They are very efficient on ice, mud or snow. They use these for transportation and help carry mail and freight to the village. One will be here shortly to take you to the village."

Cape Prince of Wales. The village is at the center of the photograph.

Arrival at the Village

I stepped off the plane and shivered as a cold wind cut right through me. I climbed back into the plane wishing I had dressed more warmly. Ten minutes later, the Army weasel and driver arrived. Bob and the driver helped transfer our baggage and some sacks of mail to a rack on the top of the weasel. I climbed into the seat beside the driver, and Virginia and Tommy rode in the back.

We approached the village along the sandy beach and passed small, rustic buildings with sod grass piled to the windows— in a few cases, to the roofline. Some of the houses were made of driftwood logs, some plywood. None were painted. Fifteen or twenty men and women stood outside their homes watching us pass. Wide ruffs framed their faces and fanned in the wind. The parkas of the men extended below the waist and were covered with plain white cloth while those of the women were of colored print with decorative hems below the knees. They were bulky parkas, which I assumed had the fur turned inward. Some children, wearing Sears Roebuck look-alike parkas with the hoods pulled over their heads, ran alongside the weasel. I felt like I was in a parade and we were the main attraction.

We came to a stop a few yards from the school at a side entrance facing the beach. After thanking the driver and offering pay, which he refused, I opened the door, but my attention was quickly diverted to the plopping sound of low breakers on the beach just thirty yards away. A man about five-ten, in his late twenties, dark-haired, broad-shouldered, and standing erect with head held high, approached the weasel. He was wearing a baseball cap. His ruff of wolf fur was lowered around his neck. He smiled as he held out his hand and said, "Hi! I am Toby Anungazuk. I am school janitor." He then pointed to a shorter, sharp-featured man, also smiling, about the same age, standing beside him, and said, "This is Roland Angnaboogok. He is chief of Wales Village Council. We will carry your bags." I suspected he knew I was the new teacher.

"Thank you. I'm Wilford Corbin," I said. "This is my wife, Virginia, and son, Tommy."

"We will take your bags all the way inside teacher quarters." Toby spoke with a slight guttural accent, distinct from any I had heard in Nome or anywhere else. I imagined his speech was probably like that of natives fifty miles across the strait on the Siberian side. But the last names he pronounced disturbed me the most. I knew immediately, that if other last names were similar to these two, I was going to have difficulty learning and pronouncing them.

We entered the building, walked through a ten-foot narrow passageway and stepped into a ten-by-twelve-foot room with cabinets to the ceiling on the left and radio equipment on the right. Here, the men set our baggage on the floor. Toby grinned as he looked at me and said, "The other teachers are getting ready to leave. Their baggage is in the schoolroom. I go help carry. You go in the quarters now."

Virginia and I stepped inside the living room of the teacher's quarters and met the former teacher and his wife, who were making last-minute preparations to leave. They both seemed excited. The teacher said, "Toby will show you around. We have to go now. We only stayed here one year and our stay wasn't all that pleasant. Charlie K... threatened to kill me several times." He pulled back his jacket, displaying a gun in a shoulder holster. "You'll have trouble with Charlie!"

More discouraging thoughts!

I envied their leaving, but knew that we had no choice but to stick it out at least one year, so we could save enough money to pay for our way back home. Soon the former teachers were gone, and we busied ourselves the rest of the day getting acquainted with the facilities and some more of the people. We gave no further thought to our predicament till later that night when we lay down to sleep. Virginia cried, and I felt like doing the same.

As soon as the former teachers were gone, Toby began giving me a tour of the facilities. "This is old building. It was built in 1903," he said. "The walls are insulated with tundra grass six inches thick. Sod grass is packed to the windows along the out-side for insulation."

The building consisted of the teacher's quarters, two schoolrooms, a post office, school kitchen, storage rooms, shop and office. The office contained the medicine cabinet and radio communication equipment. There were three sets of sashes and panes in each window and at least two doors to go through at each entrance. There were three entrances, one by the post office, one through the office and another through the shop. Access to the schoolrooms from the teacher's quarters was either through the office or through the kitchen. A doorway connected the schoolrooms.

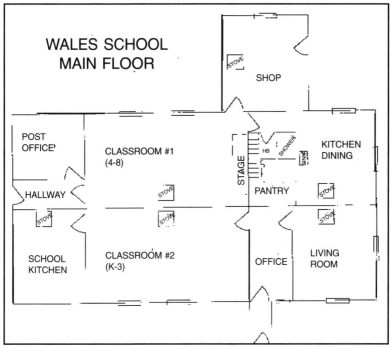

The teacher's quarters consisted of a living room and a kitchen with a very large pantry. A shower stall was in one corner of the pantry. The toilet with the honey bucket was in a nook at the base of the stairs. There were two bedrooms upstairs. In the east bedroom was a 200-gallon wooden water tank, directly over the kitchen stove. Copper tubing curled through the firebox in the stove and upward through the water tank, then back down again through the stove. The purpose was to circulate heated water to melt ice or snow in the tank. A supply line came from the tank to the kitchen sink. Another line went to the shower stall in the pantry. We could take a shower when the ice or snow in the tank was melted. I soon learned to conserve water because every chunk of ice, snow or bucket of water had to be carried upstairs and dumped into the tank. The wastewater from the shower and kitchen sink poured underneath the building. Toby said, "Under the building is like a lake."

"Doesn't that ever cause some kind of trouble or smell?"

"No. It stays that way all the time; hardly ever freezes."

The building was heated with six H.C. Little oil-burning stoves, a stove in each of the main spaces downstairs. The oil was fed through copper tubing from six fifty-five gallon oil drums, connected in tandem in a small, one-room building, fifty feet from the south end of the school, the end next to the teacher's quarters. Toby said, "The oil supply building is old school building. It was built in 1890. It was where the first Wales teacher taught. He was white man missionary-teacher, name of Harrison Thornton. I think he came here from Massachusetts."

Beside the old school was a smaller building with a gasoline operated, four-cylinder, 1.5kW Kohler electric generator. It furnished enough power for one light bulb in each room and to operate the short-wave radio transmitter and receiver. Back-up kerosene lamps were placed in each room in case of light-plant failure.

Toby took me to the attic above the post office, schoolrooms and school kitchen. There was barely enough room to step inside, as the attic was piled high with everything imaginable: old books, beds, rugs, stoves, tables, school desks, living room suites, sewing machines, kegs of butter in brine, cases of dried milk and soups.

All foods were labeled USDA NOT FOR SALE. He said, "We have no room for anything."

"I agree," I responded. "Something needs to be done about this."

Behind the school was a mountain of oil drums — hundreds, perhaps thousands, of them — piled ten feet high. Toby said, "All the drums are empty except maybe a half gallon in each barrel."

"Why doesn't the government take back the empties when they bring in the new supply?" I asked.

"Every year when ship arrives, it is sometimes stormy and they don't wait around to load empties. They go on to other villages and the empties just keep piling up here in village. Some starts leaking on the tundra grass. This is what happens every year."

Toby spoke good enough English, however broken, and seemed most helpful and considerate. I sensed that he was concerned that I get off to a good start, that we not get homesick and leave. He said, "The man teacher didn't get along very well. He had some trouble with Charlie K..., but I don't think Charlie, he would bother him. Charlie is really a good person."

Toby told me about his trip to the "Outside." Outside is a word used by most Alaskans to refer to the Lower Forty-Eight. "I came back to Wales last year from a trip Outside," he said. "I was in Eskimo show for big Eskimo show company. We gave shows in the big cities. I had to do the kayak flip in a tank twice a day. Angnaboogok was in the show and some others. They did the Eskimo dance and the blanket toss. It was good money. But all the Eskimos didn't like the food. There was not much meat. In Philadelphia, where our mobile homes were near a park, some of the boys shot this deer, but they just got in trouble. Somebody, I think, heard the shot. They came and got the meat. We had put it in garbage can where maybe they wouldn't find it, but the policemen found it and took it away."

"Did they charge them with anything?" I asked.

"I think the show owner talked to some authorities about it. Maybe the show owner paid a fine. We never found out. We just told the authorities we can't live without good meat."

We walked into the office, where Toby handed me the key to the medicine cabinet. It was six feet wide, with shelves from the floor to the ceiling, stacked full with bottles of drugs, first aid supplies and equipment. There were three shapes of tooth pullers, also books, including the large *Ship's Medicine Chest*, which had instructions on what to do in any case of medical emergency. Toby said, "The cabinet should be kept locked. Somebody, or children, might get something out."

He pointed to a box in the corner of the office and said, "That's the 'baby box.' The midwives come and get it when a woman is ready for the baby to come out. Inside the box are the supplies that are needed. The midwives will come and bang on your door when they need it. Sometimes it's in the middle of the night."

I opened the lid and looked inside. The box was packed neatly with sterile items, towels, etc. On the other side of the office, large radio transmitters and receivers, of the same make as those the radioman in Anchorage had shown me, covered two large office desks.

Toby followed as I walked through the ten-foot passageway to the office entrance then down two steps onto beach sand. Ten feet away was a waist-high seawall made of four-by-twelve timbers. I asked, "Is this to prevent waves from splashing against the building?"

"That hardly ever happens," he said. "We only have two-foot tides here." I noticed the surf gently sloshing along the water's edge and low breakers plopping over a submerged sandbar farther out.

We went back inside the building at the main entrance and entered a hallway. On the left side, a sign above a window read "Wales Post Office". Toby introduced me to the postmaster. Dwight Tevuk, about five feet, eight inches tall, slight of build, and in his mid-forties, wore glasses and a green Sears-type parka. He was sorting letter mail and packages that had just arrived. His rapid speech and fluent English surprised me. He would later prove to be an admired friend and advisor. He later told me that he assisted Roald Amundsen after his dirigible flight over the North Pole to the Seward Peninsula in 1926. He had worked for curators from the Denver Museum during the 1930s, '40s and early '50s, and was consulted by James Michener while Michener was in Nome to do research for his book, *Alaska*.

While Toby showed me around the school, Virginia explored the kitchen to familiarize herself with the supplies and equipment. She found that the former teachers had left several cases of food, enough to last a month. There were canned meats and vegetables with which neither of us were acquainted but which we would eat, for it would be six weeks before the ship could bring our year's supply of groceries. In the kerosene-burning refrigerator were about ten pounds of frozen salmon.

During our next few days, several women came to visit and introduce themselves. They sat on the couch, still wearing their parkas with fur turned in. The colorful outer cloth cover had decorative beadwork on hems and cuffs. The women spoke in broken English, while sometimes smiling and sometimes laughing. They apologized for the whims of the Wales weather and each gave their version of how the people had adapted to it. A few were elderly, with faces like leather and teeth worn flat from years of crimping the toes and heels of mukluk soles. They seemed to adore our sandy-haired, three-year-old son, Tommy, who enjoyed the attention and went outside to play with their children.

To get acquainted with the village, I first walked to the village store, where I met the manager, Alfred Mazonna, age about 40, who had large white teeth and a broad smile. Alfred was five feet ten, about 250 pounds and enjoyed talking and laughing with people, which was probably one reason he was elected to be store manager. "You'll come here lots when it gets dark this winter," he said, laughing. Five or six other men eyed me as they sat on benches and empty butter kegs. I could tell there was a lot of business transacted at the village store from the look of those well-worn butter kegs around the hot potbelly stove. This was not a great deal unlike the village store on Ellijay Creek where I swapped eggs for kerosene oil for our lamps in the thirties and forties.

The next day I walked to the Army base, beside the beach about a mile north of the village. The base was composed of three Quonset huts and a small motor pool. The officer in charge said, "We're abandoning this base in the spring. Construction workers have finished the Air Force Distant Early Warning site on top of Cape Mountain, so there's no further need for our small radar site up there." He pointed toward a camouflaged area in the rocks, about a hundred yards up the side of the mountain. Although the Army personnel were officially restricted from most contacts with the village, they proved to be a valuable resource for us that first winter.

Since my main reason for being in Wales was to serve as teacher, I decided I should first set a school starting date. I asked Toby to call a village council meeting for that purpose. Thirty minutes later he came to me and said, "I talked to Angnaboogok. He is village council chief. He said he will have the meeting tonight."

That night after the reading of the minutes and other preliminaries, Village Council Chief, Roland Angnaboogok, asked me, "Do you have something to bring up?"

"Yes. I would like to start school on Monday, September fifth —one week from today."

After a twenty minute discussion of my proposal, all in Eskimo, Roland turned to me, grinning, and said, "We decided it's up to you when to start school. You are the teacher."

"OK. I thank you. Will you pass the word in the village that we will start school next Monday at eight o'clock?"

The men smiled. Several responded with "Ee-ees," which means "Yes."

The following morning, I found the roll of prospective students, then asked Toby to help me learn to pronounce the children's last names. He consented and pronounced "Angnaboogok", "Ongtowasruk" and "Oxereok" for me several times. He laughed at my attempts to copy his deep guttural accent, which I knew sounded more like I was clearing my throat. I cut the lesson short. The children each had two names, an English first name and an Inuit last name. No middle name. The other last names were Anungazuk, Mazonna, Okpealuk, Seetook, Tevuk and Weyapuk. Only the children of two families, those of Willie and of Roland Angnaboogok, had the same last names.

The school at Wales was organized differently from any school I had known in North Carolina. Although the school served grades one through eight, I soon learned that a grade number had less meaning to the people at Wales than the age. The children attended school from the age of six through eighteen or nineteen. This meant that seventh and eighth graders were as old as seniors in high school back home! The students repeated at least four of the nine grades regardless of their ability. How would I cope with teaching so many grown bodies in the elementary grades? And what would I do come promotion time at the end of the year? For sure, this was one area where I would be learning.

I turned to acquainting myself with the school materials. The classroom shelves were full of books. Closets were stacked high with cases of papers, pencils, games, and workbooks, even trash and scraps left there by former teachers. I had never before seen so much "stuff" in a school. Enough, I thought, to supply a school five times the size of Wales!

I looked in the office files and was again reminded of the myriad of monthly government reports I was required to make to

Nome, Juneau and Washington. But my main purpose for being here was to teach. School must start!

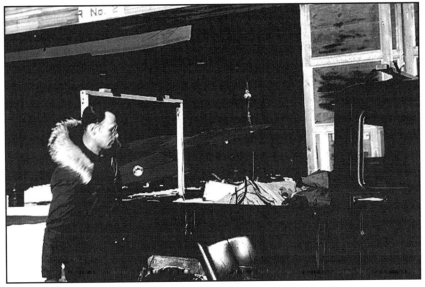

Bob Jacobs, Alaska Airlines bush pilot, 1955.

School Days

During my seventeen years as a student, from first grade through college, I learned more about teaching than any other profession. I watched teachers try to disseminate knowledge while struggling with disruptive students and others who seemed not to care. Some of my teachers seemed longing to be anywhere but the classroom. I sympathized with them and resolved that the teaching profession was not for me. It was only after I came home from the Navy in 1948 that I learned that teaching was the most wide open profession. I could get the G I Bill and attend school at nearby Western Carolina Teacher's College, where a number of my veteran friends were already enrolled.

So there I was on Sunday, twenty miles from the International Date Line, preparing for the first day of school and feeling insecure. I looked out the office window across the strait and saw the mountaintops on East Cape in Siberia, where it was already Monday, and mused, "Monday will arrive here tomorrow, the first day of school for me at Wales."

I walked into the schoolroom early that Monday to await the children's arrival. I had books, paper, pencils, and workbooks on the desks for each student. I had arranged the smaller desks for the lower grades at the front of the room and the larger desks for the upper grades at the rear. I had all of the week's lessons planned for each subject each day for all eight grades--forty lessons a day! I was ready for school to start--or so I thought!

The children began arriving at a quarter to eight. I met them at the front door and smiled and said "hello" as they entered. Although they smiled back at me as they walked past, none of the children said "hello" or "good morning." In fact, they only smiled shyly and said nothing except some soft words in Eskimo to one another. About a third of the students took off their parkas and hung them on hooks in the hallway. The others kept their parkas on as they went to their seats. The smaller children went to the smaller desks and the larger children went to the larger desks. Each student seemed to know exactly where he or she was supposed to sit. When all were seated, I counted forty-three students, the exact number on the list compiled by the former teacher. The children ranged in age from five through eighteen. They sat quiet and motionless, staring at me with all eighty-six beady, inquisitive eyes that clearly said, "Now we're here. Your move is next!"

I broke the silence by clearing my throat. I said, "I'm going to call the roll, and I would like for you to answer and raise your hands so I can begin learning your names." An older girl, tall and slender with long black hair, and wearing a knee-length green print dress over jeans, in the back of the room, interrupted and spoke rapidly in Eskimo. The other students turned and faced her as she spoke. I assumed she was interpreting what I had said. When she stopped talking I asked her, "What were you saying to them?"

She smiled and said in rapid English, "I was just telling them what you said."

"That's good. What is your name?"

"I am Harriet Tevuk," she responded with a sheepish smile.

"Thank you." I responded. "OK, now I'm going to call the roll," I repeated, then opened my roll book and called each child's first and last name with the pronunciations I had been practicing. Some children smiled and raised their hand. Others said an awkward "here," except for two small first graders who did not answer. Harriet raised her hand and smiled as she said, "Those two don't know their English names."

To learn children's names was always difficult for me, and now was even more so since the last names of all the children were in Inuit. During recess I said to Toby, "I am relieved that the children have English first names. It's the Eskimo surnames that are giving me trouble."

He laughed and said, "It was not many years ago when Wales people began using English first names. Long ago, when Wales Eskimos born, they each were given one name only. But few years ago the United States government made us change that. I think it was back in the 1930s when they made us change our names. They said for every man to use his Eskimo name as his last name and put white man's name in front of it. Then they said to have all his children and his wife to have his Eskimo name for the family last name, but to always use white man's first names, each one different."

"How do the people like this new naming system?"

"Well, it's good to put on papers, and for school to use," he said, smiling. "But we have our other names also."

"You mean the village people still have other Eskimo names?"

"Yes," he said with a grin. "And they already gave you Eskimo name, and one for your wife and for Tommy also."

On that first day, Toby walked through the room several times as if observing to see that school went smoothly. He once stopped beside me and said in a soft voice, "I can help interpret for you anytime if you want."

I detected he might have thought that I could well use his help. I said, "I may need you to interpret at any time, but some of these girls seem to be pretty good at interpreting." To me, it seemed that school was getting off to a good start.

The next day was about like the first. I moved from grade to grade, using older children, mostly girls, to interpret and to help the younger children. I used a teaching method similar to that of the two-teacher school of my elementary years. I assigned plenty of seat work and oral reading from books in English. Sometimes, two or three read out loud simultaneously.

During the middle of the second week of school the children became more vocal, louder and speaking almost entirely in Eskimo. I occasionally heard an English word. The children began getting out of their seats more often, and tended to walk around the room. They were paying less attention to me. Sometimes, Toby, who was usually nearby, would intercede, speak to the children in Eskimo, and they would calm down again, but only for a short time. I realized that I was losing control, that the situation was getting out of hand. Some older girls were attaining the position of the alpha teacher, speaking in Eskimo in harsh terms to some of the third- and fourth-graders. Order in the classroom was becoming too hectic, and what was I to do about it? There were just too many students in too many grades in one small room.

I stayed awake much of that night, worrying. The next day was even worse. After school, I radioed the Nome office and spoke to the educational supervisor, Warren Tiffany. While trying to disguise my anxiety, I informed him of the pandemonium that was breaking out. After considerable discussion, he said, "Do what you have to do. If you need to divide your school into sessions, do that.

You could teach grades one through three in the morning and grades four through eight in the afternoon." Boy, was I relieved to hear those words! It was the most welcome advice I have received from a supervisor before or since.

The next morning, with the help of Toby and some older boys, I moved the desks for grades one through three into the other room and sent the older children home with instructions to return at twelve for lunch. I kept three older girls who were willing to help tutor in the lower grades. Each older girl took a grade to teach. I suggested what to teach, and intervened only occasionally. I felt that school might now be getting underway, that finally I was teaching.

The afternoon session went like clockwork. The older children felt more important and unburdened without the little ones around. They understood English pretty well and I could teach them the way I was comfortable to teach. I found them to be fast learners. They especially loved math and reading. That night I slept much better.

Virginia's job was mainly supervision of a few volunteer adult women and older girls in the school kitchen, preparing and serving the noon meal. All grades were at the school during lunch hour. Virginia also monitored the older girls in sewing classes three evenings a week. The school furnished cloth for the girls to make dresses (itigluks) and such. After her first sewing session she said, "Those girls know more about sewing than I do."

While the girls were in sewing class, the boys went to the shop to carve ivory from walrus tusks they brought from home. Toby did the actual teaching of the ivory carving class. I was fascinated to watch the boys carve figurines of seals, walrus, polar bear, whales, and billikens, the Eskimo rendition of squat, smiling comic figures. The artistic talent and dexterity of the group was truly evident, and I marveled at their creations.

The children came to school warmly dressed. Early in the school year almost all the clothing they wore was similar to that sold by Sears. The only difference in attire between the boys and girls was that the girls wore dresses over long pants. At first this seemed odd to me because girls where I had previously taught wore dresses over long stockings and never wore pants. But I soon got accustomed to the Eskimo girls' mode of dress and assumed the weather also compelled them to wear a second or third pair of pants underneath their dresses.

As the days grew shorter and the weather colder, more and more children wore fur parkas, fur mittens and several layers of cotton or wool pants. Toby said they wore fur socks inside home-made mukluks with soles made of oogruk (large seal) hide, shaped by their mother's teeth and sewn onto fur leggings with thread twisted from reindeer sinew.

All fur was tanned in the home, using urine, the traditional process, which Toby said was better than tannic acid. So I had my parka, mukluks, and mittens made by the same method. The smell was different than anything I was used to, but I soon learned that the Eskimo clothing would keep me warm even in chill factors of 100 degrees below zero.

From the start of school until September 15, we had a cold, windy drizzle nearly every day. Then I noticed the top of Cape Prince of Wales Mountain had turned white with snow. During the following week the snow line dropped down the mountainside, lower and lower each day, until on the 21st, all was white in the village. After school, Toby commented about this. "Freeze-up is coming early this year."

For the next ten days the north wind blew over open water and brought a steady snow that formed drifts three to four feet deep around the school. Suddenly, about the first of October, the wind changed to blow from the south, and the weather warmed. Again, rain fell and froze, forming an inch of ice on top of the snow that had already fallen. The following day the wind direction shifted back to the north, bringing with it more snow. But the

strong winds kept the snow blown off the ice, except near obstacles such as buildings or rocks. The surface of the snow remained ice-covered and slick for most of the rest of that winter and made walking difficult.

Nora Ahwinona, the elderly wife of the Eskimo Covenant Mission preacher from White Mountain, an Eskimo village sixty miles southeast of Nome, once saw me fall. She laughed and said, "Now you will have to hold a party. It is Eskimo custom that whoever falls must give a party."

When I came into the schoolroom early on the morning after the rain, I observed unusual thumping noises on the wooden floor as children were walking to their seats. Several students were still wearing ice skates. I noticed that their skates were homemade and fashioned from pieces of saw blades and driftwood, then lashed to their mukluks with strips of rawhide, probably with the help of a parent. But I felt they shouldn't be allowed to walk around the schoolroom wearing skates. I decreed, "You cannot wear skates in the schoolroom. You will have to take off your skates."

Walter Weyapuk, a fifth grader, apparently speaking for the group, said, "But it is too much trouble to put on skates and take off skates. It takes too long."

"But if you keep your skates on in the schoolroom they will scar the floor and Toby won't like it. Also they will make too much noise when you walk around the room," I protested, but realized the considerable skill and time required to lash their skates firmly enough, but not too tightly, to their mukluks. I said, "I will let you keep your skates on only if you will stay in your seats during classes and not walk on the floor." I assigned the duties of sharpening pencils and retrieving supplies that required walking inside the schoolroom to the few students who weren't wearing skates. I was pleasantly surprised to see no students leaving their seats while wearing skates, except during recesses and when they left after school to go home.

Although the students were adept at skating, uphill and down, on the village's hard, ice-covered snowdrifts, I did not possess such skills and fell on my backside more than once. Soon, however, I devised a better way to walk without injury. I removed the felt padding from inside my new mukluks, then stuck thumbtacks, which were plentiful in the school's supplies, through the bottoms of the skin soles. Then I replaced the felt padding. I had about twenty or thirty sharp points sticking out the bottoms of my soles.

I found I could walk expertly up and down ice-covered drifts without falling. The children marveled at my ice-walking expertise. But my secret was short-lived, as I think a child observed tracks of my thumbtacks on the ice and spread the news of my mukluk modification to some village adults, including Nora Ahwinona. Nora, who had made the mukluks for me, came and admonished me in front of the children. "You will ruin your mukluks by putting tacks in them." I thought no more of the matter until thirty-four years later when I visited eighty-nine-year-old Nora living in Nome. She laughed as she reminded me of the "awful thing" I had done to my mukluks.

Some of the children brought sleds to school to slide down the slopes during recess. When the wind was strong, they sailed on sleds or on skates by holding pieces of cardboard in front of them. Or, if the wind was very strong, they sometimes sailed on foot with their arms outstretched. I noticed they could turn left by lowering their left arms or turn right by lowering their right arms. Four boys once sailed so far from the school that they failed to walk back to class in time. They came in the schoolroom fifteen minutes late. To me this was another discipline problem that would only get worse if it wasn't stopped. When the stragglers settled into their seats, I turned to Toby so students could also hear me ask, "What do you think I should do about students coming back tardy from recess?"

"Maybe you should scold them," he said.

"Scolding, you say?" I was dumfounded, then I got him aside and quietly asked, "You say I should scold them? How do I do that?"

"I think scolding will work," he responded with a half-smile. "Scolding is way Wales Eskimos always make children behave. One teacher one time was putting children in the attic to make them behave, but it did not work. They only misbehave some more. Also, I think some of the village people did not like it when children were in attic. That teacher also sometimes was paddling and that was no good."

"How should I scold them?" I was curious.

"You should tell them not to come back in schoolroom late from recess," he answered matter-of-factly.

I doubted Toby's technique would work. I had more faith in taking away recess periods or other privileges. Besides, scolding was not one of the courses taught at the college. But I decided I would give Toby's "scolding" technique a try. I walked into the schoolroom and said to the students, in as firm a voice and with as straight a face as I knew how, "All right, some of you students have been sailing too far away from the school at recess, and it is taking you much too long to come back into the room after I ring the bell. You must come back to your seats when the bell is rung."

The room got as quiet as a funeral procession. Every student eyed me. Some turned and looked at Harriet, who spoke briefly in Eskimo, smiling. I turned and saw Toby standing in the doorway, also smiling. I felt then that perhaps I had mastered the technique of scolding, Eskimo style. To my surprise I had no more students returning to the schoolroom tardy from skating at recess, and I began to believe that scolding was the only disciplinary method I would need for the remainder of my Alaskan career. As my teaching career continued, I learned that Eskimo children are very responsive to, and respectful of, stern advice given to them by their elders. They responded much better to "scoldings" than children I previously taught or would teach in the future. In fact, during my years in Alaska I never saw or heard of any form of correction of children by Eskimo parents except "scolding."

Toby Anunqazuk, School Janitor, Wales, Alaska 1956

Will Our Supplies Arrive?

In October, the days became noticeably shorter. The cold north wind blew almost without ceasing. Mush ice formed in the surf. Toby said, "freeze-up is coming soon." People in the village worried that the BIA ship, *North Star*, with our groceries, school supplies and stock for the village store, might be delayed or, worse yet, might not come at all.

Each night for two weeks before the ship's scheduled arrival at Wales, I talked daily by radio to the ship's radioman, Darby, as the ship supplied villages down the northwest coast of Alaska. Darby was also concerned that the early freeze-up would disrupt the *North Star*'s tight schedule. He especially wanted to keep tabs on weather conditions in the Bering Strait. During one conversation, while his ship was lightering at Kotzebue, I detected unease in his voice when I overheard him say, "Wales is the most difficult to supply of any village up here, because of the constant high winds and the fast moving current in the Bering Strait. We're also running behind schedule and we're afraid the ice will start freezing any day now."

Three days later, I was standing by the radio when Toby burst excitedly into my office. "I've been listening to the *North Star* talking. The ship is nearly finished lightering at Shishmaref, and they will be coming to Wales next. But the mush ice is already starting to form." He wasn't smiling and his voice had a solemn tone.

No sooner had he spoken, when a radio call came from Darby, "KWP Two-Four Wales, KWP Two-Four Wales, this is the *North Star*, how's your weather there in the strait? Over."

"*North Star*, Two-Four Wales, the wind is about thirty-five miles per hour and we have pretty good-sized swells.

The natives tell me mush ice is starting to form. Over."

"Two-Four Wales, this is the *North Star* back." He paused. "We have just finished lightering at Shishmaref and we're heading your way. We'll be ready to start offloading onto the skinboats tomorrow morning at eight. Tell the village to have the men ready. Over."

Since Shishmaref is the neighboring village only seventy miles to the north, the ship moved into the strait during the night. At daybreak, the large ship was a welcomed sight, anchored just two miles offshore. Our groceries were aboard and the ship was now ready to offload cargo onto three thirty-foot skinboats to be brought ashore. I thought, "It will be good to get our groceries and have a variety of good foods for a change."

At 7:30, I radioed Darby, "Your ship sure looks good out there."

"OK, Will. I think some of the men are still in the mess hall eating breakfast, but we'll be ready shortly. The weather looks good. The sea is almost calm."

Just then Toby walked into the office. He was ashen-faced and almost out of breath. He said, "Mush ice is too thick; skinboats can't go through it!"

"Are you sure? The water looks calm to me." I was shocked.

"Yes, but mush ice is too thick," he repeated. "Angnaboogok and others say skinboats can't go through it. Can't unload supplies. It would take too long to go through the ice to ship."

I was stunned. How would we manage if our supplies weren't brought ashore? The ship was so close, but yet so far away! I guess my voice was cracking when I radioed Darby, "The natives tell me that the mush ice is too thick to lighter. They say their skinboats can't go through it."

"Stand by," he responded. Thirty long seconds later he said, "The captain says we can't wait here long. We've got lots of villages to supply south of here. He says we can't wait more than one more day. He says we're already running more than a week behind schedule. If we can't unload the cargo for your village here, we'll have to unload it at Nome."

I looked at Toby. He was speechless. His supplies were also on the ship.

I then radioed Mr. Jenkins at the Nome office. He calmly said, "I already heard about your problem. If the ship can't unload supplies there, they'll have to be unloaded here at Nome." I knew immediately that if our year's supply of groceries, fuel oil for the stoves, and gasoline for the electric generator had to be airlifted from Nome by bush plane as weather permitted, the school would be strapped for supplies all winter. No way could I imagine Bob Jacobs flying to Wales in his small bush plane with an adequate cargo of groceries, school supplies and, yes, one fifty-five-gallon barrel of heating oil at a time. The school could not operate without fuel for heating, and I was not prepared to live on blubber and seal oil; and I knew for sure Virginia wouldn't.

Toby had said the Wales weather during the short days of winter might be bad for weeks at a time. We couldn't just walk down to the corner grocery store. There wasn't one. I also realized that the cost of extra handling of cargo would be ours to pay and that the expense of having our groceries flown in from Nome on many flights would be tremendous, if not prohibitive.

Several times that day I walked in the cold breeze to the edge of the beach to observe the mush ice as it gently rode the low swells. The ship was an imposing sight at anchor, with its bow facing north. The current there was moving south. My radio schedule with Darby was at ten, twelve, two and four but there was no change in the icy conditions. That night, I was again talking to Darby when an Army weasel drove up outside. Gene Brewer, the CO of the Navy outpost, walked into the office. He said, "We've been listening to your radio conversations. We heard that the *North Star* will leave in a day or two if the natives can't lighter your cargo. We have two amphibious vehicles that we could use to bring the supplies ashore, but we're not allowed to do this except in case of an emergency. You would have to be the one to declare the emergency."

I quickly said, "The Eskimos tell me they can't go through the mush ice with their skinboats to bring in the supplies for the village. They say the mush ice is too thick. I think if there ever is an emergency, *this is it!*"

"In that case we'll have two amphibious vehicles ready to go at eight tomorrow morning. If our vehicles can go through the ice, we'll try to get your stuff ashore. Tell the natives to be ready to work first thing in the morning."

"Thank you!" I responded. "That is very good news to us."

I radiocd thc good ncws to Darby, hoping it was not too late and that the ship hadn't already decided to get under-way. He said, "The captain is standing right here. He said that, indeed, is welcome news. We'll be ready to offload at eight o'clock tomorrow morning."

Sure enough, the next morning the amphibious ve-hicles were in front of the school, with one driver in each. Four men climbed into each vehicle, which drove easily through the mush ice to the ship. The vehicles made only five round trips each and delivered ashore all the cargo for the village and school. It was a cooperative effort, as every able-bodied person, from first grade up, worked to carry containers to storage rooms in the school, the teacher's quarters and the village store. All workers were paid ten cents per item carried. For each drum of oil and gasoline rolled to the school, the pay was a quarter. The year's supply of groceries and fuel for the school and the store was soon stashed in storage rooms and pantries. I recorded this day as a school day and counted all students present. We were ready for the rest of the winter and the *North Star* could now go south.

Walrus!

The Bering Strait, located between the mountains of East Cape in Siberia and Cape Prince of Wales in Alaska, serves as a nozzle that moves air, water and ice rapidly through. This passageway connects the warmer waters of the Pacific with the colder waters of the Arctic Ocean, setting up powerful, and sometimes violent, oceanic and atmospheric conditions rarely witnessed anywhere else on earth. Survival by the Eskimos here is an art, which they have long since mastered.

The Saturday after the *North Star* moved south toward Nome, the mush ice that had been forming moved away from the shore. Conditions again became favorable for hunters to launch skinboats in the strait, and I hoped I could join them for the adventure. The opportunity came when Dwight Tevuk knocked on my door early that morning.

"My crew is getting ready to go out in skinboat now," he said. "Sereadlook spotted walrus with a telescope from the mountain. The walrus are on the ice way out. You can go with us if you like."

I quickly said, "I'll get ready. Should I bring a gun?"

"No. We have guns, but you can bring your camera. You should dress warmly and wear your hip boots. The men are about ready to go."

I dressed hurriedly, grabbed my camera and an extra roll of film, then walked to the beach. Dwight, Toby and six other men were assembled around a thirty-foot skinboat. They were loading guns, ropes, sacks, harpoons, cans of gasoline and two extra motors.

"Old Man" Clyde Ongtowasruk, in his mid to upper

seventies with a full head of white hair, was there. I nodded to him and said, "Hi." He smiled with large white teeth showing and said something in Inupiaq and laughed.

Dwight said, "We are ready. We go now." The men talked in Eskimo as they pushed the boat into the water. I helped push, wading in water up to my knees. Dwight said, "You get in now."

I climbed aboard near the middle of the boat, as did Old Man Ongtowasruk from the other side. He moved toward the rear. The other men continued talking while they pushed the boat into deeper water. When the water reached their thighs, they also climbed aboard, then grabbed paddles, which they pushed against the seabed. The boat drifted into deeper water. The men paddled a few feet, till the boat slowed on a submerged bar, where they again pushed with their paddles against the bottom. Dwight said, "This is the last sandbar to cross." He said something else in Eskimo, whereupon the men laid their paddles inside the boat. The boat began drifting as Toby tinkered momentarily with the motor. He then swung the propeller into the water and pulled the starter cord. The motor cranked after the third try. He revved the motor and turned the boat northwest into the strait, then sat down.

Dwight sat on the left side of the bench beside me. Four men were on two seats up front, two were seated behind me and one sat on the seat beside Toby. High-powered M-1 rifles stood against the outside ribs, their barrels pointing up and away. I was ready to enjoy the adventure and sat quietly at first, while the conversation around me was all in Eskimo. I suppose they were discussing important issues such as the wind, the current or the pack ice farther out. As we passed over low swells, the skin on the sides of the boat bent in and out against the ribs. I felt the skin of the boat under my feet move, so I moved my feet to the top of a rib.

I noticed the skin was lashed with strips of rawhide around the gunwale, and asked Dwight, "What kind of skin is this boat made of?"

"It is walrus skin," he said. "We make it from the female walrus."

"Why not from the bulls?"

"The bull walrus skin is too thick. Even the female walrus hide is thick, but we split it. We use both the outside skin and the inner skin for making the boats."

"How many hides made this boat?"

"It takes about five or six walrus for making a boat."

"It looks like a lot of work to make a skinboat. All these seams look watertight. Who sewed them together?"

"The women do it with rawhide," he responded. "It is the women's job to split the hides and do all the sewing. The men make the frame. We stretch the skin and lash it to the frame."

"How long does the skin last before you have to make a new boat?"

"Three years," he responded. "After three years, the skin is no good. Then we put on new skin."

"Seems like people would get wooden or fiberglass boats."

"Well, it's been tried before, but jagged ice is bad for wooden or fiberglass boats. Skinboat is much safer. Jagged ice will rip the boats made of wood or fiberglass but only makes puncture hole in skinboat."

"What do you do when you get a puncture hole in the skin and you're out in the water?"

"We carry things for patching holes. If that happens--if we get a hole, we just pull boat on ice floe and sew up the hole. You see those patches there." He pointed toward what to me appeared to be patches where bullets or harpoons had penetrated. "It happens only few times. But mostly the skin just bends. Eskimos make skinboats for hundreds of years, maybe thousands." He sounded proud.

I thought, "Wow! And here I am in the 20th century, riding a boat the type of which has survived the ages in the sea at the same place where the first man is believed to have crossed from Asia to America."

Frank Oxereok, a wiry built Eskimo in his mid thirties who was sitting in front of me, had apparently been listening to our conversation. He turned to me smiling and said, "Also, if we get stranded, we will eat the boat."

"*Eat* the boat?" I was flabbergasted.

"Yes," he said smiling broadly. "We eat the boat," he repeated then pulled a small knife from its sheath on his belt and cut an inch-long piece from the edge of the skin beside his seat. He put it in his mouth and began chewing then said, "Umm, good!" The other men laughed.

In front of my feet was a sealskin that had all the holes sewn tightly together with thick rawhide thongs and was full of something. It looked almost alive. I pointed to it and asked Dwight, "What's that for?"

"That is sealskin poke. It is full of air. It is for getting animal that has been shot in the water. You see that coil of rope beside it? One end of the rope is tied to the poke and the other end is tied to the ivory tip of that harpoon there. So when a walrus is harpooned, the ivory tip will go under the walrus skin and separate from the harpoon. The harpoon floats, then we pick it up. The rope and sealskin poke are tied to the walrus and we throw them both in the water. The poke will float so we can tell where is the walrus if it sinks. If it is still alive, we will know where it will come up for air and we can shoot it again. If it dies and sinks, the sealskin poke will not sink. Then we pull the walrus back to surface."

"Sounds like a good system."

"Yes, it's been used by Eskimos since long time ago. But when walrus is harpooned, be careful! Don't let feet get tangled in rope. One time we lost a person who got his feet caught in rope. The walrus was alive and pulled him overboard and under the water."

As we moved farther out I saw thousands of birds. Some were sitting on the water, while others were flying in formation overhead, coming across the strait from Siberia, going south for the winter. Dwight identified the birds with their English names. I asked, "How did you learn the names of all those birds?"

"Well, I used to help collect different birds and animals for the Denver Museum in Colorado. I did this long time. I started helping Alfred Baily, head curator, from back in the '20s. He used to come here."

I pointed to a group of small red and white birds that were frolicking on the surface forty yards to our left and asked, "What are the names of those over there on the water?"

"Those are red phalaropes," he responded.

Suddenly the surface of the water changed drastically. The boat began pitching, as I noticed the water we had just left behind was glassy with low swells, while the water we were entering was like a rolling river. It was weird! I looked right then left. "What is happening?" I asked.

Dwight was smiling. He said, "We are entering the Japanese Current. It goes fast through the strait here. We always reach the current at this point about five miles from shore. The water here is moving fast to the north."

"Wow!" I thought. "The interface at the edge of the current is sharp."

Toby turned the boat slightly westward, while the boat flopped and bent with each wave it crossed. Dwight said, "We are now in the current and it is taking us north."

My gloved hands and my feet were getting cold. I looked around at the others and realized I was not as warmly dressed. I put my hands inside my parka pockets. Dwight asked, "Are you cold?"

"No," I lied. Although my toes were getting cold, I was determined to stick it out. I was determined not to be a hindrance whatever the consequence, and refrained from jiggling my feet up and down. But I resolved to wear fur socks on my next trip out here.

We continued in the same direction for some fifteen or twenty minutes more as the mountains of East Cape in Siberia loomed larger. We passed small chunks of ice on the water while one man up front pointed the way for Toby to guide the boat. The man beside him also stood and was looking through binoculars.

We passed between some large floes where the surface of the water was calmer and the boat rode smoother. The man with binoculars turned and said something in Eskimo, then pointed west. Toby turned the boat in that direction. The conversation of the men, now all in Eskimo, became more rapid and animated, except for Old Man Ongtowasruk, who spoke slowly and calmly.

I asked Dwight, "Do they see some walrus up ahead?"

"Yes," he answered. "He say he see maybe fifteen or twenty. They're bull walrus on some floes. We are getting near to them. You can stand up and see them up ahead."

I eased up to a standing position and saw a dark

brown mass on a large ice floe, then sat back down. Toby slowed the motor. The men, except Toby and Old Man Ongtowasruk, gathered their guns from racks along the sides. They stood and assumed a firing position. Dwight said, "You can take some pictures." I stood in a crouch and snapped a couple, then sat back down.

Toby slowed the motor to a purr. They exchanged more conversation, but gradually their discussion became subdued, until only Old Man Ongtowasruk was talking. I glanced at him. He was now in the seat in front of the motor. I whispered to Dwight, "What is he saying?"

Dwight spoke in a low tone, "Well, he say which walruses to shoot. He also will tell us when to shoot them."

Toby turned off the motor as the boat slowly drifted toward the walruses that seemed unaware of our approach. We drifted closer. We came to within fifty yards, then forty. Some walruses appeared drowsy. They were weaving their heads back and forth. Others were apparently asleep. No noise. The boat turned at a right angle to the walruses. The men continued pointing their guns. Old Man Ongtowasruk lowered his voice to a murmur. He then raised it with a sharp command. I assumed he said, "Fire," as seven M-1 rifles spoke a deafening cacophony of quick rounds. Four walruses dropped limply on the ice. The others lumbered

into the water. Four or five resurfaced within a few feet of the boat. The men put their guns back in the racks. They picked up paddles and began frantically splashing the water. Dwight said, "We use the paddles to keep the walruses away from the boat. They try to put their tusks in the boat and tear it up." He suddenly stopped waving his paddle then picked up a harpoon and threw it into a bleeding walrus off the right side just ten feet from where I sat. With the harpoon attached to the walrus's back, he picked up the coils of rope and the sealskin poke and quickly threw them overboard. He said, "That walrus is dying. We can now pull it up if it sinks."

The men paddled the boat alongside the ice floe. We stepped onto the floe and pulled the boat on top. The men laughed. They began talking, and I assumed they were assessing the situation and deciding their next course of action. Dwight snagged the sealskin poke with a hook, then pulled the walrus to the surface. He first spoke in Eskimo, then to me in English, "This walrus is dead."

Toby tied one end of a block and tackle to the walrus's tusks while Frank anchored the other end twenty feet away toward the middle of the floe. With each of us pulling, the walrus gradually slid out of the water, then onto the ice with the others. When the men stopped pulling, they again laughed and talked in Eskimo. They seemed proud that a difficult task was accomplished so easily, that food would now be available for their dogs and their families, that tusks could be carved into trinkets and jewelry for sale to craft stores in Nome, Anchorage and Seattle.

The work of butchering and loading the five three-thousand-pound walruses now began. Dwight said, "We will butcher fast because the ice is drifting north. You see Cape Prince of Wales Mountain is now far away. Don't get too close to the edge of the ice. Some might break off." I hop-stepped away from the edge.

The men rolled the walruses onto their backs and separated their hides from their carcasses. Dwight cut a small cube of pink hide, then put it in his mouth and began chewing. He smiled as he said, "This is called *koke*. It is Eskimo delicacy, but white men never eat it."

Frank offered me a piece, which I refused. Others also ate while they worked, laughing and talking. Each walrus was carved into fifty- to one-hundred-pound chunks.

The openings to the walruses' stomachs were tied shut with the contents remaining intact. "What are you going to do with that?" I asked.

"We keep the contents of the walrus stomachs," Dwight said. "It is best part. It is only partly digested clams. You will like it too." He laughed.

I wondered if he was really serious. I recalled a guest Virginia and I had recently hosted at our school, a Mr. Weyman Carroll, whom we later named our second son after. He was a collector of animals for zoos around the world. He had flown to the village to check on the possibility of obtaining a pair of baby walruses for the New York Aquarium. He said, "Keeping adult walruses in captivity has never been successful to date, but they have recently analyzed the walrus's milk and now know the formula, so they want to try raising them from babies."

The first night of his visit, Virginia asked him, "What would you like for dinner tonight—reindeer stew, ptarmigan dumplings, fried salmon, baked goose, murre egg...?"

"Oh, I eat anything," he interrupted. "I've eaten meals in remote villages all over the world, and I make it a point to eat the same foods the villagers eat."

"Did you ever get sick from eating foods in faraway places?"

"Yes, but I always go prepared. I carry emergency supplies with me. I have antibiotics I can take for all kinds of sicknesses. Once when I was in a village a few miles northwest of Kaga Bandora in Central African Republic, the village medicine man became acutely sick. The people in the village had lost hope that their shaman would ever get well. I convinced the chief to let me shoot him with penicillin. I did and the man got well within three days. I became an instant celebrity. Then the chief declared a feast to be held in my honor. The food was good until I asked, 'What is this meat we're eating?' He said, 'We had this old man died last week.'"

I came back to what Frank had just offered me and said, "I don't think I will try it this time!"

The men squeezed the contents of the intestines onto the ice. Dwight said, "We only save the intestine walls. They are good for making things. It makes the best rain parkas. They're better than rubber. It doesn't get you sweaty, but it keeps you dry and warm."

"How about those hides? What do you do with them?"

"Well, the *koke* is good to eat, but we ship most of the bull walrus hides out to Seattle. It brings a good price."

"What do they use the hides for?"

"They use the bull walrus hides in factories to polish silverwares."

As Toby chopped the tusks off a walrus head with an ax, I noticed one tusk was broken and asked, "How did that tusk get broken?"

"Maybe fighting is how. I think they fight in mating season." He then pointed toward some hides. "You see those scars there. It's also from fights. The bulls always fight. It's mostly in mating season when they fight."

The live walruses had been gone from the area for some time when we lowered the boat back into the water. Toby gave each of us a foot-long iron hook with a handle. He smiled and said, "This is for carrying meat to umiak. We will take everything except those big necks. The necks are mostly just bone and we can't use them."

While we were loading the boat, I noticed Frank carrying some eighteen-inch-long bones to the boat and asked Toby, "What is he carrying?"

"Those are *ooziks*. It's the male bone. Bull walrus have bone instead of what you call it?"

"Penis?"

"Yes. We send them to Nome. They bring good price from tourists."

I recalled that Mr. Jenkins had retrieved one from his front room closet, saying, "This is a bull walrus penis, which is worth more than a tusk. On the radio we refer to them as 'baseball bats'. That's what we'll say on the radio when we want you to ask the store manager if he has some ooziks he can ship to Nome." I never learned why the ooziks are so valuable.

Soon the boat was loaded. Most seats were covered. The boat rode low in the water. Dwight said, "We get in now. We have drifted far to the north and have long way to go home."

I slithered into the meat to my thighs. It felt so warm! Dwight smiled as he sank in the meat beside me.

"What will you do with all this meat?" I asked.

"Well, it's mostly for dog food. Dogs need lots to eat. We always depend on walrus meat for enough dog food to last all year."

When everyone had taken places in the boat, Toby and Frank clamped two other motors to the back of the boat. I commented, "It's good to have extra motors."

"Yes," said Dwight. "We need the extra motors to go against the current. We have long way to go now. Look! You see mostly only top part of Cape Mountain." I saw that the current had indeed moved us a long way from home and realized why the men had worked so quickly and efficiently.

Soon Toby and Frank had all motors humming. Toby controlled two and Frank the other. The men stood to better view their course between ice floes. They were in meat above their knees. Two hours later we approached the first sandbar, where Toby and Frank raced all three motors with a loud roar and the boat surged forward. The men then quickly turned the motors off and raised the propellers from the water while the boat glided fast over the submerged bars, then slid to within ten feet of the water's edge. The men laughed. I stepped out and waded ashore.

Six or eight of my school pupils came running. They were excited and speaking in Eskimo, all speaking at once. I heard repeated several times *eskoolty* and *eskooluk*. I even heard *eskooluktuk*. I later learned they were talking about me. One student asked, "How did you like it out there?"

"Fine," I said.

Another asked, "Did you get cold?"

"No," I lied, then turned to Toby, "Do you want me to help unload?"

"No, we will do it. Also we have lots of children to help put the meat in the caches. You should go home."

Several women arrived at the boat with large containers. I went home.

Walking on Water

The morning after our first blizzard from the north, I was reading a story to the third grade, when a man walked past the schoolroom window in even stride, without snow-shoes, on top of a six-foot drift. Was I seeing things? How was he doing that? From past experience in deep snow, I thought surely he should have sunk to his thighs! I lay my book on the desk, then walked outside, where a frigid wind stung my face. I stepped on the snow, but I didn't sink into it either. It was packed rock hard. I quickly returned inside, and some students looked at me as if to ask, "Why did you go outside?"

After school I commented about the deep, hard, new-fallen, wind-packed snow to Toby, then asked, "Do the people in Wales ever use snowshoes?"

"Wales people don't use snowshoes. We never need them here. The wind packs the snow hard. Wales people only have ice shoes that are made like snowshoes but a lot smaller for walking on the mush ice."

"Ice shoes?"

"Yes, they are used mostly in seal hunting. Old people used to walk on mush ice to get seal that was shot."

"Do you have a pair?"

"No, I don't have ice shoes. Mostly no one use them anymore. But I think some old people might still have them."

"Do you know someone who has ice shoes? I sure would like to see someone walking on mush ice."

"I think Joshua Ahwinona has ice shoes. You might ask him if he would demonstrate it for you. I think he can do it. He already demonstrated to some Army boys."

Joshua Ahwinona was a stocky, physically fit, sixty-nine-year-old Eskimo from White Mountain, who served as minister in the Covenant Mission Church next door to the school. Both Joshua and his wife, Nora, seemed to enjoy our visits with them. They were fun loving and would do almost anything for you that you might ask. Each time I visited, either Joshua or Nora offered me a fishy-or sealy-tasting delicacy, but I usually refused. Not so, our son Tommy! Nora baby-sat Tommy during the hours Virginia worked and often fed him morsels of Eskimo foods, so that when he came home at the end of the day he smelled of blubber and spoke Inupiaq. They renamed him "Little Eskimo."

I knocked on the door and heard Joshua say, "Come in!"

I entered and found them sitting at the dining table. Joshua chuckled, then said, "I knew that was you at the door. That's why I said 'come in'. If it had been Wales people, they would just come in without knocking. Wales people never knock." He laughed. "We're eating muk-tuk. Would you like to taste some?"

"No, thank you. Toby let me taste some a few days ago. It's too oily and I doubt I would ever learn to like walrus blubber," I said. "I just came over to ask a favor of you. Toby tells me you have some ice shoes for walking on mush ice."

"Yes," he said, smiling, then got up from the table and stepped sprightly to a closet and retrieved two pairs of hand-crafted objects, one small and one large. "I made these both. These long ones are snowshoes. These smaller ones are the ice shoes for walking on mush ice. I use them sometimes to walk on mush ice to hook a seal I have shot. I brought the snowshoes to Wales too, but I never need snowshoes here." He chuckled. "The wind in Wales always is just strong and packs the snow hard. The wind is much worse than White Mountain where I'm from. The weather there is much better."

He handed me an ice shoe to examine. It was two feet long, masterfully constructed of wood and strips of rawhide made in the same pattern as his snowshoes. I handed the ice shoe back to him and said, "Toby tells me you might demonstrate walking on mush ice. I would like to see you do it sometime."

"So you would like to see old Eskimo trick of walking on water, like Jesus?" He laughed.

"I sure would!"

"Well, yes, I can do it if ice conditions are right for walking. But it's usually real cold when mush ice is forming. Saltwater ice is different than freshwater ice. Freshwater, when it freezes, just cracks and might break right through if you step on thin ice. Saltwater turns to mush before it freezes. Freshwater freezes at thirty-two degrees. Saltwater freezes about fifteen. A piece of saltwater ice is much stronger than a piece of freshwater ice, same size. Some saltwater ice, when you walk on it, just bends. But if you walk on mush ice, you have to walk fast and you have to keep walking. You can't stop walking when you're out on mush ice. If you stop you would sink into the water. I used to watch my father walking on mush ice when he went to get seal he would shoot. He would walk very fast and just push up some mush ice behind his shoes. He taught me. I don't think white man should try it." He laughed.

I am disappointed that I never saw Joshua walk on mush ice. I only heard the account of a Sergeant Hark, who said, "It was the most amazing feat I ever saw."

Winds of Wales

One afternoon early in November, I stood in awe beside Toby in front of the school, as we watched five monstrous icebergs swirling slowly off shore. A steady north wind was pushing them closer toward the village. Other groups of people were also on the beach, watching the spectacle. Toby said, "The icebergs are coming toward the beach and will be grounded. That big one has stopped moving already. It is being grounded now." The side of one was blue like the sky. He said, "That blue ice is fresh water. Maybe it came from glacier down south. If shore ice freezes around it, it will stay all winter and some peoples may go there for ice to make water instead of going to lake."

"Do you think they will stay grounded all winter?" I asked.

"Maybe they will stay all winter because they are stopping moving. New ice will soon freeze around them. But the wind evaporates the ice even when the temperature is below zero. The wind here in the strait is very strong. The average velocity is twenty-one miles an hour and will just make the icebergs smaller by spring. And rounded." He was looking far into the distance as he spoke. His mind seemed focused on the long dark winter ahead.

Later, I had occasion to observe first-hand the effect of wind on ice. It was during a flu epidemic that mainly affected small children. A cold north wind was blowing and the temperature was well below zero while I visited homes morning and night, under doctor's orders to give shots of penicillin. One evening at Dwight's house, I noticed he had parked a fresh sled load of foot-thick blocks of jagged ice just outside his front door. During the night the wind direction changed to blow from the south and rocked the building for most of the night. By morning the wind had somewhat abated and the temperature had warmed to zero. When I returned to Dwight's house, I noticed his blocks of ice were still in the sled, but were reduced to small, rounded statues the size of coke bottles! Inside, I mentioned this to Dwight, "The wind last night has almost blown your ice away."

"Yes, I noticed it while ago," he chuckled. "The wind does that even if the temperature is very cold. I didn't know the wind would pick up that strong. Now I will just have to go back to lake for more ice."

One week later, the south wind blew again, with hurricane force that lasted throughout the night. When Toby walked into the school that morning, I noticed a somber look on his face. He said, "Lawrence Etukeok lost all his dogs last night."

"How? What happened?" I was shocked. I recalled that Lawrence had just built a fourteen-by-fourteen-foot plywood dog barn to shelter his dogs from the cold winds.

"It was from the wind," he responded.

"The *wind?*"

"Yes, all nine of his dogs were hung by their necks! He tied them inside his new dog barn. He tied them separated from each other with short chains so they wouldn't fight. The storm turned the barn upside down. It stopped against the back of store building and the dogs were hung by their necks—all of them, dead!"

After school that day the wind had almost stopped blowing when I went to Lawrence's house to see if there was something I could do, such as perhaps help him get a loan to buy a new team of dogs.

Lawrence, a robust man in his forties with a full head of bushy white hair and a deep voice, was quite fluent in English. He once told me that he and his wife were more receptive to white man's ways than most Eskimos in Wales. He said he and his wife always used English when speaking in the presence of their four-year-old daughter. "She will have a better life if she speaks English," he said. "It is better children learn it when they are young."

Lawrence was sitting with a cup of coffee at a small table beside a window where he could see his barn lodged against the warehouse of the village store. *"Coo-pe-uk oo-ah vene?"* he asked, pointing to a chair across the table where I should sit.

His wife placed a cup of coffee in front of me as I sat down. I said, "Toby says you lost all your dogs last night."

"Yes, they were hung by their necks when the wind turned over my barn. Lost all nine of them," he said matter-of-factly and chuckling. He didn't seem the slightest bit depressed. How could he be laughing at such a great loss?

"But what will you do now that you have lost all your dogs?"

"There's plenty dogs in the village," he responded. "I'll just carve more ivory and buy more dogs."

"But how about your dog barn? That lumber cost a lot of money."

"I'll take it apart and rebuild it again next summer when the ground is thawed. Then it will freeze to the ground and can't blow away. I waited too late this year to build the barn. I built it on top of the snow and it never got stuck to the ground. In summer I'll pile sod against the sides like all Eskimo houses. Even your school is fixed that way, with sod piled under the windows all around the outside."

Later that month around noon during school hours, I noticed the south wind was starting to blow again, and getting stronger by the minute. By two o'clock that afternoon the building was shaking. I opened the school door to take a look outside. The visibility was less than three feet! Powdery snow hit me in the face and swirled throughout the hallway. I shut the door quickly and walked back into the classroom, where the children were at their desks, working in workbooks. Their conversation was uncommonly subdued. Were they becoming apprehensive of the howling storm outside?

At five minutes till dismissal time, I looked up and was startled by a gathering in the back of the room. Six grim-faced men were standing along the wall. I hadn't seen them enter. Two men were holding a long rope. They were looking straight at me. Why the rope? And why are they looking at me? What had I done? Just then Toby approached me from behind. He said, "The men have come to take the children home. The wind is very strong now."

I walked to the back of the room and greeted the men. Their pants, parkas, mukluks, and eyelashes were white with powdery snow. Most were fathers of some of the students. Each man had a serious look on his face. Roland Angnaboogok smiled as he said, "We have come to take the children home. It's very windy now. One time before, we had one small child was blown on the ice, never to be seen again. We don't want to take chances anymore. We tie the children together with rope so they won't get blown away."

"OK. Very good!" I was relieved to learn the men had come to help. I also felt they knew what they were doing. I turned and dismissed the children, who jammed books and pencils inside their desks, then scurried from their seats to retrieve flashlights and parkas and mittens to get ready to leave.

The men stretched the rope from the front of the schoolroom into the hallway near the front door. The rope was forty feet long and had shorter ropes with snap hooks attached every two feet along its length. When the children had donned parkas and mittens, the men hooked the short ropes around their waists, so that all the children were harnessed along the entire length of the rope.

When everyone was ready to leave, Roland spoke in Eskimo, then grabbed the front of the rope and turned toward the door. Toby opened the door and held it open while Roland led the way outside and the other men took positions at intervals along the rope to stabilize the procession as it walked into the raging blizzard. Out of curiosity— or was it stupidity?—I decided to go along as far as the first house, to observe, so I grabbed the rope between two students near the tail end.

As I went out the door Toby asked, "Are you going too?"

"I'm just going a little way," I said, then stepped outside where the wind was to our backs blowing at least a hundred miles an hour, maybe more.

I held the rope and leaned backwards hard to keep my footing. I could see only two people in front and back of me.

The children walking beside me were light on their feet and giggling, and I began to wonder why I was doing this stupid thing. I suppose some of the men wondered the same.

When we reached the first house, a sister and brother were unhooked from the rope. One man held open the house door, while another shoved the children inside, then closed the door. I was reminded of school buses in North Carolina, but this was not a school bus. I had seen enough. I said to Jonah Tokienna who was standing near me, "I believe I'll go back now."

"Can you find your way back?"

"Yes," I said as the rope became taut and the procession started moving. I let go of the rope, then watched as the child on the tail of the rope disappeared into the fury. I turned. I took one step and collided broadside against a strange building. Where was I? What had I gotten myself into? What should I do now? There was no rope to hold to. I stopped and stood motionless. I was horrified. But I knew I must not panic. Better not to step at all than to take a wrong step. The swirling snow stung my face and lodged in my eyelashes. I decided to stay in touch with this building, to walk alongside and maybe soon determine where I was. I felt my way along the wall with my hands. I walked slowly past a window but there was no light inside.

Where am I and why am I here? I wondered. "I must keep my senses," I told myself. I continued groping along the side of the building and was surprised and somewhat relieved when I found I had reached the front of the village store and the main trail, which led to the school. Now I knew where I was and the direction to the school. But to go there from this point, I realized I could no longer feel my way along a building. I left the storefront and leaned hard against the wind with my head down. I looked only at the trail. I could see nothing except my feet and frozen footprints on the trail that was kept cleared by the driving wind. I concentrated only on that footpath and the direction I thought should lead me back to the school. Soon I reached a hard wind-packed snowbank, which I recognized and crawled across. I glimpsed the front of the church and knew the school was now across one more snowbank, twenty steps away.

After going inside and closing the school door, I dusted off the powdery snow and said to myself, "Whew!" I resolved to never again take such a stupid adventure.

Inside the schoolroom, Toby was sweeping the floor and picking up paper and pencils. "The wind is very strong," I said, while disguising my voice to sound casual.

"Yes," he said. "One time we had a child was blown away—never to be found. If you get blown out on the ice, you can't get back. You just slide. The wind makes the ice out there slick and there's nothing to hold to. Maybe you slide to Siberia or some place."

During that winter the wind blew away three dozen soccer balls. They were last seen heading toward Siberia. Two cases of cotton flags were ripped to shreds. The next year we received a nylon flag. As for soccer balls, I decreed, "No more soccer playing in strong winds."

One morning after another blizzard that lasted throughout the night, this time from the north, the children in the lower grades came into the schoolroom strangely charged, talking loud and fast in Eskimo. The noise continued while they went to their seats so I asked, "What's all this commotion about?"

Frank Oxereok Jr., a first-grader with his eyes open wide as saucers, stood with his hands outstretched and said, "Nanuk, Nanuk! Big, big?" He then pointed outside. "You go see!"

"OK, let's go out and see," I said, since I felt it was useless to try to start school with the class in such a clamor. I proceeded to walk out the front door as every child followed. When we were outside, the children raced past me to a point on the beach just forty feet from the school. Several students pointed along the hard, wind-packed snow at polar bear tracks, while talking in Eskimo and looking at me.

The tracks were each two feet in diameter, four feet apart and pressed an inch into the hard snow with claw prints pointing south.

Toby, obviously aware of the excitement, walked to our location and began a lecture in English to the children, his best foreign language (English) lesson of the year. They listened intently as he spoke, "These are largest polar bear tracks I ever seen. Maybe a big male. The bear went through the village in the storm last night. It walked south with back to the wind. Polar bear always walk with back to wind in strong storms. Some men are now following the tracks."

"Have polar bear ever walked through the village before?" I asked to prod Toby to continue his lesson.

"Yes, only a few times they have walked through the village. But it was only in blizzards."

"They walk through the village **only** in storms?"

"Yes, some animals go walking in storms. Reindeer also go walking when it gets real stormy, but they walk into the wind. Reindeer just lower their heads and walk into the wind. This is different from polar bear. Polar bear walk in storms the other way, with back to the wind."

The children resumed talking excitedly in Eskimo as we walked back to the schoolroom. I noticed my tracks and those of the children were hardly visible, but the polar bear tracks remained on the ice near the school for most of the remainder of that winter.

The wind piles the snow deep on the lee side of the school.

Polar Bear Hunting

After a week of strong, cold northwest winds, Toby said, "Willie Angnaboogok just while ago killed a polar bear and brought it to his house. It's the first polar bear killed this winter, and we have a village custom that the first man who kill a polar bear must cook a pot of meat for a polar bear feast. The village council wants me to ask you if they could have it at the school. Teachers before let them have polar bear feast at the school. Only the men and the boys are allowed to be at the feast."

"What are the activities at the feast?" I asked.

"We just sit around and talk and laugh. The man who killed the polar bear must tell the story about the kill. The man's wife always cooks the meat and brings it to the school, then she leaves. I think you will like to be at the feast. You can taste the meat." He smiled.

"Sure. Anytime," I said. "When do they want to have the feast?"

"They want to have it tonight. Maybe about seven-thirty. Willie's wife is cooking the meat now."

"Do you think Willie would mind if I went to his house to take a picture of the polar bear?"

"I think he will not mind if you take some pictures. You could go see."

I went into my quarters and donned my mukluks, parka, and mittens. I grabbed my camera, flash attachment and some extra flash bulbs. When I stepped out the door I almost bumped into Katie Tokienna as she walked by me fast. She was coming from the direction of Willie's house, cradling a pot of meat under her arm.

The sky was clear and the sun was below a purple horizon in the southwest. A stinging, cold wind was blowing from the north. Eight boys and girls, ages twelve to fourteen, were on the beach beside the school, playing soccer. Their cheeks, chins and noses were bright red. As I began walking the seventy-five yards toward Willie's house, the children stopped playing, and ran to catch me. One asked, "Are you going to take picture of polar bear?"

"Yes."

They joined me. About halfway, we met two young women walking quickly. They carried containers heavy with meat. The news that Willie had killed the first polar bear of the season was obviously well known in the village.

I said, "Hi!"

They smiled and said something in Eskimo, then giggled as they walked by us.

When I reached Willie's outer door, I knocked and a woman's voice inside yelled something in Eskimo. One of the children pointed toward the door and said in halting English, "You go in."

I entered a small room with a low ceiling, then walked past heaps of frost-covered skins, meat and hunting equipment. The children followed as I knocked on the inner door and again heard the woman's voice. I opened the door and stooped to go through the low door. The children followed. Inside, a sudden rush of cold air from the outside met the warm, moist air of the room, raising a fog that suddenly changed to a flurry of snowflakes that settled to the floor. Willie's wife said something harshly to the children, which I easily interpreted as, "*Shut the doors!*" The children promptly shut both doors, then found places to stand inside the small room. She looked at me laughing and said, "Lots of visitors!"

The room smelled of meat simmering in a two-gallon aluminum pot on the small wood-burning stove. It reminded me of the same smell years ago of beef steaming on my grandmother's stove. I turned to Willie, who was sitting on the edge of a low bunk with his parka off and his face red from the day's hunt in the frigid wind. "I heard you killed the first bear this fall."

He smiled, then pointed to the hide at the foot of his

bed. He said, "I got it twenty miles up the beach."

"Toby said you are going to give a polar bear feast at the school tonight."

"We're cooking some meat now," he said, motioning toward the pot on the stove.

"If you don't mind, I would like to get your picture with the hide."

"I can hold up the part of the head for you," he said then kneeled beside the hide and held it by its ears.

At 7:30, Willie's wife brought a large pot of boiled polar bear meat, perhaps fifteen pounds, to the schoolroom, where approximately twenty men and some boys had already gathered. She sat the pot in the middle of the schoolroom floor and said something to the men in Eskimo, then giggled as she went out the door.

While the men and boys were eating, Lawrence Etukeok said to me, "This is way to eat meat." Using his left hand, he put a large piece of the meat to his mouth, then with the knife in his right hand, he cut off a good-sized bite. "White man cut meat in plate," he said chuckling. "Eskimos cut it this way. You try it."

I accepted his challenge. I took out my pocketknife and, with my left hand, I picked up a two-inch cube of meat. I put the meat to my mouth, then bit into one corner and cut off about three-fourths of it. Fortunately, I didn't cut my mouth. Everyone laughed as I chewed the tough, fishy-tasting piece, which seemed to get larger the longer I chewed. I decided not to try eating the remainder of the piece of meat. As soon as I felt no one was looking, I put it into my left front pocket. The "feast" was nothing more than a get-together with the men sitting around eating and talking in Eskimo, while the boys sat quietly listening.

I asked Toby, "What are they saying?"

"He say he shot the bear up the beach about twenty miles while it was eating on a seal."

The following day during recess, Willie pulled the polar bear hide on a sled to a point on the shore ice about fifty yards in front of the school, where he began chopping a hole in the ice with a steel-tipped pole. Curious, I walked to his location and asked, "Why are you chopping the hole in the ice?"

He smiled as he said, "I put hide under ice."

"Why don't you sell the hide?" I asked, thinking I might buy it if he was going to throw it away, providing the price was reasonable.

He said, "Yes, I will sell it."

"How much do you get for a hide that size?"

"I get six hundred dollars for it, but I have to clean it first. I would spend long time scraping the hide, so I put it under the ice and let the little sea animals clean it for me. It only takes them about a week to clean it and they clean it better than I can."

"But how will you know where the hide is? The ice will just freeze up again."

"I tie this rope through the eye holes, then after a week I chop down beside the rope and pull it out of the water."

At 2:00 one afternoon in late December, Dwight rushed into the classroom and said, "I'm closing the post office. If someone comes, will you tell them I'll be back tomorrow morning? Five polar bears are sighted eating on the dead whale up the beach. We are going up there by dog sleds to get them."

"Could I go along?" I asked, thinking of the excitement and the pictures I could take.

He responded sharply, "No, you should not go. It's too dangerous. Polar bear will attack when they are with food, and sometimes we have to act in an emergency. We will talk fast, only in Eskimo, and you will not understand."

"But I could help work."

"You should not go," he repeated. I was disappointed, for I was ready to get dressed for the cold and tell Virginia to watch the schoolchildren the rest of the day.

Toby didn't go either. After school he said, "When polar bear are eating some food, they are afraid of nothing. They will attack anything and all the shooting must be straight."

"Dwight said they are eating on a dead whale that washed ashore up the beach. When did it wash ashore?"

"It came ashore last spring after it was drowned."

"The whale drowned?"

"Yes, it was drowned trying to go north through the strait. Sometimes the pack ice gets jammed up tight in the strait and the whales trying to get through can't come up for air. The ice is too thick, and they drown. Sometimes we get our whale meat that way, from whale drowning and washing up on the beach. Sometimes the meat is not spoiled and we go get some of it. Polar bears, foxes, and birds get the rest of it."

"Is the meat on this whale any good?" I asked.

"No, this whale was killed last spring. Been dead too long. Good only for the animals to eat. That's how we sometimes get polar bear when they come ashore to eat on the dead whales. But they only come ashore after strong northwest wind in winter has been blowing for many days."

George Ootenna was the oldest, most revered man in the village. He had spent most of his life on the tundra herding reindeer, and if you wanted to get the weather forecast for a week in advance, you asked Mr. Ootenna. He spoke not a word of English and was the village storyteller. When he scheduled storytelling events at the school, nearly every person came to listen to his stories, which sometimes lasted for hours.

I asked Toby, "Would it be all right if I could tape record his stories sometime?"

"I think not!" he said. "He wouldn't like it. Most peoples don't like someone to take their stories and make money from them. They think that is not right to do."

"Then would it be all right for me to tape a session of George's storytelling and give the tape to the village council?" I asked.

He thought briefly, then said, "I think that may be acceptable to do. I will check with village council to see if it is all right to record on tape his stories."

The next day after school while Toby was sweeping the floor, he said, "I asked village council if it is all right for you to record Ootenna's stories and they say it will be all right if you give them the tape. They want to come to the school Friday night to listen to stories."

Storytelling

After school on Friday, Toby and some older boys positioned the desks and chairs against the walls, clearing the floor for the children to sit. Adults sat on desks and chairs, while young people and children sat on the floor. A few stood in the doorways. I think all 128 inhabitants of the village had crowded into the schoolroom and waited in silence for the stories to begin.

I placed the tape recorder on the edge of the stage and plugged in the electrical cord. I opened a box with a new reel, which I snapped into position as "Old Man" George stepped to the front of the room and smiled. I said, "Hi!"

He smiled back and said, "Ee-ee," then laughed. He sat on the edge of the stage and turned and said something in Eskimo to Toby, then he laughed again. Toby turned to me and said, "He said he is ready to start now."

I switched the recorder on, and George began to speak. Except for an occasional whimper of a baby, the room was quiet, as George held the people spellbound. He gestured as he spoke with a voice of a seasoned orator. After an hour and fifteen minutes he stopped talking and looked at me, signifying that he was finished. I think every eye in the room was on me as I stopped the recorder. I lifted the tape and replaced it in the box. I put the box in a manila envelope and sealed it with a piece of tape. I wrote on the envelope the date and "Not to be opened for five years," then presented the envelope to Roland Angnaboogok, chief of the Wales Village Council.

Roland smiled and said, "Ka-ya-nah. We will keep it in the village safe."

A few days after I taped George's stories in the schoolroom, I met him and Roland at the store sitting on butter kegs. I was surprised when Roland smiled and said, "George will tell you a story, and I will interpret."

I quickly said, "Great! I would like to hear it."

Roland spoke in Eskimo to George, who laughed. George spoke in Eskimo for nearly a minute then stopped. Roland said, "Ee-ee," then looked at me and slowly began interpreting: "George says once he was out on the ice hunting. He managed to slip upwind to a polar bear real close to him on ice floe. He says he was going to shoot it but noticed that the bear was looking in the water. So he wanted to see *why* the bear was looking in the water before he shoot it. He says all of a sudden the bear slipped off the ice into the water at the same time a seal came to the surface for air a few yards away. Very soon the bear pulled the seal back under the surface. You know, when a seal has its head above water it cannot see back down in the water, so it couldn't see the polar bear coming. The bear knew to go under the water to catch the seal when the seal is coming up for air."

Roland turned and said something in Eskimo to George, who then spoke for another minute. When "Old Man" George stopped talking, Roland smiled, then turned back to me and continued interpreting: "He says the bear caught the seal and brought it to the top of the ice floe and slammed it down to kill it. You know, polar bear won't eat warm meat. Polar bear always wait for meat to cool before he eats it. So the polar bear went over and lay down on the ice, waiting for seal to cool before he eats it.

"George says he decide to watch the polar bear eat the seal before he shoots it. But then he noticed the bear had raised its head looking upwind and began smelling something. He says he looks in the same direction the bear was looking and saw a wolverine coming toward the bear. You know, polar bear will stay with its food. He will not leave his food. He says he watch the wolverine as it come on the same ice as the polar bear. The polar bear got up on his feet and the wolverine began walking around and around the bear. The bear kept looking at the wolverine while it was walking around and around. He says pretty soon the wolverine jumped on the polar bear's neck and held on.

The polar bear was leaping and throwing its head around trying to get the wolverine off. Blood began pouring from the polar bear's neck and the wolverine was drinking the blood. Soon the polar bear just went down on the ice, ne-ki! Dead! He says he then just shot the wolverine."

I turned to George and said, "Great story! That was indeed a great story."

Roland said something to George in Eskimo, and George replied, "Ee-ee-ah," which is "yes" in Eskimo. He then spoke some more and laughed.

"What did he say?" I asked Roland.

"He says he brought home a polar bear, a wolverine and a seal, all with just one shot," he replied, smiling.

"Is that true?" I asked. "Did he really do that?"

Roland turned to speak to George who answered briefly. Roland turned to me and said, "He say 'it is true'."

I looked at "Old Man" George, who looked me seriously in the eye and said, "*Ee-ee-ah*," then looked away.

Forty years later, the village of Wales opened a museum with artifacts and exhibits depicting the history of Wales. It is named The George Ootenna Museum.

Communication Difficulties

Toby's job description was purely janitorial, but I believe his main concern was the children and that they receive a good education. Although "teacher's aide" was not in Toby's job description, he was to me "teacher's aide," and I welcomed his advice and help. He often spoke to the group or to an individual child in Eskimo, then explained to me in English what that communication was about. Sometimes he interceded to admonish or instruct an individual or the entire group. And sometimes he interpreted what I had said to the children.

Once, while trying to communicate with little Victor Ongtowasruk, a first grade student, I found myself getting absolutely nowhere. I had asked him a very simple question, which should require only a simple "yes" or "no" answer. But he only stared at me with a frozen expression. I repeated the question gently, in the most concise, broken-English terms I knew, and that I was certain Victor should understand. But, again, I received no reply. Instead, he seemed only to get upset. I was dumbfounded that he didn't respond. I looked at Toby. He was grinning. He said, "He's answering you!"

"What!" I exclaimed, "Victor is *answering* me?"

"Yes, he's answering you," Toby replied, laughing. "He's answering you with his eyes."

"With his eyes?"

"Yes. Us Eskimos sometimes talk with our eyes. We open our eyes a little more to say 'yes' and close them a little to say 'no'." He demonstrated to me, then turned to Victor and said something in Eskimo. Victor smiled! My unspoken response was "*Wow!*" From that day forward I noticed children and adults many times trying to speak to me with their eyes. I tried speaking to them with *my* eyes, but I was usually laughed at when I did. Although I practiced a few times in the mirror, I could not perfect the technique of Eskimo eye talking.

In winter the students seldom asked to "be excused" to use the outside toilets, which, I suspect, was partly due to the cold outside temperatures. Occasionally, however, the smaller children did ask to go to the toilet, in which case they came to me and asked, "May I go pee?" I was shocked at first because, in North Carolina, it was always, "May I be excused?" But I soon became accustomed to *"May I go pee?"* and it never really disturbed me until sixteen-year-old Harriet Tevuk, one of the tutors of the lower-grade students, came to me and shyly asked, "May I go pee?" Then I *was* shocked, but said, "Yes," hoping that her question did not have the same connotation to her as it did to me—that she was speaking to me in my language, not hers. I also felt then, as I felt many times at Wales, how ironic it was that I, as teacher, spoke only one language while my students spoke mine *and* theirs, and, as little Victor with his eyes had taught me, a third language as well.

Since the Eskimos never developed a written language, their communication was almost entirely verbal. Thus the history of past village events was passed down by word of mouth, primarily through their elders, such as George Ootenna, Lawrence Etukeuk or Dwight Tevuk, who were deemed among the wisest, most experienced storytellers. When I asked Toby a question about Wales history he often referred me to one of those three. So when I asked Toby to tell me the story about H. R. Thornton, the first teacher in Wales, he said, "You should ask Lawrence Etukeok. He can tell you better."

Lawrence spoke good enough English and enjoyed trying to teach me Inupiaq. On occasions when I visited Lawrence, he often spoke to me during the first few minutes only in Eskimo. Once he asked, *"Coo-pe-uk oo-ah vene?"* (Do you want a cup of coffee?) while motioning with his hands. I answered in a few Eskimo words I had previously learned, *"Ee-ee ah coo-pe-uk wong-ah."* (Yes, I'll have coffee.)

He laughed and indicated his approval as he said, "This is the way to teach. By speaking Eskimo language is better way to learn it. You teach me English, and I teach you Eskimo."

I said, "Toby said you are the best storyteller in the village. He suggested that you might tell me about the first teacher to come to Wales."

Lawrence looked at the floor, then back up at me with a serious look on his face. He said, "OK, if you want to hear it. I can tell you the story. But it's not a good story." He motioned out his small, east-facing window toward the mountain. "You can see tombstone up there on mountain." He paused. "It happened long time ago—maybe sometime around 1890. They buried him up there. And some of teacher's people brought the tombstone by ship later.

"Well, Thornton was the first teacher who was teaching here in Wales. He brought all his food by ship. He was also a missionary. He would share some of white man's food same as Wales people share their food with each other. You know, we share our food with anyone who wants it. If you want food, all you do is ask and we give it. We never refuse a person food. All winter long, Mr. Thornton and his wife would give some of his food to some of the children. But come spring he was running short of food and maybe he was thinking he wouldn't have enough food to last till ship come again. So he quit giving food away. Then he refused some boys some food.

"Some boys—there were three of them—decide to slip in teacher's house and steal a few of white man's food. But teacher's wife saw the boys steal the few foods.

"Now stealing is a very bad thing among us Eskimos. We don't believe a person should steal. There's no need for anyone to steal because if you need anything, we give it—if we got it.

"When this happened, it was late spring and the boys were afraid they would be reported of their crime to the village council. The boys knew it was very wrong to steal. The boys knew they would be in trouble when the leaders of the village returned to Wales.

"They decide to kill the teacher and his wife so they couldn't report of their stealing food. They set up a whale gun on a tripod out from door of teacher's house. One boy went and knocked on teacher's door. Then he ran. When someone inside touched the doorknob, they fired the whale gun into the door and the bomb killed the teacher. The teacher's wife was not hurt. Some women later found her hiding under a bed and came to stay with her.

"This happened few years before Nome was built. And was when most of the men of the village were on trading trip to other places by skinboat. Some went to Siberia. Some went to Kotzebue. Soon the word got out who killed the teacher, and when the leaders of the village returned from the trading, they were told who did it. Then the village council had a meeting. They decided what should be done. They said, 'the boys should die for what they did.' And they were to be given their choice *how* to die.

"One boy said he would let his uncle shoot him on the mountain at the cemetery. He did it up there.

"The other boys said, 'Since we killed a white man, we will be buried like a white man. We will dig our own graves and be shot.' So they would dig a few inches, then wait for ground to thaw, then dig some more. It took several days to dig it, then they were shot and put in the ground.

"Later in the summer the word got out to the U.S. Marshals what had happened. The marshals came to Wales by ship and anchored offshore. Then a small boat full of men started to come ashore. Everyone in the village saw the boat coming and were afraid what would happen. Someone said, 'It's the marshals!' They ran from the village up and over the mountain. All the village people ran except some old ones and little children.

"When the marshals came ashore, they were told by an old man through an interpreter what had happened.

"The marshals said, 'You should not have killed the boys. We would have taken them to court in Nome and given them fair trial.'

"The old man told the marshals, he said, '*We* gave the boys fair trial!'

"The marshals got back in boat and left, and nothing more was done about it."

I later asked Dwight Tevuk to also tell me the story of the death of the first Wales teacher and received identically, almost word for word, the same story as told by Lawrence.

The only tombstone at Wales bears the inscription of Harrison R. Thornton, 1858--1893.

The Mail and the Killing Flu

It was Saturday morning in late January, the day the mail plane was scheduled to come to Wales. Bad weather had canceled the mail delivery for the last six Saturdays. People were anxious to get mail and the Christmas packages they had ordered more than six weeks before. But today the weather was improving. As soon as it was daylight, I stepped outside to check the wind, ceiling and visibility. Conditions looked good. I went back inside and turned on the radio.

Soon I heard, "Two-Four Wales, Two-Four Wales, this is Alaska-Nome. Do you read? Over." It was Bob Jacobs, the Alaska Airlines mailman and bush pilot. I hurried to the radio and pressed the button on the microphone. "Alaska-Nome, this is KWP Two-Four Wales. I read you loud and clear, Bob. Over."

"Two-Four Wales, this is Alaska-Nome. Morning, Will. I've been trying to get in touch with you. How's your weather up there? Over."

"Nome, Two-Four Wales back. The wind is about twenty-five miles per hour, visibility about ten miles, ceiling about three hundred feet, overcast, except I see a hole in the ceiling up by Hogback Mountain. Over."

"OK, Will. I'm going to load up and try to get up there today. Over."

"Nome, Two-Four Wales. Can you pick up half a carcass of reindeer in Teller for me? Over."

"Wales, Nome. OK, Will. I'll probably get up there in a couple hours. Over."

"Nome. Wales. Roger. Over."

"Nome clear."

"Two-Four Wales clear."

Every home in Wales had a battery radio, and most people heard every word of short-wave communication I made with the outside world. They knew when the mail plane was coming, if there were passengers and, often, what the cargo was. I knew excitement was building in anticipation of the arrival of the plane. I walked into the post office to tell Dwight the mail plane was coming.

"I already heard about it," he said, as he shoved a parcel into a bag, then snapped the lock. He looked up and smiled. "There's lots of mail to go out. I have packages and furs. And peoples also sending lots of letters to relatives."

"Do people have many relatives in other villages?" I asked.

"Yes. When peoples get married, the boy usually goes to live in the village of the girl, and they write and send things. But some of them gets homesick and go back to their old village." He stamped another letter which someone had just passed through the window, then put a package in a mail sack.

"I have noticed ten or fifteen empty houses in Wales," I said. Are these houses deserted because some people got homesick and left the village?"

"That's one reason, but mostly the empty houses are because of the 1918 flu. And the population never increase since that time."

"What was the population of Wales before the flu?"

"Back then, before the 1918 flu, the village population was over 400. But since that time it stay about the same, about 120 or 130." His voice trailed. He tied and snapped locks on two more mail sacks.

"Do you remember the 1918 flu?" I asked.

He looked me in the eye, then said, "Yes, I was twelve at that time. The mail come more often at that time than today because it was always come by dogsled in winter. It come by boat only in summer. But the flu was in spring—I think April. At that time when the mail arrived in the village, the mailman was found dead on the sled. People did not know what killed him. There was a big funeral in the church. I think everyone come to the church and was crowded.

"Later, when someone had opened a letter, it told

about the sickness that was killing peoples in Brevig Mission and Nome and other places. The letter told that peoples were dying everywhere.

"Then people in Wales also started getting sick and was dying. Two men went to Shishmaref to warn Shishmaref people what was happening. The men stopped outside the village, maybe hundred yards. They yelled a message from a distance. They told them about the awful disease that was killing the people in Wales and other places. The men told the Shishmaref people to put up guards around their village and not to let anyone come in the village. One of these men was dead when they got back to Wales. But Shishmaref people never got the flu."

"That was a heroic thing to do," I said.

"Yes, and on Diomede Island they never got the flu either. But here in Wales many people were sick and dying all over the village. Mostly the older people died. In some houses all were sick, even the younger ones. Some of them died too."

"How did you make out during the flu?"

"Someone told me that if you put a wool cloth over your face to breathe through, it was better. I was sick but I breathed through a wool sock over my nose and mouth. It was better.

"At that time all my folks were sick too. I was the only one able to work, and when I went to lake for ice to melt for water— on the way—I noticed that lots of dogs had not been fed. Some of them were loose. I met my cousin. He was sick and crawling. He said all his family were dead. He said he was going to his uncle's house. When I was out at the lake getting the ice I heard louder barking of dogs. On the way back, I saw the dogs were eating my cousin. I saw mostly only just his clothes were left.

"Later, some people started getting better, but over half of Wales population were dead. And they were decaying in the houses. Not enough peoples strong enough to carry out the dead. Then a work crew came from Nome. They dug a mass grave in the sand dunes up the beach and buried all the dead. That's where you see the wooden cross. Finally peoples' life started getting better, but the population of the village never increase since that time."

"That was really bad," I said. "How did your family

come through it?"

"I lost both my parents, one grandmother and one younger brother." He turned to gaze away.

Changing the subject, I said, "The mail plane should be here pretty soon. I ordered a half carcass of reindeer from Johnny Kakayruk at Teller."

"Reindeer is good meat. Everyone likes reindeer," he said. "We used to have a herd of reindeer here at Wales too, but one time about eight years ago the herders all came into the school for the Christmas program of the children. They left the herd and a storm came up while they were in the village. But a storm is when the herders need to stay with the herd. You know, reindeer start moving when a blizzard comes up. That's when the herders should be with the herd because the herd starts walking right into the blizzard. They face the wind and keep walking. After the school program, when the men went back to the herd, they couldn't find them. The reindeer were never located. Some, I think joined with caribou. You find caribou are now mixed with reindeer. And I think some reindeer got caught by wolverines. One wolverine sometimes kill five or six reindeers in one night and drink the blood. Then all you see is a hole in their neck."

Later I was in the office when I heard loud shouting from children outside, "Airpla'ick! Airpla'ick!" Then a small boy opened the office door and shouted, "Airpla'ick!" Suddenly the plane roared over the building, then circled to land in front of the school. I went to the post office to help Dwight and two other men carry the outgoing mail.

The following Monday after school, I sat at my schoolroom desk while Toby swept the floor. He stopped sweeping then looked up and sat on a desk. He said, "We were lucky to get the mail Saturday."

"I agree."

"Sometimes in winter when days are short, we wait for mail long time. But it will be long time before the village of Little Diomede, in the middle of the strait, get their mail."

"When is that?"

"It will be sometime around March when the daylight is longer and the place on the ice is smooth for landing the plane."

Later, I talked by radio to the teacher on Little Diomede. "How do you folks manage to tolerate life there without getting mail for so long a period of time?"

"We're doing just fine," he answered. "If you don't expect mail you really don't miss it. In fact, I'm beginning to enjoy life without mail."

But this day, Toby continued, "When the ice gets smooth and the days get longer, Martin Olsen, Eskimo bush pilot in Nome, will fly out to Little Diomede. He has two planes. Sometimes he charters for Alaska Airlines and will fly over there when it is safer to go and when it is more daylight. He's the only pilot that will fly to Diomede."

"Is that the only way the people of Little Diomede get their mail?" I asked.

"No, sometimes a boat goes over in summer, when the ice is gone."

"Has anyone ever walked across the strait on the ice?"

"Yes, it was long time ago," he said. "I think it was sometime around 1905. It was Kay-a-khat who did it. He was Katie Tokienna's father. He was Eskimo from Siberian village on East Cape. He was married to Katie's mother and was living here in Wales. One time, I think he got homesick and couldn't wait for ice to break up to go by boat to visit his people. He decided to walk over and take the mail. He went with few dogs and pulled a sled. He was out there three days walking, because the ice was drifting north. But he made it. He came back by boat that summer. Katie's father was the last man who walked across. It was last time mail went across on the ice. Ice conditions in the strait are more solid around March and not much movement. Sometimes by last of February it gets pretty solid across."

"Could someone do that today? I mean walk across on the ice?"

"Maybe. But the ice pack is not as thick now as it used to be. Old people say it used to be more solid across. I think back in 1800s people went back and forth across on the ice and took mail and things every winter. There was more ice then. It was more solid. Less moving ice than now. I don't think anyone should try to walk over anymore." He smiled. "I think if you would like to visit Little Diomede, you could go with Martin Olsen when he flies out to take the mail."

"That's a good idea." I said. "I'll ask Martin the next time I see him. I really would like to see the village. Do Little Diomeders ever walk over to Big Diomede, the Russian island?"

"Yes, three years ago three men walked to Big Diomede. I think they went over to visit some relatives. But the Russians held them for six months and wouldn't let them go home. Then they finally let them go. You can't go over to Russia!"

One week later, Martin was in the village and I asked him if sometime he might stop on his way to Diomede and take me along. He said he would but that it would probably be April before he would go.

Curious to hear more of the 1905 "walk across the strait" by Katie Tokienna's father, I went to her house, where I found her plying an ulu to a seal. Sixty-year-old Katie was energetic for her age and taller than most Inuit women. She was proud of her Siberian Eskimo heritage and didn't mind telling you how things ought to be. I mentioned to Katie that Toby said her father was the last man to walk across the strait. She smiled and said, "Yes, I was small then, but I remember when he done it. He was a strong man, my father. We were all proud of him. He took the mail with him and came back by boat when the ice went away."

View across the Bering Strait from the cross at the mass grave site.

Let the Dance Begin

My duty to deliver messages I received by radio and dispense medications from the medicine cabinet as prescribed by the BIA doctor in Kotzebue gave me an excuse to walk around the village and visit in the homes. I enjoyed these responsibilities and that's how I often spent my after-school hours. It helped me relieve tensions from long days of confinement in the classroom.

Early that first winter, as the days became shorter and the air temperature colder, I noticed less and less outside activity by adults in the village. I saw only an occasional man returning from a hunt, feeding his sled dogs, or bringing in ice or snow to melt for water.

At night the men were usually in the corner of their combination kitchen, dining and living room, at a small table that served as a shop bench where they carved ivory into trinkets, bracelets or watchbands. They sawed the ivory in a vise with a hack saw, then shaped it with a file or drill, smoothed it with sandpaper, polished it with metal polish, scratched images of animals into the surface and filled the scratches with India ink.

Aside from the regular household work of preparing food, the women were usually knitting or sewing. They made socks and gloves from balls of yarn and sewed pants, parkas, mukluks and mittens from furs or skins, using sinew they had stripped from legs of reindeer and twisted into thread. They crimped oogruk hides with their teeth to form the toes and heels for the soles of mukluks. They decorated the cuffs and hems of parkas and the tops of mukluks with intricate patterns of glass beads or checkered designs of black and white fur or cowhide. Most of the parkas and mukluks and all of the ivory carvings were shipped to Nome, Juneau or Anchorage for sale in clothing stores and craft shops.

To me, it seemed that most of the adults did nothing but work. Toby noticed this also. He said, "The people need to do other things. Not just work. They need some recreation. Teachers before always let us use the school for some recreation in winter. It is better for people to get out of their houses, not to stay in the small houses all the time."

"What kind of recreation?"

"It was usually dances. The village council would like for the village to have dances. And teachers before allowed us to have dances in the school."

"When do they want to have the dances?"

"Well, I think Saturday nights would be the best time to have the dances. That's when the village usually had them."

"That's fine with me. How often do they want the dances? Saturday nights?"

"Well, yes, I think every Saturday night in the winter. That's so people can get out of their houses more and get exercise. Besides, the people like it. The older ones like Eskimo dancing. Some of the younger ones like square dancing. The square dancing was taught them by some former teachers. It was taught mostly at school time. The school has square dance record player and records. Sometimes you might have square dance also."

After school on Wednesday of the first week in November, while Toby was sweeping the schoolroom floor, he said, "The village council say they would like to start the dances."

"Saturday night?"

"Yes, I think it would be good to have dance Saturday night. I will ask village council."

The next morning he said, "I mentioned to Angnaboogok about having dance Saturday night. He said it was OK." The following Friday afternoon, just as I was about to dismiss the students for the day, Toby came into the room and spoke to the students in Eskimo, then turned to me and said, "I have asked some of the older boys to help move the desks to make the schoolroom ready for the dance."

When school was out, six boys helped Toby move the

desks and chairs against the wall. They moved two tables to the other room. Thus, the middle of the room was cleared of all furniture. After Toby finished sweeping and mopping the floor, he smiled broadly and announced, "We are now ready for big Eskimo dance."

At 6:30 the following night, young and old arrived at the school. No small children came. The atmosphere was festive and exciting in anticipation of the activities that were about to happen. I noticed some of the women admiring each other's fur parkas and the dangling strips of beaver or wolverine fur. Several wore parkas that appeared to have been ordered from Sears. Many wore mukluks that looked new.

Peter Ibianna, the only bald-headed Eskimo in the village and perhaps the only completely bald-headed person on the Seward Peninsula, arrived early. He carried a large sack from which he emptied six drums and some wooden sticks onto the stage. The sticks, about two feet long, had been whittled from driftwood. Each drum, about eighteen inches in diameter and also fashioned of wood, was in the shape of a frying pan with a six-inch handle. The translucent skin of walrus stomach was stretched over the frame and attached with a rawhide string.

Peter spent the first few minutes moistening the drums with water and making adjustments to the rawhide strings. Then he sat on the edge of the stage with his feet dangling and held a drum by the handle with the skin on top. He began tapping lightly underneath the frame with a stick. Four other men picked up drums and sticks, joined him on the edge of the stage, and began lightly tapping their sticks on the drums.

Soon Peter began singing slowly and softly in Eskimo to the beat of the drums. The other drummers followed his singing and drumming. The words of the song were interspersed with an occasional loud shout, while seven or eight women and men stepped onto the floor and began stomping their feet and waving and jerking their arms and heads to the beat of the drums. As the dance progressed, the singing and drumming became louder and the dancing faster. After a few minutes the drumming and singing abruptly stopped. Then the dancers moved off the floor to catch their breath, laughing and talking in Eskimo. Soon Peter again began tapping lightly on his drum and singing another song. The other drummers followed his lead and other dancers stepped onto the floor. Each dancer had a different style and each song had a different beat.

After Toby finished one of his dances I asked, "What are the songs about?"

"Well, the songs mostly tell a story," he said. "Some songs are about animals. Some are about hunting and everything. The movements of the dancers are to tell the story of the song."

I noticed one song had the word "*coo-pe-uk*" and asked, "Does that song have something to do with coffee?"

"Yes," he said, smiling. "*Coo-pe-uk* is Eskimo word for coffee. It's about long ago when ship did not come and bring coffee for trade and people did not have coffee for long time."

I tried a couple of the dances and was good-naturedly praised by several adults but laughed at by some of my students. I felt I was making a fool of myself, so I gave up trying to dance.

The spirited drumming and lively, creative dancing lasted until late at night and was an appropriate ending to each week in the darkness of the long winter months.

A week before Thanksgiving, Toby said, "The village like to have feast at Thanksgiving. Teachers always let us use the school for Thanksgiving feast. and everyone always come to the feast."

"You want to have the feast on Thanksgiving Day?" I asked.

"Yes, Angnaboogok, chief of village council, already said it would be good to have the feast on Thanksgiving Day."

"What do they do at the feast?"

"They bring foods. All kinds of delicacies, and Eskimo ice cream. You will like the Eskimo ice cream. It's a mixture of berries, seal oil and snow."

When feast day arrived, the people again came to the schoolhouse wearing new dresses, parkas and mukluks. It seemed that the entire population of the village was in the school. Some sat in chairs and many sat on the floor, which Toby had made especially clean the previous afternoon.

I said to Toby, "It looks like perfect attendance at school today."

"Yes," he said. "I think everyone come, except Clarence's mother. She was sick and can't come."

The women spread foodstuffs on paper towels on desks, tables and the floor. From the school kitchen, they got small bowls in which they placed different foods as well as Eskimo ice cream.

I said to Toby, "Looks like they brought plenty of Eskimo ice cream."

"Yes," he said, then turned to his wife, Martha, and said something in Eskimo. She responded. He turned back to me and said, "Martha made some Eskimo ice cream for you. It has not much seal oil in it. You will like it."

Martha smiled, then handed me a spoon and a bowl of Eskimo ice cream. She spoke very little English but said, "Maybe you like."

Although I spoke no Eskimo, I said, "*Ka-ya-nah.* But I would like to taste some real Eskimo ice cream." I pointed to her bowl. She giggled.

She took my spoon, then dipped a small portion from her bowl and handed it to me. She said, "OK, you taste."

I found the mixture tasted more like cod liver oil than berries, but I managed to swallow and forced a smile.

"Umm, not bad," I said. Martha laughed. I proceeded to cut the aftertaste by eating from the bowl she gave me. The tartness of the berries, without the seal oil, was more suitable to my taste.

I noticed the schoolroom was quieter this day than any day since school had started. Everyone sat around eating and smiling. A few men talked in low tones while the women appeared only to be eyeing the costumes of others. Only a few hushed words were spoken by young people. If a small child made a whimper, a mother's soft voice stopped that. Even the school children were quiet. Wow!

After eating, speeches were made by some of the councilmen as well as "Old Man" George Ootenna, who received the complete undivided attention of everyone, including the little children. Without a doubt, he was a remarkable speaker in his language.

One week before Christmas, Toby said, "We usually have our winter games around Christmas."

"Winter games? What kind?"

"We have all kinds of outdoor jumping, running and racing. It's good to have outdoor contests in middle of winter when it gets cold and dark. That's when some people want to stay in houses, so the games help them to be outside . We have contests for the different age groups of men, women, boys and girls. And we also have the annual sled dog race at the same time."

Because of the cold and the darkness, and because I did not receive a schedule of events, I only managed to enter the five-mile run for the men. Toby had said, "The race starts at the school at 11:00 a.m. It goes north along the beach to a 55-gallon oil drum and back." When I stepped outside to go to the race, the temperature on the wall thermometer outside the door registered thirty-nine below! The sky was clear and the sun was below a purple horizon to the south. A breeze from the north drifted snow by my feet, but I felt I was ready to go. I wore my new eiderdown parka with a wolf ruff that Nora Ahwinona had attached the day before. I wore my new sealskin mukluks with rabbit fur socks over wool socks and cotton socks next to my feet. On my hands I wore wool gloves inside wolf head mittens that were tied together with a loop around my neck, so that if they came off my hands they would not get blown away. I wore insulated long underwear and two pairs of loose-fitting pants. I felt I was adequately dressed for the cold.

Although I was a smoker at the time, I had been walking a lot and doing some running to prepare myself for this race. As I walked to the starting line, I remembered that the last time I ran five miles was in high school track.

I joined about twelve men of varying ages. I turned to Joshua Ahwinona, who was twice my age, and said, "Maybe we won't freeze our lungs."

He laughed and said, "You won't freeze your lungs. You will just get hot. Even when cold air goes in your hot body it just gets warm. You will even want to pull off your coat if you run hard."

My confidence increased a bit.

Suddenly, the chief of the village council fired a pistol into the air and off we went. Several men passed me. I only jogged, as did some of the others. I kept a steady pace and, sure enough, shortly, I began heating up. At the two-mile point I was perspiring profusely. I pushed the hood off my head. I noticed some of the other runners had done the same. Then I put my hood back on, then back off again. There seemed to be more fog coming off my head and out of my mouth than the others, but I kept running.

Before I reached the halfway point, I met most of the runners coming back, including Joshua. After the turn around I saw he was nearly out of sight! The wind was to my back and I really got hot, even with my hood down. I unzipped my parka and noticed heavy fog was drifting off my shirt. But I kept jogging to the finish line. I came in last! A few weeks after that run, I quit smoking.

Twenty Below in the Bedroom

In the Bering Strait, the average daily wind velocity is twenty-one miles an hour. It blows almost continuously, either from the north or from the south, and usually lasts for days, sometimes weeks, blowing in the same direction. It rarely blows from the east or west. No one ever asks "Is the wind blowing?" The only questions asked are, "Which direction is it blowing?" and "How *strong* is it blowing today?" Only rarely during our two years at Wales, was the wind calm so that the flag on our flagpole was limp. When the wind stops blowing, it's usually for a brief few hours or for the purpose of changing directions. On occasions when it stops blowing, everyone in the village wonders which direction, north or south, the wind will blow next. That is, except "Old Man" George Ootenna, who had the uncanny ability to forecast the weather for five days in advance.

In summer, driving rain is usually mixed with salty spray off whitecaps on the sea. In winter, the north wind often brings temperatures as low as fifty below while the south wind is warmer and brings blizzards with wet snow.

One day after school Toby told me about an emergency I might have resulting from a bitterly cold, north wind in winter. He said, "Sometimes when the north wind is blowing hard, it might cause the oil for stoves to freeze up in the school and your quarters."

"You mean our oil freeze up?" I asked. I was picking up some broken English, which I sometimes find myself continuing to use, forty years later.

"Yes," he replied. "When it gets real cold and the wind is strong from the north, the oil sometimes cannot flow through the oil lines from the tanks. The oil gets too thick. When that happens, all the stoves in the building will go out. The stoves in the school and your quarters will get cold. It usually happens at night when it is real cold and the wind is strong."

"What do we do when that happens?" I asked.

"All stoves have tanks for oil on the back of them. What I do is bring oil inside the building to put in the stove tanks. First I close the valves on the supply lines coming from the tanks in the oil storage house and connect the lines from the tanks on the back of the stoves. I keep a bucket and shovel out in the storage building. If the oil freeze up on weekend or when I'm not at the school, you can go out to the oil storage building and open the lid on top of tank and get some oil with the shovel."

Later in January, I noticed the north wind had been blowing for over a week. The outside temperature was steadily dropping. One night as we went to bed upstairs, the wind whistled and moaned around the eaves of the building as Virginia tucked Tommy into the crib beside our bed. She then crawled into bed with me. She commented, "The wind outside is blowing hard but the sled dogs are not howling like they usually do when the wind is blowing hard."

"Maybe it's too cold out there tonight. Perhaps they just lay down and curl up and let snow drift over them to stay warm." I thought of the advice Toby had given me earlier. He had said, "Never walk close to where dogs are tied. They may be underneath snow so you can't see them and they might attack if you step on one. People have been attacked that way by dogs before."

At two o'clock the following morning, I woke up cold as Tommy was climbing into the bed between us. Virginia complained, "It's cold in here."

I crawled out of bed in my long underwear. The floor under my bare feet felt like ice. I grabbed my flashlight and focused the light on the wall thermometer. The mercury in the glass was near the bottom! I sensed that the worst had happened. "I'm afraid our oil has frozen up," I announced. "It's twenty below in here!"

"Could you go get Toby?" Virginia's voice trembled.

"No, I wouldn't want to bother him this time of night. I'll go out to the tanks to bring in some oil for the stoves."

I quickly slipped into wool pants, fur socks, mukluks, parka, wool gloves and fur mittens, then announced, "I'm ready. I'm going out now."

"But we're cold!" she whined. "We need more covers."

I picked up the five-by-seven-foot, three-inch-thick reindeer rug that was on the floor beside our bed and placed it on top of the covers and said, "This ought to help."

I went downstairs without my flashlight since enough starlight was reflected through the windows from the outside whiteness. I exited the building through the shop door, which the north wind usually kept clear of drifting snow. Outside, I felt the excruciating cold as blowing snow stung my face. My mukluks screeched with each step. It seemed to me to be about as cold as it could get. If the temperature inside the house was twenty below, it was no less than fifty below outside, and the gale force wind made the chill factor feel at least a hundred below.

I opened the door to the oil storage building and saw everything inside was frosty white. I found the shovel and the five-gallon bucket. I tried to open the lid to the oil tank but couldn't turn the latch with my mittens on. I slipped them off and opened the lid, but my hands went instantly numb. They had no feeling. "Gosh," I thought, "I've got to get the oil, and I must not panic." I put my hands back inside my mittens. They stayed numb. I barely could hold the shovel but managed to push the blade of the shovel into the oil. It looked like sand. Black sand! I hurriedly put three heaping shovelsful into my bucket, then closed the lid. I left the oil storage building. I leaned hard against the wind on my way back to the house. When I stepped inside, I closed the door, then glanced into the bucket. I was amazed to see the bucket of "black sand" change instantly to oil!

With my hands warming but starting to ache, I closed the valves then disconnected the lines from the storage building to both the kitchen and bedroom stoves. I then connected the lines from the small tanks on the back of each stove and poured half the oil into each one. I opened the valves to let oil flow into the fireboxes then lit the oil with lighted pieces of paper. When I crawled back into bed, Virginia was shivering as she asked, "What did you do?"

"I got the stoves going," I answered, then snuggled into the bed under the covers against her and Tommy. Sometime later I fell back to sleep.

By morning our quarters had warmed. I walked into the schoolroom, where the stoves felt like ice and the wall thermometer registered twenty-two below! When children began arriving, I sent them home, "No school today! No heat."

When Toby arrived at a quarter till eight, I told him what had happened and that I was sending the children home. He said nothing. I walked back into our quarters and sat down at the kitchen table with a cup of coffee, thinking "This is a good day for vacation."

Ten minutes later, a smiling Toby walked into our kitchen and said, "I have all the stoves going now."

I almost spilled my coffee. "You have the stoves going? How?" How could he possibly put oil in five stoves and light them so quickly?

"I just put some gas with the oil and got it flowing again."

"You put *gasoline* in the oil tank!" I was stunned. "But Toby," I said. "We get memos from Washington and from the office in Juneau warning us to never mix gasoline with oil. They say we must never, but *never*, mix gasoline with the oil. They say it is too dangerous!"

"Yes, they always say that. But we always thin the oil with some gas and we never have trouble with it." We didn't.

Tragedy Strikes

I got up early on the first Saturday in February, our scheduled mail day. Three weeks had passed since we last received mail. I noticed the north wind had stopped blowing and the skies were clearing. Perhaps the mail plane would come today. I tuned my radio to the Alaska Airlines frequency in Nome in case the mailman might call for a weather report. I stepped outside, and noticed the weather was warming and our flag on the flagpole indicated only a slight breeze from the south. I then walked into the post office, where Dwight was canceling some letters.

He laughed and said, "The weather is pretty good right now, but the south wind is already starting to blow."

Twenty minutes later, I went outside again and noticed the flag was standing straight out, pointing north and flapping. I estimated the wind speed was now a stiff thirty miles per hour, with gusts perhaps to fourty.

"KWP Two-Four Wales, KWP Two-Four Wales, this is Nome. Do you read me? Over." The distinct and clear voice of Bob Jacobs, our mailman, was calling.

I quickly grabbed the transmitter mike, "Nome, this is Two-Four Wales. Over."

"Two-Four Wales, Alaska-Nome. How's your weather, Will?"

"Alaska-Nome, Two-Four Wales. Bob, our ceiling and visibility is unlimited. The wind speed is about thirty, but it's increasing. Over."

"Two-Four Wales, Nome back. Yeah, we're getting the same winds here in Nome, but visibility is good. I think we'll head up your way. Another plane will be coming with me. We have a lot of freight for your school and the village.

You'll need to meet us to sign for the freight. We'll be leaving here in about thirty minutes. Over."

"Roger, Bob. Two-Four Wales clear," I said, trying not to sound excessively elated. I heard him click his mike in acknowledgment, then I stepped outside again to look at the flag. It was now flapping and popping. I judged the wind speed at more than fifty miles an hour! I went back inside.

Soon I heard the pilots talking to each other, as they were headed our way. Bob was giving instructions to a rookie pilot, Larry. I soon learned from their conversation that Larry was flying to the strait for the first time. Bob was telling him about the terrain and conditions along the way.

I turned up the volume on my receiver, then walked through the schoolroom to the post office and reported to Dwight. "Two mail planes are now on their way. They must have lots of mail and some freight."

"Yes, I heard it on my battery radio. But the wind is picking up." He then motioned toward my office. "I hear Bob calling you again."

As I walked toward the radio, I heard Bob say, "Two-four Wales, if you hear me, Will, we'll be landing there pretty soon. We have a pretty good tailwind. I have some school freight for you to sign."

I stepped outside and estimated the wind speed had increased to about seventy miles per hour. Even though the visibility remained good, I wondered how these planes could land in such winds. Many village people had obviously been listening to the conversations on their battery radios and were also out to watch the landings. Someone pointed to the south. A boy yelled, *"Air-pla-uk, air-pla'-uk!"* The planes appeared fast into view around the point of the mountain and flew by the village in a flash, then made a 360-degree turn to land facing the wind. They dropped gently straight down onto the ice, landing a half mile north of the school and a quarter mile out from the beach.

We began walking toward the plane, which was not easy as the wind was hard to our backs. When I stepped onto the ice, I immediately fell and slid. I got to my feet, but found walking — that is picking my feet up and setting them down — on the glassy, slick shore ice was out of the question. I noticed Dwight and the other men were standing with their legs straight. In other words, they were skating. Or rather, I should say, *sailing,* as they were being pushed by the wind across the ice like sailboats on water. There was no doubt that this condition was not new to them. So I followed their example as I watched them tack left by extending their right arms and tack right by extending their left arms. In like manner, I managed to steer to meet the planes, then sat on my haunches to finally slide to a stop.

Both pilots remained at the controls to keep their engines revved at near flight speed to hold the planes on the ice as the wind was not decreasing. I opened the door of Larry's plane as it vibrated back and forth on the ice. I stooped and walked to the cockpit to sign for some freight.

"I don't see how we can take off in this wind," he said, his voice trembling, while he gripped the controls so tightly the knuckles of his hands were white. He was in a state of fright, and I really knew nothing I could say would calm him except, "There's nothing to worry about. When you take off, the plane will just go nearly straight up." I quickly signed for the freight, then left his plane, as some of the men unloaded the freight and held it with their hands and between their legs to keep it from being blown away. I entered Bob's plane to sign for more freight. I stepped to his cockpit and said, "That new pilot is afraid to take off in this wind."

"He'd better take off if he wants to keep his job. I've already told him how to do it," he said in firm voice, while also concentrating on keeping his plane on the ground.

After the freight was off the planes, we moved a short distance away, then turned and watched the planes take off. They rose vertically like sea gulls and gained altitude, but made no progress toward Nome. If anything, they drifted backwards!

I picked up a bag of mail and began walking with the other men toward the school. I fell and slid a few feet, then got back on my feet.

Dwight saw me fall and said with words muffled in the wind, "We can't walk toward the school. The ice is too slick. We need to go this direction to get ashore where we can walk." He pointed toward the shore about a quarter mile northeast of the village.

As we struggled toward the shore, I saw the planes were

making no progress toward Nome. They only gained altitude till they became but specks high above.

When we arrived back at the school, Dwight pointed above Cape Mountain and said, "Just now, you see the planes going over the mountain." I looked up and saw the tiny dots go out of sight over the mountain toward Nome.

Later that day I talked to Bob. He said, "It only took us forty-five minutes to fly to Wales but we were two and a half hours getting back to Nome."

The following Saturday, Bob and Larry were again flying out to the cape. This time, only Bob was to bring the Wales mail. Larry was carrying six young Air Force boys to the DEW Line site at Tin City, where a contingent of forty men maintained the radar dome on top of 2,000-foot Cape Prince of Wales Mountain.

The landing strip at Tin City is on top of a sheer cliff, the south end of which drops six hundred feet to the ice below. When the wind is from the north it plunges off the south end of the landing strip like water off Niagara Falls. That day we were having a steady twenty-knot north wind, but the weather was clear.

I listened to the two pilots talking to each other as they approached the cape. Bob was again giving instructions to Larry, which he repeated more than once, "You've got to come in high to the strip at Tin City with this north wind. There's always a downdraft off the runway there when the wind is from this direction. Stay high on your approach, then when you get over the end of the runway, you can let down. Approach it high!"

Minutes later, I was in another room and heard Bob continue to give instructions. Soon he buzzed the school then landed and taxied to within a hundred feet of the school. When I arrived at the plane, Bob came to the door. His eyes seemed twice as big as normal and his face was pale. His voice quivered as he tried to speak. He sat on the floor in the doorway with his feet dangling and put his hand to his forehead as if he felt faint. I was thunder-struck! He said, "Boy! Will, I just saw the worst sight I have ever seen in my life! Larry just now crashed off the runway at Tin City with six Air Force boys."

"What?"

"He came in to the runway too low, got in the downdraft, and hit the cliff. Head on! The plane burst into flames and fell down on the ice. They were all killed. No one could survive that. It was awful!"

During our stay at Wales, four more white men would lose their lives due to the wind or the current in the strait, but not a single native.

The Seal Hunt

As frigid temperatures in the Arctic expand the ice pack and the north wind drives it southward through the strait, a band of shore ice is created along the Bering and Arctic coastlines, up to six feet thick and in most places miles wide. At Wales, however, the shore ice is narrow and open water that is suitable for hunting seals may be found within walking distance of the village, especially during a period of offshore breezes. Such was the case in February. In almost every house I visited frozen seals lay around the living room to thaw before they could be butchered. Sometimes a child used a seal for a seat.

After school one day I commented to Toby, "I notice the hunters are getting lots of seals now."

"Yes, February is very good month for seal hunting when you have offshore wind. Right now we have wind off shore and it makes some open water. The wind keeps the big ice pack out from the shore ice, maybe a hundred yards, maybe more. The men stand on the edge and get seals."

"How do they retrieve them from the water when they shoot them?" I asked.

"We have a wooden float with hooks on it. It has a line on it. We just throw it out into the water over the seal and hook it and pull it in. We also have kayak or small umiak if the seal is too far out to throw the hook. Then we paddle in boat to get it."

"Could I go with you sometime when you go out there to hunt?"

"Yes, if you like," he said, "but if you go, you should have Eskimo clothing. When we are out there on edge of ice, we just stand there all day and wait for seal to come up for air, and it is very, very cold. All Eskimos have parka to pull over. We don't have buttons or zippers for wind to go through. We have sealskin pants and everything, all waterproof."

"Waterproof?"

"Yes, the women sew everything waterproof. We also have a drawstring, and the women tie it around our wrists, around our waists and around here." He pointed around his face. "If we fall in the water, our clothes will turn to ice, but we don't get wet except on our face. We won't freeze."

"I don't have sealskin pants, only mukluks, and an Eddie Bauer eiderdown parka, the best they make," I said. "It has a zipper up the front with overlapping flaps and buttons. I also have that wolf ruff around my hood that Nora sewed on."

"Wolverine ruff is much better than wolf ruff," he responded. "Wolverine fur keeps your face warm, but I think you can go out. If you get cold, you can just come back. But you should wear several pairs of pants and some wool if you got it."

The following Saturday, Toby came to our quarters and said, "We can go out to hunt seals today. I see there is open water out there, and there's not much wind. You can see fog rising out there." He pointed southwest. About a mile from the village, a flume of pale steam was rising from the strait. "Oxereok has small umiak out there. We can use it."

I dressed as warmly as I could, grabbed my gun and camera and stepped outside, where the temperature registered thirty-five below. The sun was shining through the steam that indicated open water at the edge of the shore ice. A gentle five-to ten-mile-per-hour breeze was drifting the steam toward the southwest.

We walked to the edge of the shore ice, which was indicated by large ice blocks in haphazard piles blown there by onshore winds. Open water appeared beyond smooth young ice about fifty yards farther out. Toby retrieved Oxereok's tiny canvas boat, which he began dragging onto young ice that had recently formed. I followed. Toby said, "The young ice is sticking to the shore ice. We go farther out to open water and keep the boat with us in case the young ice breaks off from the shore ice and drifts out."

When we reached open water at the edge of the young

ice, the pack ice, a thick jumbled mass, was a couple of hundred yards farther out in the strait, moving slowly toward the north. The water between us and the pack ice was glassy, with undulating swells and an occasional soft sloshing sound at the interface of ice and water. Pods of frost crystals were forming on the surface of the water for ten yards out from where we stood.

"Is that water freezing? I asked.

"Yes, it is freezing," Toby answered, "and we can soon walk on it."

Sure enough, ten minutes later he said, "Now it is solid enough and we can walk on it. The young ice keeps growing and we keep going farther out on new ice every fifteen or twenty minutes. The seals will come up for air only where there is water. We stay near the water." He then stepped onto the new ice, which bent slightly under his feet as he dragged the boat. I followed behind him as we again walked to the edge of the water.

He said, "We must keep the boat with us because sometimes, when we start home, we find that the wind has moved the ice we stand on and we are drifting out. We then have nothing but open water between us and the shore. This has happened before. Sometimes Eskimos come out with dogs and sled and have no boat with them. And when they finish hunting and start home, they find the ice they are on is drifted out. So they are drifted out on the ice, and this is bad. They have nothing but open water between them and the shore ice. Then they can't come home. When this happens they just have to wait for the wind to change and blow them back to shore. They sometimes wait for days and have only seal to eat and snow for water. They can only curl up at night to sleep with their dogs. This has happened."

Young ice continued freezing and we continued to move farther into the strait to hunt. Occasionally a seal surfaced for air, but too far away to shoot.

Toby said, "Old people always say that long ago, before Eskimo had guns, the seals were not afraid of people. They would come up nearby and you could just harpoon them from kayak. Now the seals know about guns, and they stay farther away."

One seal, however, did come to the surface for air about

fifty feet away. Toby shot it, then tossed a five-inch wooden ball with protruding steel hooks attached to a seventy foot nylon cord and snagged the seal on the first try. He pulled it to the edge of the ice, where he placed his boat then stepped into it and lifted the seal onto solid ice. He tied a rope around the seal's nose as steam rose from its carcass. He slung the other end over his shoulder and smiled as he said, "Now we should go home. You can bring the boat to where we got it." I was relieved to be going home after standing on the ice for the past two hours in forty-below temperatures.

I began dragging the boat and turned my head to the side as the wind was no longer to our backs. We were now facing the wind, which stung my face and forehead. It was much stronger than when we came, and the sun had sunk below a purple horizon in the southwest. We walked past the point on the young ice where we first began hunting. It was now seventy-five yards from open water. I was thankful the young ice hadn't drifted out to sea while we were on it because I questioned whether the small boat could have held us both.

When we returned to the point where we found the boat, Toby turned it upside down and tied the rope to a stake in the ice. He said, "This is to keep wind from blowing boat away."

As I walked toward home, the wind nearer the land

was stronger and my chin was getting cold. I thought it might be starting to freeze. I stopped walking and turned my back to the wind. I laid my gun and camera down and tried to tuck the wolf ruff under my chin and fasten a flap over it. I found I could not do this with my mittens on, so I slipped them off my gloves, but my fingers instantly lost feeling. I thought, "Will I ever learn that the only clothing fit for this place is what the Eskimos and the animals wear— fur clothing without zippers, buttons or flaps?" I gave up trying to adjust my parka and put my numb hands back inside my mittens. I picked up my gun and camera and resumed walking in misery.

By this time, I noticed Toby was dragging the seal far ahead. I walked faster. I ran a while. I walked backwards. I ran some more. Finally, I arrived inside the warmth of home where Virginia met me. She said, "Look at yourself in the mirror."

"What's wrong?" I asked.

"Your chin is white!" she said. I looked and saw my chin was not a pretty sight. (It later turned black and peeled off.) My fingers ached and throbbed intensely.

The next morning, Sunday, I stepped outside the front entrance of the apartment and noticed that the offshore wind had stopped blowing. The temperature had warmed considerably. I heard noises like loud squeals and thunder coming from the strait. What was that? Just then, Pete Sereadlook came walking by, going to church.

I pointed into the strait and asked, "What's that noise out there?"

He stopped and said, "The pack ice is hitting against the young ice. You could go out and watch if you like."

"Would it be safe out there?"

"It will be safe. It's the pack ice coming toward the shore that's making the noise. It is crushing the young ice. If you go out, you can stay on the shore ice. It will stay solid but don't get too close to the moving ice." He smiled and walked on.

I walked to the edge of the shore ice, where I stood and watched the pack ice pulverizing the young ice where Toby and I had hunted the day before. Like a monstrous bulldozer, with a blade miles wide, it came steadily toward me, pushing before it a ten-foot-high mound of broken blocks of the young ice up to two feet thick.

I stepped backward when the pack ice reached the shore ice, as louder squeals and thunder were coming from deep in the water and from all along the pressure ridge. I wondered if that's where the movement would stop and what would happen next. I moved further back as blocks of the oldest, and thickest, of the young ice rose upward and slid toward me on top of the shore ice. But the pack ice, with blocks the size of houses, came no farther. It only screeched and groaned as it rubbed against the shore ice and began moving northward at the speed of a lazy stroll.

Seal thawing in house.

The Doctor Calls

The first childbirth in the village during our first year at Wales was without incident. On that occasion, Virginia woke me in the middle of the night, saying, "Somebody's banging on our front door downstairs."

"I'll get up and go see," I said. "Maybe it's the midwives and they want the baby box." I heard more loud pounding on the door as I was dressing. When I opened the front door, I found a half-smiling husband, who said in halting English, "Midwives want baby."

I knew what he meant and pointed to the baby box in the corner. He picked up the box, cradled it under his right arm, said, "Thank you," then left quickly.

The next morning, Toby announced that a new baby had been born in the village. That afternoon the midwives brought the baby box back to my office and replenished it with sanitary and medical supplies they would need for the next delivery.

Two months later, on a Friday around noon, Toby came into the classroom and said, "The midwives came for the baby box. I gave it for them. Dorothy Tevuk is now starting to have labor."

Soon after I turned school out, one of the midwives came into my office. She had a worried look on her face as she said, "It is pain. Doctor, you talk."

"Maybe Toby interpret," I said.

"*Ee-ee*," she said, then hurried past me into the schoolroom to get him.

I turned on the radio. The doctor was talking to someone in another village but was soon finished. I pressed the button on my mike and called, "KWG Four-Nine

Kotzebue, this is Two-Four Wales. Over."

"Go ahead, Wales," the doctor answered.

"We have a nineteen-year-old woman trying to give birth to her first child and she's having some kind of trouble. One of the midwives is standing here. Stand by while I get some more information."

I turned and made eye contact with the midwife, who spoke rapidly and frantically for about twenty seconds to Toby in Eskimo. When she finished, Toby turned to me and said, "Well, she say it is very serious and she don't know what to do."

I pressed the mike button and said, "Doctor, the midwives say something is seriously wrong and they don't know what to do. Over."

He asked, "How's your weather out there? Can we get a plane out to pick her up?"

"Our weather is bad. Light snow. Visibility, less than a quarter of a mile."

"In that case, you'll have to do the best you can with her out there till the weather opens up and we can get a plane to go out and pick her up." He then asked for a more detailed description of Dorothy's problem, which Toby relayed to me from the midwife. The doctor, in turn, gave suggestions for the midwives to follow. Toby heard the doctor's advice, then interpreted it to the midwife, who said, "*Ka ya nah,*" and left hurriedly for Dorothy's house to join the other midwife.

"Looks like the midwives are having trouble," I said to Toby. "You know, the medic at the army base said he could help with medical problems if we ever needed it. I believe we might use him now. Would you walk up to the army base and ask the medic if he could come down here?"

"Yes, I'll go," he said and hurried out the door to walk to the base, about a mile north of the village.

Thirty minutes later, an Army "weasel" drove up outside and Sergeant Hark — a man about six feet tall, of medium build, twenty-five years of age, neatly dressed in army green and polished boots — burst into the office. He said, "I saw Dorothy on my way here. I believe she is in serious trouble. I've never been in any situation like this before, so I'll tell you what we need to do. I'm going to ask for some boys to roll out a telephone line from Dorothy's house to the school. I'll stay at her house and talk to you on the phone while you talk to the doctor on the radio."

"Good idea," I said. "That will be a great help."

Soon the Army boys had the telephone hookups ready for use and I made contact with Sergeant Hark on the telephone. I relayed conversations between him and the doctor for ten or fifteen minutes, but radio contact was fast fading and becoming difficult. Soon I could barely hear the doctor above the static. I could hear him in the background but couldn't make out what he was saying.

When I thought he might be finished, I said, "Four-Nine Kotzebue, this is Two-Four Wales. Doctor, I did not read your last transmission. Break, is there someone who might relay? This is Two-Four Wales standing by." I laid the mike down.

A teacher at Savoonga on St. Lawrence Island had been listening. He said, "Break, Two-Four Wales, this is Three-Two Savoonga. I can hear both of you. Do you read me? Over." I heard him faintly.

"Three-Two Savoonga, this is Two-Four Wales. Your signal is faint but go ahead. Let's try. Did you get the doctor's last transmission? Over."

"Two-Four Wales, Three-Two Savoonga back. The doctor was saying he wants you to try to get her to push down more. The doctor said he would continue to stand by his radio and I'll also stand by here to relay if you need me." I passed the message on to Sergeant Hark over the phone.

Soon Sergeant Hark informed me that labor contractions had ceased and that she was becoming tired and distressed. He needed more advice from the doctor, but when I tried to make contact, I found signals had deteriorated and communication was no longer possible. I could hear neither Kotzebue nor Savoonga. I then called "in the blind" for anyone who might hear me to answer. I only heard static and couldn't tell whether anyone heard me. I put the mike down and thought I detected the doctor trying to call me, but I wasn't sure. I faintly heard a Coast Guard ship trying to call, or was it my imagination? His signal was too weak for intelligible communication so I didn't answer.

Obviously, medical advice from a doctor was now out of the question. I informed Sergeant Hark that we were now on our own. I did not know how much time we had to work with, but felt each second was precious, as a life or two would probably depend on the action we took. Yet neither Sergeant Hark nor I had any experience in obstetrics.

Thinking it might be of some help, I opened the medicine cabinet and picked up from the bottom shelf the large, heavy volume of *The Ship's Medicine Chest*, which described procedures to follow in most medical emergencies. My thoughts were interrupted as I heard the drone of an Army weasel drive up and come to a stop just outside the office door. The lieutenant in charge of the base came inside quickly without knocking and said, "We want to take *you* to the base. We have been listening on our base radio to the trouble you are having while trying to talk to the doctor. We can tune our big transmitter to your authorized frequency, 3385KC. We're really not allowed to do this, so you will have to do the talking and use your call sign as if you were talking from the school radio. Some boys have already begun rolling out a telephone line from the base to Dorothy's house."

"But there's too much interference on the radio," I said.

"We'll get you through," he responded.

I quickly donned my parka and climbed into the weasel, which took me to the base. We entered a Quonset hut and stepped inside a large room filled with monstrous pieces of equipment with dials and gauges. This, I thought, was, without a doubt, state-of-the-art Cold War stuff. I knew I had just walked into the Free World's first line of defense against a threat from across the strait. What would I do here? I felt reassured as a corporal handed me the mike in one hand and a cup of coffee in the other.

He said, "You can start talking to the doctor. But you've got to use *your* call sign as if you are talking from the school. We've tuned this transmitter to your frequency, 3385 kilocycles. It's ready to go."

I pressed the button on top of the mike and started calling, "Four Nine Kotzebue, Four Nine Kotzebue, this is KWP Two-Four Wales. Do you read me? Over."

The answer came back quickly, as loud as if he were in our room! It was the clearest I had ever heard him speak.

The doctor said, "I read you loud and clear. You almost

knocked our hospital off the foundations. What have you done?"

The lieutenant smiled and shook his head and finger then said, "You can't tell him where you are."

I said, "We've been working on the radio."

I stayed at the base radio room the rest of the night, relaying communication between Sergeant Hark and the doctor. I was served coffee, doughnuts and anything else I needed. The doctor remained near his radio in the hospital at Kotzebue, as well.

By daybreak, it was determined that the baby was dead and only part way out. Sergeant Hark and the doctor continued working till nine that morning, when Dorothy's condition became stabilized and a plane arrived to take her to Nome Hospital. I thanked the lieutenant, then left the army base and walked to the village as the plane was leaving for Nome. I met Sergeant Hark walking toward the base. He said, "Dorothy would have died last night if we hadn't gotten in contact with the doctor when we did. That doctor really knows what he is doing."

During our first winter in Wales I experienced few dull moments. Other than working with school matters, I was kept busy passing out pills from the medicine cabinet, walking around the village shooting doses of penicillin or dealing with an occasional medical emergency, but none were as life-threatening as was that of Dorothy.

One day, Nellie Anungazuk, Toby's tall, twelve-year-old daughter, cut her hand with an ulu. Toby brought her to the office. She was crying. It was a deep cut across the palm of her left hand from the base of her little finger to near the base of her thumb. The muscles underneath the skin were drawn into knots.

I called the doctor on the radio and described the cut. I said, "Doctor, I have a twelve-year-old girl here in the office who has a large cut across her palm." I added, "I've never sewed up any cuts before. I would like to get her out to Nome to have it sewed up there, but our weather is bad. What do you advise us to do in the meantime? Over."

"Sew it up!" came the emphatic response. "You have suturing supplies in your medicine cabinet, don't you?"

"Yes doctor, but if I sew it up you'll have to give me

detailed instructions on how to do it. I've never sewn up any cuts before."

"You have Novocain, don't you?"

"Yes, doctor."

"Then shoot some Novocain around the area of the cut in several places. The Novocain will reduce the pain. Then try to match the palm prints as best as you can and suture the skin back together. Then you can swab some Merthiolate on it to keep down infection and bandage it up. That's it!"

"Thank you, doctor. I'll try."

I washed my hands at the kitchen sink, then gathered some iodine, sterile gauze, adhesive tape, suturing supplies, Novocain and a syringe with a needle. Nellie whimpered when she saw the needle and started crying as she glanced at her palm. I reached for her arm to position her hand and get a better look at the cut, but she pulled back and continued to cry. She wouldn't let me touch her.

Toby spoke to her in Eskimo which sounded to me to be part scolding and part calming. I suggested to Toby, "Let's try to get her to lie down on her stomach on the floor." I stepped into the living room and brought a pillow from the couch and handed it to Toby. He put the pillow on the floor, then said something in Eskimo. She consented to lie on her stomach on the floor with her head to one side on the pillow.

Toby spoke again, and she put her left hand on her back. He held her arm while I squirted Novocain in several places in and around the cut. She gave no resistance. With the suturing needle, I pulled the thread through each side of the cut and tied the skin together in about twenty different places. I matched her palm imprints the best I could, as the doctor had advised. When the medical operation was completed, I wondered how well I had done.

Six months later, the doctor came to the village for a routine visit. While he was in the schoolroom giving physical checkups to the children, he asked, "Where's the girl whose cut hand you sewed up? I would like to see it."

I turned to Nellie and said, "Go up there to the doctor. He wants to see where you cut your hand."

She walked sheepishly to the doctor and held out her hand. He looked it over and said, "That's a good job. I couldn't have done better myself."

I have wondered about that statement many times since: One, did he really mean what he said? Or, two, should I have become a doctor instead of a teacher?

On several occasions the doctor prescribed for me to administer enemas and explained how to give them. One day Toby came to our apartment and said, "This old women is sick from tuberculosis. She wants you to give her an enema."

"Is this the same woman I tried to get to go to the sanitarium in Anchorage?" I asked.

"Yes, it is the same. But she refused to go. Some old folks never would go to the hospital."

"I sent her some TB medicine by her son last fall, but she sent it back."

Toby said, "I think I should go with you to interpret because that family speak not much English. She never would speak it."

I retrieved the enema equipment from the medicine cabinet and filled it with warm, soapy water in the kitchen. I slipped on my parka and mittens, then we started walking in the bitter cold to her house.

On the way Toby said, "She would never go to Anchorage hospital. She never would take white man's medicine. She always say white man bring disease and trouble. She never learned to speak English."

When we arrived at the house, six or eight of her folks were there. I greeted them in English. They smiled. Toby spoke to them in Eskimo, then one of her sons said something to his mother in Eskimo. "*Ee-ee*," she said, yes.

He then helped her out of the bed, and I gave her the enema. She smiled and said, "Thank you," then something else in Eskimo. Her son helped her get back into bed. I talked a minute or two with some of her folks, then went back to my apartment.

About twenty minutes later, a knock came on my door. It was Toby again. He said calmly, "The old woman is dead."

"What? She *died*? Was it because of something *I* did?" I was stunned.

"It was not anything you did," he responded sadly. "As soon as you left, she said, 'Now, I am ready'. So they took her out in the cold. This is old Eskimo way. Freeze to death is easy—like going to sleep. You know, when you were there, she said 'Thank you,' and that was the first time ever she spoke a white man's word!"

My doctoring days weren't over. One day after school Toby said to me, "Etukeok's wife wants for you to pull her tooth."

"No, I don't pull teeth," I quickly answered.

He said, "I think there's some pullers in medicine cabinet. She wants you to pull it."

"I've never pulled any teeth. I don't know how."

The next afternoon after school, Etukeok's wife came into the schoolroom where Toby and I were both working. She said something in Eskimo to Toby. Toby responded in Eskimo then turned to me, "She wants you to pull her tooth."

"But I've never pulled any teeth."

"She say, 'You can talk to doctor. He will tell you how.'"

She walked over to me, smiled, opened her mouth, and pointed with her forefinger at a lower tooth about halfway toward the back of her mouth.

"OK. I'll talk to the doctor about your tooth tonight and see what he says, but I don't think I'll be pulling your tooth."

Toby said something in Eskimo to her. She turned to me smiling and said "*Ee-ee*," then left.

That night I made radio contact with the doctor in Kotzebue: "Kotzebue, this is Two-Four Wales. I have a thirty-five-year-old woman here who keeps insisting that I pull one of her teeth. Over."

"Pull it!" he responded sharply.

"Kotzebue, Two-Four Wales back. I have never pulled a tooth before and I don't know the first thing about it."

"Do you have pullers?"

"Yes, we have three different pairs here in the medicine cabinet."

"Then pull it!" He didn't quibble.

"Doctor, the pullers are different shapes, and I wouldn't know which puller to use."

"Which tooth is it?"

"A lower tooth about halfway toward the back."

"That's probably one of the bicuspids," he said, then asked for a description of the shapes of the pullers which I gave to him. He then told me which puller to use and said, "Get a firm grip all the way down to the gum. Don't squeeze too hard or you might crush it, then twist it slightly to break it loose. Have some pressure outwards. Not toward the upper teeth, because when it comes out suddenly, you don't want the pullers to hit the upper teeth and break them. Just do it that way and you'll probably do all right."

"Kotzebue, Two-Four Wales, Roger. Two-Four clear." I put down the mike with a sick feeling in my stomach and turned around as Toby and Etukeok's wife entered the office. She had probably been listening on her home radio.

Toby said, "She is ready to have it pulled."

"I'll try," I said, trying to sound calm. I opened the medicine cabinet and chose the set of pullers I believed was the one recommended by the doctor, then turned to face her. She opened her mouth and put a finger on the tooth she wanted pulled, then took her finger away. It had a black, grayish hole in the center. I slipped the points of the pullers over the tooth, then applied a firm grip and began to make a slight twist with the pressure outward, as the doctor had advised. To my utter surprise and relief, the tooth broke free from the gums and was out! Wow! I was relieved that this task was complete. With the thumb and forefinger of my left hand, I took the tooth from the pullers and handed it to her. She smiled through blood as she said, "*Ka-ya-nah.* Thank you. *Ka-ya-na* very much." She picked up a piece of paper towel from my desk, put it to her mouth and left.

Toby laughed, "Now you may just have to pull more teeth."

Sometime later in March, I was at the village store when Alfred Mazonna, the store manager, said, "I am going to have all my upper teeth pulled." He laughed and moved his finger across his upper lip.

"Why?" I thought surely he was joking. Or was he just teasing?

But then he said, "They're no good. I'm going to get a plate made in Nome. You can pull them." He laughed.

This time I was positive that he was kidding. I suggested, "If you're going to Nome to get a plate made anyway, let the dentist down there pull your teeth."

"It would take too long that way," he said. "I would have to stay there long time for mouth to heal before they could make plate and put it in. Anyway, the BIA is calling a meeting in Anchorage of all the Alaska Native store managers. I can get plate in Nome and go on to Anchorage, same trip."

"Have you been to Anchorage before?" I asked, thinking he was serious after all. Perhaps I was given a recommendation by Etukeok's wife.

"No, I only been to Nome once before," he answered.

During the next three weeks I pulled all his upper teeth. About a month later he left for Nome and the Alaska Native store managers' meeting in Anchorage. He was gone about ten days.

The afternoon of Alfred's return to Wales I went to the village store to see him with his new dentures. I was also curious to learn of his impressions of the big white man's town. He was sitting behind the counter when I walked in. He gave me a big bright smile as if to show he was proud of his new teeth. He then laughed as he looked down and shook his head.

I knew then that he had seen a world unlike anything he had experienced before. I asked, "Well, what do you think of Anchorage? Tell me, how was it?"

"No wind!" he said and repeated, "No wind! It was no good down there with no wind."

"Well, what do you think about Anchorage?"

"Down there you don't even need flashlights to walk around at night. Everything all lit up, the streets with lights, and why do the policemen carry guns around? What will they shoot? Nothing there to hunt." He laughed again.

I sensed that he might be just pulling my leg and said, "I don't know what they will shoot."

"At the banquet they had about five silverwares, and I asked the store manager from the other village sitting with me, 'Why do they have so many eating spoons and things?' He said, 'Maybe it's in case you drop one.' We laugh about it."

"Well, I suppose it's just something nice they wanted to do for the Eskimo store managers of Alaska." I said.

Then he began deeper ribbing of me about white man's world as he asked, "Do white man believe Eskimos live in ice houses? Books show pictures of igloos made with ice."

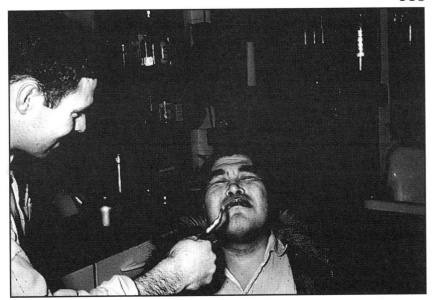

"Some people believe it," I said.

"But if we live in ice house, we would just get cold. Then if house got warm, it would melt." He giggled.

"I agree," I said, and detected that he had probably been as shocked to visit the white man's world as I was when I first landed at Wales.

Then he said, "You know, long ago white man came to Alaska and put up flag on pole and say, 'Now this is my land', then in 1867 another white man came and put up another flag and *he* say, 'Now this is my land.' You know, Eskimo not smart like white man. We never thought to put up flag was way to get land. We should have put up flag." He laughed and shook his head and looked down at the floor.

The successful pulling of Alfred's teeth, however, later proved to be my last. It happened when another man, age about fifty, asked me to pull one. He opened his mouth and showed it to me. It was a lower jaw tooth that was hollowed out from decay. Only a shell remained. I pressed the pullers as far into the gums as I could, got a firm grip and began applying pressure. The tooth burst into many pieces. All that remained of the tooth was the root. There was no way I was going to get that tooth out!

I felt terrible, but managed to say, "It broke and now

there's not enough tooth to get hold of with the pullers. Maybe you should have a dentist get it out."

"It's OK," he responded with a smile. "It feels much better now."

I thought that he might just be trying to soothe my wounded ego. About three months later a dentist came to the village and finished where I left off. I was never asked to pulled another tooth.

The Northern Lights

It was on the dark of the moon in March 1957, the year of intense solar activity and extensive testing of nuclear bombs by the United States and Russia, when Alfred Mazonna at the village store asked, "Did you see the northern lights last night?"

"No! Were they out?"

"You missed a big show. Brightest I ever saw," he said. "The sky was clear. Everyone in the village was out watching. Even all the Old Ones said it was the brightest they ever saw."

I was disappointed that I had missed it, but my hopes were raised when he added, "Maybe they will be out again tonight. Sometimes they come out several nights in a row. If it's not cloudy tonight, you should look."

"I will," I said and made a mental note to not forget.

"What do you think causes the northern lights?" he asked, laughing. "You have education, you are *eskoolty.* You should know."

I said, "A scientist on AFRN (Armed Forces Radio in Nome) said this is the IGY (International Geophysical Year) of increased sunspot activity that happens every eleven years. He said solar flares throw out atomic particles, which come to the earth and are caught by the earth's magnetic field, then drift into the atmosphere near the North Pole and light up the sky. He also said the large number of atomic bomb tests by the United States and Russia have added a lot more radiation to the atmosphere, so they say we can expect to have some spectacular northern lights this year."

Alfred smiled and said, "But *we* believe it's the spirits of the dead people come back up there to sing to us. They were singing last night."

At 8:00 p.m., the sky was clear, the temperature was

twenty-five below, and a gentle breeze was blowing from the north when I stepped outside and received the shock of my life. The whole sky was lit like a neon city. The village was as bright as moonlight and there were no shadows. Half the southern sky was an undulating curtain of violet with folds grading into lavender and a bottom hem of bright red. Yellowish-green rays painted the western sky to the zenith. In the north, streaks of pale yellow and white were gently waving like a flag in a breeze.

I walked to a group of eight or ten young people standing on the shore ice in front of the village store. Farther up the beach were two other groups. Several older people were standing outside their houses. Everyone was gazing skyward and looking at the sky in different directions. Occasionally a person pointed into the sky. The conversation of those nearest me was low-key and in awe of the scene above.

Toby's twelve-year-old daughter, Nellie, came to me and smiled as she said, "Listen, you can hear the lights singing."

"You say the lights are *singing*?" I asked.

"Yes, if you will listen, you can hear them."

I strained to listen and, sure enough, I detected a slight whistling sound. Or, was it my imagination? Perhaps my ears ringing? She said, "Also if we yell they will get brighter and come closer." She then spoke in Eskimo to the others closest to us and they began yelling. So I yelled, as did another group of young people nearby. This prompted loud screams from some children farther up the beach. Sure enough, the heavens got brighter. Was yelling the cause of it? And were the lights now closer?

After two hours of watching the light's changing colors, brightness and positions in the sky, I began to wear down. I noticed others retiring to their homes. I went inside our quarters and upstairs to bed, where Virginia was not yet asleep. She said, "The lights are really beautiful. I've been watching them through the window. It was too cold to go outside."

I positioned my pillow so I could also see out the window and I resumed watching the heavenly show from the bed. But I soon fell asleep. I awakened at three the next morning to see the sky pulsating like a beating heart and shooting streaks of pale-green and yellowish-white from south to north. A half hour later, I was again fast asleep.

Spring Arrives

I was in the classroom at noon one Friday in late March, when a bush plane buzzed the school. Who could that possibly be? It couldn't be the mail plane, because our scheduled mail day was on Saturdays, weather permitting. Only rarely did a plane other than the mail plane come to Wales. Could it be a charter flight with a visitor from the BIA office in Nome or Juneau to check on me and school operations? No, they said they would let me know when they were coming. Was it a visitor from the Lower Forty-Eight? Perhaps more than one visitor? And would we sleep on the roll-out couch in our living room tonight and give visitors our upstairs bedrooms?

My questions were quickly answered by Dwight Tevuk, when he rushed into the schoolroom excited and out of breath. He said, "Martin Olsen is out there! He wants to see you."

"Thank you, Dwight," I said. I then recalled six months before when I had asked Martin if I could ride with him to Little Diomede sometime on one of his mail flights when he wasn't loaded. I had mentioned I would like to go over and back sometime to see the nearest neighboring village. He had agreed to take me, but he said he would have to wait till springtime when the weather would be better and there would be enough daylight to go there from Nome and get back in one day. He also said it would probably be March before the winds would blow enough snow to form a smooth landing area on the jagged ice between the two islands of Little and Big Diomede. He said there was no beach on Little Diomede on which to land a plane.

Martin Olsen was half Eskimo and half white and was congenial and ready to do a favor for anyone, so I was absolutely certain this was the reason he had stopped at Wales. I felt safe to be flying with Martin to Little Diomede because he was the most respected bush pilot on the Seward Peninsula. He was the only bush pilot in the Nome area who would fly to the island, which is located only three miles from the fortified Russian island of Big Diomede.

My adrenaline began flowing, as I realized that a trip to Diomede Island was, indeed, a rare opportunity. I quickly assigned the children to do the next page in their math notebooks. I thought this should keep them busy while I was gone. I didn't tell them where I was going. I hurried into our quarters and asked Virginia to watch the children. She said she would. I dressed warmly, because the outside temperature was well below zero, and a brisk north wind was blowing. I grabbed my camera.

When I walked outside, I saw that Martin had taxied to within thirty yards of the school. His motor was idling and he was smiling when I reached the plane. He said, "I'm going to Little Diomede. Do you want to go?"

I was already half inside the plane before he finished speaking. For me, this trip was going to be exciting. As soon as I caught my breath, I said, "I figured that's where you were going when Dwight came in and told me you wanted to see me." I took my seat beside him.

He taxied the plane onto the shore ice, then turned north and revved the engine to a heavy vibration. We were quickly airborne. He banked west as the Diomede Islands came into full view, twenty-five miles ahead. We flew over the pressure ridge, where the moving pack ice had driven large broken chunks of ice on top of the shore ice. We flew at 300 feet altitude over a long, straight break in the ice the size of a B-29 landing strip. Martin commented, "The wind is causing that break in young ice. It looks like that ice may be only two or three feet thick."

As we flew, I noticed Martin constantly looking to right and left. "We might see a polar bear. Look over there," he said, pointing. "There are some polar bear tracks." He followed the tracks a short distance, but they were heading south. We saw no polar bear, so he again headed westward. We flew over thousands of jigsaw patterns of ice, thick and thin, large and small.

After some twenty-five minutes, we approached the

island. Martin pointed to an area of open water and said, "See that man down there? He is hunting seals. Those red lines are blood trails where the hunters have been dragging seals to the village. Eskimos bleed the seals before they drag them home and the blood makes trails you can see from the air. The Diomeders hunt on the east side of the island where there is open water. On the other side the ice stays solid. That is where we will land, between the two islands, Big Diomede and Little Diomede."

We flew around the north end of Little Diomede and came into view of the steep, rocky face of Big Diomede, the Russian island, looming straight ahead. Martin commented, "On one trip out here I could see some people over there. They have Russian army outpost on the island. Little Diomede Eskimos used to go over there to visit relatives, but not any more. Little Diomede Eskimos say they sometimes see Russian soldiers over there walking around. Last time three men from Little Diomede walked over, the Russians held them captive for six months before they let them come home."

Martin turned the plane south between the two islands along the International Date Line. He flew past the village, then made a complete 180 and flew alongside the island, as he planned to land close to the village. The plane went down fast! I felt light on my seat and thought, surely we're not going to land this far from the village. We dropped to within ten or fifteen feet of the ice, then he raced his motor and pulled away from the island. I looked at him. He exclaimed, "I'm not going to try that again!"

"What?" I asked.

"That is a strong downdraft next to the island," he said. "It might give us trouble. You never take second chances like that." We landed about a mile and a half west of the island. We were probably in Russian territorial waters (or ice). Because of the strong winds we were experiencing, Martin stayed at the controls while waiting for Diomeders to come out to meet the plane. He said, "It'll be a while before the villagers get out here. We're sitting right on top of the International Date Line." He pointed out the left side and said, "Friday here." He then pointed to our right and said. "Saturday there."

"Could I get out and take a picture?" I asked.

"Sure, go ahead."

I stepped out in Friday and took a picture facing Big Diomede and Saturday. I then went around the tail of the plane across the Date Line to Saturday and took a picture looking back toward Little Diomede and Friday.

Soon the Diomede Eskimos picked up their mail and we were off again toward Wales. When I arrived back at the school, Virginia had already dismissed the children. Some of them were out to welcome me home with questions like, "How did you like it out there?" and "What was it like at Little Diomede?"

I heard a couple of students say "*Ee-see-ah, ick-ee.*" More about *Ee-see-ah* and *ick-ee* later.

Martin Olsen was killed twenty-three years later when he crashed on a flight from Shishmaref to Nome with a load of reindeer meat. The cause of the accident was not determined, but some say he may have miscalculated the weight of the cargo. Today, an airline company operating out of Nome is called Olsen Air Service.

Today's flights between Little Diomede and the mainland are commonplace, even in winter, with the use of helicopters and vastly improved bush planes, communication and weather service. Besides, the Cold War is over and Russia is no longer considered a threat.

Spring Cleaning

Each fall when new shore ice forms, the village council marks a spot halfway between the north and south ends of the village and about fifty yards from the beach to serve as village dump. That is where garbage and sewage from the homes and the school is dumped until sometime around June, when the shore ice breaks up and moves away from the village. So the school is kept cleared of refuse; except for the accumulation of junk in the attic and the mountain of empty oil drums out back of our kitchen window.

"That pile of oil drums is no good," said Toby one afternoon in May, after much of the snow had melted from around them. "We need to get rid of them."

"But the *North Star* takes empties out from the other villages. Juneau said they will pick them up here too." I replied.

"Yes, they always say that. But they never pick up empties here at Wales. Every year when they are here, the weather is usually bad and the ship gets anxious to move on. They never take any empty drums and every year another hundred or so more drums pile up. Maybe we should just put them on shore ice and let them go away with the ice at breakup."

"Where would they go? And would that be legal?"

"I dunno if it's legal. You could ask Nome office if we could do it. It would be good to get them gone. The ice could take them over to Russia or someplace. Or maybe they sink when ice melts. Those drums look bad, and besides they just in the way when dog teams need to go that way. We have plenty of men right now not doing anything. We could roll them out on the ice to garbage dump."

128

The dark streak on the shore ice in the upper center is the garbage dump and discarded oil drums. The monument is the memorial to Wales' first teacher.

"I'll try to get permission to do that," I said. "We need that mountain of drums anywhere but here. Its blocking the view from our kitchen window."

A week later, BIA Education Specialist Warren Tiffany visited the school. He was slight of build, about five-ten, and very amiable and helpful in matters of education. He enjoyed singing songs with the children, and I enjoyed his company and assistance, even if only for a day or two. He wore an attractive, light brown parka with white spots on the fur. It was made from the "parka" squirrel, prized for its warmth and tough, thin, lightweight fur. He demonstrated the unique characteristics of this fur by taking off his parka and stuffing it into the right front pocket of his cargo pants. The children laughed.

During his visit, I directed his attention to the pile of empty oil drums out back of the school and asked, "Do you think I could get permission from the government to put those drums on the ice so they will drift away in the spring?"

"Nobody would give permission to do that," he answered. "Just do it and don't say anything."

"But if you were in my place, what would *you* do?" I asked.

He smiled and said, "Those drums are no good where they are. I suggest you just do what you think best."

I mentioned to Toby what Mr. Tiffany had said, and the very next day he conscripted eight or nine men to start work. They removed the bungs from the drums and began rolling them onto the ice at the village dump. They worked about a week, with each man rolling three or four drums at a trip. When the drums were removed to the village dump, only dead tundra grass remained as evidence that some of the drums were leaking. But the scenery was vastly improved.

Toby said, "It is much better behind the school now with oil drums gone. Maybe we can do the same thing with the stuff in the attic. We need room to put new stuff in the attic when *North Star* comes."

"Good idea, Toby. I agree. Let's go up there and take a look." We went into the attic. I crawled over heaps of everything imaginable: tons of used rugs, beds, books, desks, chairs, lamps, sofas, sewing machines, radio transmitters—you name it—and some of it had probably been there since before World War I. I said, "Let's clean this place out. When can we start?"

"I think some men can start tomorrow," he said.

"Good! Everything goes except the dried foods and kegs of butter and whatever else you think we should keep. You be the judge, Toby. But let's get rid of most of it. I don't care where this stuff goes. It mostly should go to the dump."

Toby agreed. The next day some men began lowering stuff from the attic above the schoolrooms through a hole in the ceiling of the hallway beside the post office. For two days we had a noisy ceiling and hallway, with dust drifting into the classroom each time the door was opened. But the children did not mind. In fact, they seemed to enjoy the commotion as well as I welcomed the attic being cleaned out. The workers removed numerous sled loads of junk to the village dump on the shore ice. Some men kept some items they thought they could use. When they were finished, the school had an attic and storage room we could use as well.

With spring cleaning out of the way, Virginia and I made our decision to stay at Wales a second year. She said, "They will pay our way home for summer vacation if we stay another year." I agreed.

She said, "We've got to mail in our next year's grocery order because the ship will soon begin loading in Seattle for the trip north. Next year, things should be much better because we'll have more room in the attic to put our groceries. We won't have to stack stuff on the stairs and under the beds and our kitchen pantry won't be so crowded."

Baseball on the Beach

The sun was barely below the horizon at midnight in May, the month which the Eskimos say has the best weather of the year. It was daylight all night and the weather was warm. The snow on the beach was melted, and the children played baseball there at recess and after school. The games often continued for long hours into the evenings, when the children were also joined by young adults.

The game of Eskimo baseball had somewhat different rules from baseball as I knew it. Nevertheless, it was baseball, and I believe Eskimos should be given the credit for inventing the game, not Doubleday!

Although they had no rule book to follow, they used a bat, a ball, two bases (home and second) and had three

outs to an inning. Most of the other rules were different from baseball as I had known it. Among the rules of Eskimo baseball: (1) you may run, regardless if you are at bat; (2) anyone, or all, may run at anytime; (3) you get three swings at the ball; (4) going to second base (a line across the beach) and back to home base (another line across the beach) scores a run; (5) someone tagged or hit with the ball while between the bases is out; (6) three outs, change sides; and (7) you can have as many innings as you want.

I asked Toby, "How long have they been playing the game of baseball?"

"This baseball has been played by Eskimos for many years," he said. "Maybe a thousand years or more. All old people know that."

"What did they use for balls back before they got rubber balls?" I asked.

"Well, they used to play with a ball made with seal skin. The women sew it and put grass or something inside," he said.

"Everyone seems to like to play," I commented. "Even the Army boys come down and play with the young people at night."

"Yes, even some older ones, like old men and women, also sometimes go out to play at night."

"The only trouble is that the school children are also staying out late playing baseball," I said. "They don't get to bed on time. Most of them are coming to school late the next day. This is becoming a problem."

"Yes, and it happens this way every year, and the teachers and parents can't control it."

I decided to see if something could be done to get the children to come to school on time. I said to Virginia, "I'm going to bring up to the Village Council at their next meeting about children coming late to school."

"Do you think they can do anything about it?" she asked. "I noticed parents out every night, trying to get their children to go in and go to bed, but some of them won't go."

The next meeting of the village council was called for the following Monday. As part of my job description, I was required to serve as secretary to the council and keep the minutes. I sent copies to Juneau and to Washington. The talk of the meetings was always in Eskimo and would sometimes go on for hours. During the meetings I would occasionally ask Toby, "What are they talking about?" and he would tell me, then I would write something down.

At this meeting, the first item for discussion went on for some ten or fifteen minutes. When they were finished, I asked Toby, "What were they talking about?"

He said, "Well, it's about a dead dog on the beach just north of the village. It's because when the dog thaws a little, it stinks and the smell is bad when the wind is toward the village. Clarence said he would get rid of the dog." I put it in the minutes and later saw in the files that Clarence had promised each summer for the past two years to get rid of it.

Chief Angnaboogok turned to me and asked, "Do you have anything to bring up for discussion?"

"Yes," I said. "I'm getting concerned about the children coming late to school each morning. I know it's daylight now and the children like to play out on the beach late at night, but some of them are playing past midnight and are coming late to school. Is there something we can do about that?"

Toby talked awhile in Eskimo, then members of the council took turns speaking. The conversation continued for twenty minutes, then stopped. There was about a thirty-second pause, then Roland turned to me and said, "How about you just start school around ten o'clock instead of quarter to eight? Maybe they get to school on time better that way."

I quickly said, "That sounds like a *good* idea. Let's do that. Tomorrow we will start school at ten o'clock. I'll dismiss at five. Get the word out about the new starting time. If some come early anyway, they can just do what they want to do till ten o'clock."

Roland spoke some more in Eskimo. The others smiled and nodded their heads in agreement. Some laughed and several said *Eee-ee*, but I recorded none of this decision in the minutes.

We started school the rest of that year at ten o'clock and most of April and all of May the following spring.

Problems With Alcohol

Except for one occasion while I was at Wales, alcohol wasn't a problem. The subject never came up at village council meetings. I mentioned this to Toby one day after school while he was sweeping the floor. I said, "I've never seen anyone in the village drunk or drinking."

"Yes," he said, "we have village ordinance not to have any kind of whisky or drink like that. It's just no good to have in the village. It cause trouble. We don't allow beer or whisky to be in the village or anyone to bring it in."

"Does anyone ever get caught drinking in the village?" I asked.

"It *has* happened. But, mostly, that's when they come back from Nome that way. Also some of the boys sometimes try to make it with dried fruits, but we keep it down. Alcohol would be a very bad thing to have in the village. Sometimes when a village person goes to Nome and is drinking, he just gets into trouble."

At 2:30 one morning in April, Virginia woke me saying, "Someone's banging hard on our door."

I put on my clothes and went downstairs to see what was the problem.

It was Dwight. He said, "Arthur K... is shot! We need help. He is at my house. He is bleeding."

Eunice Bergland, the public health nurse who served the Nome area, happened to be in the village at the time. She was sleeping in the other bedroom upstairs.

I said to Dwight, "I'll wake up Miss Bergland and we'll be right down."

Miss Bergland, a husky, young, single woman of Swedish descent, was already awake when I told her about the shooting. She said, "I'll be right down as soon as I get dressed."

She met me in the office and quickly gathered some first aid supplies from the medicine cabinet and put them into her bag. While we were walking the 100 yards to Dwight's house, she asked, "Does this kind of thing happen here very often?"

"No," I answered. "This is the first such incident I've ever heard of in the village."

"In Nome, this kind of thing happens all the time," she said. "It's either fights or shootings, and it happens when they get a little alcohol in them."

When we arrived at Dwight's house, we found Arthur on a bed with several strips of cloth wrapped around his lower abdomen and buttocks. Dwight and his wife, May, seemed much relieved to see Eunice.

Eunice went straight to work and soon had the external bleeding under control and gave him a sedative to calm him. "We've got to get him to the hospital," she said. She led me to a corner of the room, away from Arthur, and whispered, "He's been bleeding externally four ways. I've got that stopped, but he's also bleeding internally, and that's the worst thing. The bullet went through his lower intestines."

I turned to Dwight and asked, "What happened?"

"His brother, Charlie K..., did it," he said. "It was a big gun. The bullet went all the way through."

"What should we do?" I asked.

"You should call for the marshal to come out here," he responded. "This is a very bad thing. You can call the offices in Nome, but I don't think anyone will hear at this time of night. You can try to call now, but mostly they don't turn their radio on till about 6:00, maybe even 6:30." Nevertheless, I went to the radio to call. No one answered. I went back to Dwight's house. He served coffee.

Eunice said, "I've given him two Phenobarbital tablets and he's resting comfortably now but I need to stay with him. When you go back to the school to call for the plane, would you bring my suitcase? I need to go back on the plane with the injured man."

I went back to the school at 6:00, and this time Nome answered. I told them of the shooting and that the nurse wanted a plane to come to pick up the wounded man. I also requested that the marshal come out. I went upstairs and grabbed Eunice's luggage. Virginia was awake and asked, "What happened?"

"Arthur got shot and Miss Bergland is taking care of him. I don't know how long I will be gone," I returned to Dwight's house.

At 7:45, two bush planes landed on the beach beside the school, where Roland Angnaboogok directed them to taxi close to Dwight's house. One plane brought the U.S. Marshal, and the other came to pick up Arthur. Roland, Dwight, the marshal and I carried Arthur to one plane. Miss Bergland climbed on with the patient and they left for Nome Hospital.

Dwight invited us back to his house. On the way, Roland commented, "I heard about the shooting." Inside the house, the faces of Dwight's wife and his teenage daughters expressed gloom, dismay and worry that their home-life had been so rudely disrupted. Just then the marshal burst inside and gruffly asked, "Where's he at? I mean the one that shot him?"

"He's over there," Dwight answered pointing through a small window above the dining table toward Charlie's house, about forty yards away, partially hidden by a six-foot snow bank. "He lives alone. He's the only one in the house right now."

The marshal stooped, then leaned over the table and peered out the window. He walked a few feet away, then came back and looked out the window again. "How can we get him out?" he asked.

"Just have to go get him, I think," Dwight said.

"How are we going to *go get* him?" the marshal asked sarcastically, as he glanced out the window again, then stepped back. Dwight's wife handed him a cup of coffee and he sat down in a chair. He took a sip and set his cup on the table, then stood up and peered out the window again. The rest of us were also standing and also occasionally glancing out the window, then at one another. We talked in low tones. The marshal sat back down, then got up and resumed pacing back and forth. Dwight's wife and older daughter sat on the edge of a small bed and were conversing in Eskimo in low tones. They apparently were as impatient as the rest of us for this impasse to be concluded. But time was passing and nothing indicated that it would end anytime soon. I moved over against a corner wall.

Roland came to me and quietly asked, "Is he going to go get him or not?"

"It doesn't look like he's going to," I said. "This could go on all day."

After a few more minutes with conversations muted and everyone watching the nervous marshal, Roland volunteered, "I'll go over there and get him."

We watched as Roland walked straight to Charlie's house and opened the door. It was not locked. He stepped inside and the door closed.

Time seemed to pass slowly. The marshal asked. "Will he get him out?"

"I think he will," Dwight said with a wry smile.

After five minutes the door opened and Roland came out, with Charlie walking two steps behind. As they walked toward the plane, the marshal caught Charlie and pulled his hands behind his back, then snapped on handcuffs. He then led him onto the plane. After the plane departed, I asked Roland, "What happened?"

"Well," he said, "they been drinking something, I think what they made from some dried fruits or something, and got in this argument. Charlie said Arthur kept coming to his house and banging on the door. He said he just shot through the wall to make him go away to his own house. Charlie said he just shot through the wall beside the door. He said he told him he was going to shoot. He said he kept telling Arthur to go away. He said he thought Arthur was at the door, so he shot *beside* the door. Charlie said he never knew he shot him."

"What were they arguing about?"

"It was something about their father's harpoon, who should have it. It is at Charlie's house and Arthur said it was his. Charlie said his father promised it to him."

One morning six weeks later, as school was about to start, Toby said, "Charlie came back."

"Charlie came back?" I asked in disbelief. I knew no plane had been in the village for nearly a week. "How did he come? By dogsled?"

"No, he walked from Nome."

"You mean he walked all the way from Nome? That's 120 miles!"

"Yes, he has walked it before. I think he just wanted to get back in the village. He said he's been in jail down there and didn't like it."

"What did they charge him with?"

"Well, I think they had a trial or something and decide to let him go. Anyway, I don't think he will get into trouble anymore, and maybe no more drinks. Any kind of alcohol is bad to have in village. That's why it's not allowed to be here."

"Has there ever been any trouble with alcohol in the village before this?"

"Only one time before, I think," he responded, smiling. "It was when some boys made something and was drinking it and challenged Ibionna to eat some polar bear liver. They kept saying he wouldn't eat it. Then he ate it. You know, if you eat polar bear liver all your hair will fall out. And the next morning after eating the liver, all his hair *was* out and it never grow back. That's why you see Ibionna with no hair. He's had no hair since he was a young man. You should never eat polar bear liver. You can eat seal liver. White man likes seal liver, but don't get drunk and eat polar bear liver."

I have used fictitious names for Charlie and his brother in this chapter for the sake of their family members.

Spring Hunting

It was a surprise that Sunday morning, May 6, 1956, when an unannounced bush plane landed on the beach in front of the school. "Who can that be and why now?" I wondered aloud, and went to get my parka. As I started outside, I met Dwight at the office door. He was excited and breathless. He said, "It is Bob Jacobs!"

"Did he bring the mail?"

"No, he brought two men from the Denver Museum. They are getting their baggage off the plane. They say they are going to be here three weeks during the big spring migration of birds and animals through the strait. They say they want to collect a few birds for the museum while they are here. They are looking for a place to stay. They say they brought no food. Maybe they should stay with you to eat white man's food. They say they will pay what you will charge."

"Let me go tell Virginia. I'll ask her what she thinks about it," I responded, then went into the kitchen where she was preparing lunch. "Dwight just told me the plane brought two men from the Denver Museum who want to stay two weeks with us. They say they will pay for their board. What do you think?"

"I guess it will be OK," she said, while stirring dried milk with water in a gallon jug. "But three weeks is too long. Tell them they can stay a few days till they can find somewhere else to stay."

I went back to the office, where I found Dwight standing with two men who appeared to be in their late twenties. Six large bags lay on the floor. Both visitors were smiling. "These are the men from the Denver Museum who would like to stay with you," Dwight said. He then left.

"Hi! I'm Wilford Corbin, the teacher here."

A blonde, broad-shouldered man, about six feet two, said, "Hi! I'm Kenneth King." He then motioned to the other man, who was about five-nine and of average build, and said, "This is Henry Wichers. We're from the Denver Museum of Natural History." Henry nodded and smiled. I shook both men's hands.

Kenneth, apparently in charge of the expedition, began talking fast. He seemed excited to be here. "We've been waiting in Nome for three days for a chance to fly out here. But we began to wonder if we were ever going to make it, and just this morning Bob Jacobs said he would try it, and here we are! We want to stay in Wales about three weeks. This is where Alfred Bailey, director of the Denver Museum of Natural History, came and collected lots of animals back in the '20s and '30s. He told us all about the Bering Strait and the people and about Dwight Tevuk, who helped collect most of the arctic specimens for the museum. Nearly all of our arctic collection came from the Wales area. The museum sent us up here to get acquainted with the area and to collect some specimens while we are here. We would like to stay with you if we can. We will pay whatever you ask."

"Dwight told me you were here and I just talked to my wife," I said. "We can keep you a few days till you can make other arrangements. We are quite busy with schoolwork, but we want to help all we can."

"We won't be any trouble," Kenneth responded excitedly, with a big smile. "We are thrilled to be here. This is our first trip to Alaska, but we've been reading all about the Bering Strait area. Alfred Bailey has told us all about the living conditions here, and what kind of clothes to wear and everything. We would like to go out with the hunters in their boats. Dwight Tevuk said we can go out with him and his crew every time he goes out. He said he will be going out in his skin boat to hunt when the weather is good and when he doesn't have to work in the post office."

"The weather looks good today. He may get his crew ready today. But you really need warm clothes if you're going out in the boats," I said.

"We know that," he said. "We've read up on what to wear. We brought parkas, mittens and felt shoes, the best that is made for the arctic. They're guaranteed to keep you warm to twenty below." He quickly pulled a pair of felt shoes from his bag and showed them to me.

"Yes, those are good shoes," I agreed, "but if you are going out with the Eskimos in skin boats, you'll find it's a lot different than what it is like when you're walking around on land. You'll just be sitting there all day among ice floes in a cold breeze."

I helped the men carry their bags to their room. When we walked through the kitchen, I introduced them to Virginia as she was putting lunch on the table. She said, "I've just about got dinner ready. Come back down as soon as you put your stuff in your room."

I showed them upstairs to their room, where they put down their luggage. When we were back downstairs, Kenneth asked, "Where may I wash my hands?"

I pointed to the kitchen sink and said, "You can wash here. This is the only lavatory we have." He turned on the faucet--full blast! My first thought was to say: "We never let water run down the sink like that," but I refrained from speaking, as he began washing and soaping his hands and his face and I saw the water continuing to fast disappear down the sink. Water that we had carried upstairs! I didn't think he was ever going to turn it off, and began imagining myself carrying in more ice and snow to the upstairs tank. When he finally turned off the water, and before Henry could start washing *his* hands, I decided I would tactfully give the men a short lecture on water conservation in the Arctic, but I began speaking before my concern about the pending water shortage stopped simmering.

"To me that water is like gold and we don't just let it run down the sink." I said. "Every drop of it has to be carried upstairs to a tank. What we do when we wash here in the sink is to turn the faucet on to wet our hands and turn it off to rub on soap, then we turn the water back on to rinse off the soap. After that, we turn off the faucet." I smiled when I finished talking.

Kenneth was obviously embarrassed. He began apologizing and offered, "We can help get the ice."

"Thank you," I said, feeling ashamed that I had spoken the way I did to my guests. "But that's the janitor's job. He chops the ice from the lake about a hundred yards out back, and hauls it here on his sled. I only go to bring in ice or snow when we run out of water on weekends." Henry washed his hands correctly, then we sat down to eat.

Before we finished eating, Dwight came to the door and announced, "We are getting ready to go out in boat to hunt eider ducks. We will be ready in about thirty minutes." Both men began eating faster. They soon finished, then went upstairs to change clothing. I donned an extra pair of pants, put on my mukluks and parka to go along.

I walked with the men to the edge of the shore ice, where Dwight and four others, each wearing white cloth-covered parkas, sealskin pants and mukluks, were loading guns, large crates and gasoline into a twenty-six-foot skin boat. I stood beside Kenneth as we watched two men lift a heavy crate into the boat. He took two boxes of shotgun shells from a large camera bag he was carrying and asked me, "Is this the kind of shells the men are using?"

I looked at the boxes and saw they were 00 buckshot and said, "Yes, that's the kind they use."

He said with a sly grin, "I suppose they will really like it if I give these boxes to them. I brought two more boxes I can give them later for letting us go out with them." Then Kenneth pointed to the crates the men were loading into the boat and asked, "What's in those boxes the men have been loading?"

"Those are cases of shotgun shells—about twenty-four boxes to a case."

"*Cases!*" he exclaimed. He ashamedly put his two boxes back into his bag, but promptly took them back out, and timidly walked over and gave them to Dwight. He said, "Here's some more shotgun shells you can use."

Dwight smiled as he took them, then looked at the markings and said, "Thank you." He laid them on top of a crate. He got his shotgun from his sled and placed it in a rack between the ribs of the boat with the end of the barrel pointing upward and away for safety.

Just then a line of hundreds of king eider ducks passed by offshore. I pointed them out to Kenneth and Henry and said, "That's what the men will be hunting. These ducks fly along the coast to nesting grounds farther north."

Soon we were in the boat in the water. Kenneth sat

beside me. Dwight raced his motor to turn the boat toward a mile-long line of ducks flying toward us from the south, side by side, two feet apart, low over the water. When the ducks approached the boat, the line split as ducks veered to each side. None flew directly over us. Some went by on the right and others went by on the left, as a barrage of shots burst from five automatic shotguns and ducks rained into the water on both sides. The men laughed. Dwight maneuvered the boat so each person could help retrieve the five-pound birds, shake the water from their feathers and drop them into the boat. This process was repeated many times as flocks arrived continuously from the south.

During a pause in the shooting and retrieving of ducks from the water, Kenneth turned to Dwight and said, "I notice the men are waiting till the birds go past the boat before they shoot. Wouldn't it be best if you shoot them *before* they go past the boat or at least when they are just beside it?"

Dwight said, "Well, the ducks don't fly over the boat. The ones that are coming straight toward the boat always go to their right or to their left. This makes them get a little behind the ones that are flying straight. That way, when the flock has gone past the boat, you see a wad of ducks on both sides. That's where we shoot—in the wad. It's always *after* the ducks fly past the boat that we see the wad and that is where we shoot."

Kenneth turned to me and said, "Wow! That makes sense!" He then moved his knees up and down and I suspected he was beginning to get cold. About thirty minutes later, he said to me, "I see what you mean about shoes for your feet."

"Are your feet getting cold?" I asked.

"Yes, they're cold," he answered. "How about yours? What are those you are wearing?"

"My feet are cozy. I'm wearing mukluks, the same as the Eskimos. The first time I went out in a skin boat, my feet got cold and afterwards I had a pair of mukluks made to fit."

"What are they made of?" he asked.

"They are made of sealskin—waterproof. The women make the soles from skin of the *oogruk*. They crimp the edges of the soles with their teeth to fit your feet. They sew hair seal uppers—with the fur turned in—to fit your ankles and leg. They sew on a strap to tie around your ankle." I lifted up my right foot to show him. "You see, here on the soles are the teeth marks. Some older women have teeth worn down to the gums from chewing them."

"What kind of socks do you have on?" he asked, continuing to move his feet up and down.

"I have on a pair of wool socks over cotton socks with rabbit fur socks over that. I have a couple of felt pads in the bottom of my mukluks. But most Eskimos use a pad of tundra grass in the bottom of their mukluks. They say it is warmer."

"Who can I get to make me some mukluks?"

"I think Dwight's wife will make them for you. You might ask her. When I got mine made, all I did was trace my foot on a piece of cardboard and gave it to this old Eskimo woman. But all the women here know how to make mukluks. You can ask any of them."

Two days later, the museum men found a place to stay in an abandoned house next door to Dwight. Kenneth came and proudly showed me his new mukluks, which May had made. The men extended their stay in Wales for a total of seven weeks, hunting with Dwight and his skin boat crew in the strait every time the weather was good. Occasionally Kenneth came to our apartment to buy a few cans of "white man's" food. Henry said he ate only Eskimo food. He said he became enamored with the Eskimo food and way of life to the extent that the villagers gave him the Eskimo name of *Inchumuk*. He later legally adopted this name and he is now known as Henry Wichers Inchumuk and resides in Prescott, Arizona.

The Saturday after my hunting trip with the museum men, I was with Toby, Frank Oxereok and Clarence Ongtowasruk in Toby's fourteen-foot wooden boat in open water two miles offshore. The main body of the pack ice was visible a mile farther out in the strait, moving north. Toby maneuvered the boat between scattered floes, careful not to strike a jagged chunk, which would most certainly damage the boat. Clarence stood up front pointing the way while Frank and I sat on large sacks filled with tundra grass, on a plank seat in the middle of the boat. The men were hunting the 500-pound *oogruk*, which is also known as "singing seal" because it is often heard singing even while it is under water.

Suddenly, an oogruk surfaced thirty-five yards to our right and Frank shot it. Toby then turned the boat fast to the right to get close enough for Clarence to throw the harpoon before it sank. Simultaneously, as Clarence harpooned the *oogruk*, the boat hit a piece of ice and water burst through a hole the size of a basketball in front of my feet. Water flowed around my feet and I was horrified. I knew the next thing we would all be doing was swimming in icy water while the nearest ice floe was forty yards away! Then in a flash—probably instinctively—Frank rose from his seat beside me and threw his sack cushion over the hole then stood on it as the gush of water was slowed and only a trickle seeped into the boat.

He stood there then looked at me and smiled. He seemed not the least bit concerned. Wow! I felt slightly safer but knew we were not yet out of the woods as I recalled someone saying that survival in these frigid salt waters would be brief. The men conversed in Eskimo. I couldn't tell from the tone of their voices how concerned they were. I only knew we were a long way from shore.

Toby guided the boat toward a large floe while Clarence held the line that he had attached to the *oogruk* with the harpoon and dragged it alongside. Toby circled the floe to locate the best side to land. When he stopped the boat against the floe, we climbed onto it, then pulled the boat on top and dumped out the water. The men began to pull the seal on top of the ice while I was still worried about our quandary. How would we get back to shore with the boat in such poor condition? I was worried about me, not the seal! Nevertheless, I helped pull the *oogruk* out of the water, then ventured a question to Toby, "What do we do now?"

"We fix the boat," he said.

"How are you going to fix it?"

"With a seat and some nails, we fix it." He then took a hammer, a can of nails and a hand-saw from underneath his seat. He pried up the seat I had been sitting on, then sawed it in half and nailed the two pieces to the bottom of the boat, one piece on the inside and the other on the outside. He drove the nails through and bent the sharp points down.

I felt more secure knowing we could now make it

home. But I hoped Toby would safely dodge other pieces of ice as we now had only two seats left. Frank smiled and said, "Let me have your camera. I will take your pictures." Toby and I stood beside the boat and the *oogruk* while he snapped a picture, then he handed me back the camera. I

stepped backward to take another picture while Clarence stepped back alongside me to get out of the picture. Toby said, "Don't get close to the edge." But his warning came too late! With a crack, a six-by-eight-foot overhanging piece broke from the edge of the floe underneath Clarence and me, then dropped three feet into the water. It was the longest, most frightening and most memorable three-foot ride I have ever taken in my life! Again water came over my feet but the ice stopped sinking downward and began rebounding—fast. I thought, "Now where are we going?"

I felt I was rising on a giant pogo stick as the ice threw the both of us onto our bellies on solid ice in front of Toby and Frank. They laughed and talked rapidly in Eskimo. I have no idea what was said.

Soon we put the boat back into the water, then rolled the seal into it. Toby cranked the motor. Frank and I sat on the *oogruk*. I bailed water, which seeped through the patch-work at the rate of a gallon a minute, as Toby guided the boat safely back to shore.

On shore, the men took everything out of the boat and pulled it and the *oogruk* onto the beach. Toby then sprinkled some gasoline over the boat. "Why are you doing that?" I asked.

"I will make a new boat," he answered, laughing, then threw a lighted match into the fumes. We stepped aside to watch the boat go up in flames. I had the feeling that he was superstitious about a possible repair job and remembered Martin Olsen's admonition: "You should never take a second chance!"

Three women arrived with ulus and containers. They laughed as they exchanged conversation in Eskimo. Toby turned to me, then laughed as he said, "It's the women's job now. They fix the *oogruk*."

Spring walrus hunting, the prime source of the year's supply of food for the sled dogs of Wales, is done when the pack ice is drifting north through the strait. In May, herds of female walrus are riding the ice with newborn babies. Their fine-textured tusks are prized more for carving than those of bulls, which are usually cracked, scarred or broken from fighting. The bulls ride north in June, a month later. Sometimes the pack ice, a jumbled mass of floes that swirl and rotate as they are moved by the wind and the ocean current, rubs against the shore ice while hundreds, if not thousands, of walrus are riding onboard in huddled groups. But those walrus are never taken—they continue to ride north.

I asked Toby, "Why don't you get some of these walrus while they're close to the village and you wouldn't even need a boat to get them?"

"Well," he replied, "if we kill these walrus that are riding by on the ice, they would be drifted too far north by the time we got them butchered. Then it would be very difficult to get the meat ashore. To get walrus, we need to have some open water to put the meat in boats and have good place to bring it ashore. If we have open water and walrus is sighted to the south, that is good time to get them. Then we can butcher before the ice drifts too far north."

One Saturday late in May, after thousands of walrus had already passed north on the ice through the strait, the first offshore breeze we had in weeks separated the pack ice from the shore ice, forming open water near the village. Conditions for hunting walrus became favorable. Dwight knocked on my door and said, "Three skin boats are going out now to get walrus. Sereadlook has sighted with telescope lots of walrus. Do you want to go with us?"

Feeling an instant rush of excitement, I said, "Yes, I'll get ready! What should I bring?"

"You don't need to bring your gun. We will furnish you big gun to use. You can bring your camera."

I put on my parka and an additional pair of pants, and changed to fur socks and hip boots. I caught up with the men, whose dogs were pulling the skin boats on sleds across the shore ice to open water. There, they anchored the sleds and left the dogs to lie down and wait for our return. Eighteen men, counting me and "Old Man" George Ootenna, climbed into the boats, six to a boat. George and I were in Dwight's boat.

We went south along the open lead of water between the shore ice and the moving ice. King Island, clearly visible fifty miles to our south, appeared reflected on top of itself, in an inversion, as a flat-topped tower. The pack ice was a couple of miles farther out in the strait, drifting north. Soon we were alongside the pack ice, still traveling south. I spotted a group of about twenty walrus on the ice near the edge. I pointed and said to Dwight, who was guiding his skin boat, "There's walrus!" I thought surely they would stop here and get some of them.

He smiled and motioned with his arm toward the south. I looked along the ice toward the south, but saw no walrus in that direction. Then Dwight and George conversed briefly in Eskimo. George laughed and looked at me and smiled.

Ten minutes later, we approached more walrus. I again looked at Dwight. He smiled back at me as all three boats continued steadily southward alongside the pack ice. We continued south for another thirty or forty minutes, passing hundreds more walrus, perhaps thousands. At times there were walrus on the pack ice as far as I could see. Some were near the edge, but the boats continued on. I wondered how much farther south we would go, and why.

I looked back toward Cape Prince of Wales Mountain,

which now appeared to be as close to our north as King Island appeared to our south. Discussions in Eskimo by the men became more animated and talk became faster. Two men standing in a boat in front of us pointed farther toward the south. I looked in that direction and saw a mass of brown shapes near the edge of the ice pack about a half mile away.

Soon all three boats were slowed. Dwight and George began talking fast in Eskimo, then Dwight guided our boat alongside a large floe about thirty yards from the group of walrus. We stepped onto the floe. Some of the walrus appeared to be sleeping, while others were looking at us but made no effort to go into the water. Babies were scattered among them. Dwight said, "Looks like some of the babies were recently born. Now we pull the boats on top of the ice so the walrus can't tear it up when we start the shooting."

I helped pull our boat on top of the ice. All three boats

were soon safely on top of the ice and moved a few feet from the edge. Roland passed out M-1 rifles from his boat. He gave me one, which I slung by the strap across my shoulder. He spoke in a charged-up tone, "The gun is loaded. We got these guns from the National Guard armory. It is all right to use them. The Army like for us to use them in walrus hunting."

He pointed out the safety latch and said, "All you do is move this safety latch, then you can shoot it. We will, everyone except Ootenna, stand side by side on the ice, and when we begin shooting, you shoot. Hit as many as you can. 'Old Man' George will give the signal. You can just start shooting when the others shoot. The men on the left will shoot walrus on the left. The men on the right will shoot toward the right. If you are in the middle, shoot walrus toward the middle. Aim for the neck."

Roland put something in his ears. I had no ear plugs. Everyone formed a line side by side. I stood somewhere in the middle with Dwight beside me. When he raised his gun, I raised my gun, as did all the others. George stood behind the line. He was speaking in low tones.

Suddenly, as guns around me began firing, I fired about six rounds, then lowered my gun and took a picture. Ten seconds later, the sound of gun firing stopped as scores of live walrus bellowed loudly and scrambled into the water.

Dwight said, "Looks like we got about twenty on the ice. The babies don't leave their mothers." The other walrus went into the water and remained in the area. Some surfaced next to our floe less than six feet from where I stood. About six more came up side by side less than ten feet away and stared with eyes the size of tennis balls. Glen Sereadlook shouted something in Eskimo and they simultaneously slipped silently beneath the surface. Several men laughed.

During the butchering, George gave instructions to the younger hunters. He said something in Eskimo to Pete Sereadlook, while he pointed about forty yards upwind at a live walrus on top of a small floe. It had either not submerged with all the others in the area or had recently emerged.

Pete, a tall, slender Eskimo in his mid twenties, stepped and leaped over several floes to within three feet of the walrus, which either was sleeping with its head aright or otherwise was unaware of what was happening around it. Pete took his revolver from its holster and fired one round into a vital area of the head, causing the walrus to slump limp onto the ice.

He reholstered his revolver and started butchering. I

noticed his floe was drifting slowly apart from the other ice. At first only a few feet separated his floe from the others, but I watched as the feet gradually became yards. I detected no concern by the other men, who continued working even after thirty yards of water was between Pete and the main body of ice. I assumed that a boat would now be required to retrieve him and his walrus. But he continued to butcher.

Soon Pete looked up and put his knife in its sheath and unzipped his army parka. He smiled at me as he spread it between his outstretched arms thus making a sail which the breeze caught and began pushing him in our direction. Fifteen minutes later, he resumed his butchering, his floe now snug against our own.

After an hour and a half of butchering, the loading was ready to begin. All the live walrus had long since left the area and it was now safe to put the skin boats back into the water. But the floe we were on was no longer near open water. During the butchering, it had rotated to approximately thirty yards inside the ice pack. The men, while standing on one large floe, pushed hard with paddles and with their feet to gradually spread them apart. They soon made enough space between the floes to slide the boats back into the water. They then began the loading. They divided the pile of meat, skins and tusks between the three boats and tossed the live babies on top of the bloody mass, two of them in Dwight's boat.

I asked Dwight, "What are you going to do with the babies—dog food too?"

"No, only the meat is for dog food. I think the New York Aquarium wants the babies," he said. "You can call to Nome and tell them we have them. They will send a plane out to pick them up."

When the boats were loaded, everyone climbed aboard, then pushed with paddles and feet against the floes on each side of the boats. I pushed hard with a paddle. Gradually, the floes spread apart to allow our boat to pass a short distance toward open water. This process was repeated several times as other floes were pushed apart. Soon all three boats were again in open water, ready to head home.

Dwight said, "Look up! You see the village now."

I looked up and was astounded to see that we were

beside the village! I could hardly believe my eyes.

"The ocean current brought us home again," Dwight laughed, then pulled the starter cord on his motor and delivered us on the shore ice in less than five minutes.

An hour and a half to go hunting, another hour and a half to butcher and just five minutes to return!

Cordella Angnabooguk and Lucille Tevuk with baby walrus for the New York Aquarium.

Summer in the Bering Strait

My first summer at Wales, if you can call it summer, began with a student revolt on the last day of school. After I passed out the report cards, along with twenty-three perfect-attendance certificates, the children left the building to begin their vacation. I said to Toby as he was moving desks, picking up papers and sweeping the floor, "I couldn't believe it! More than half of the children never missed a day of school. I never heard of such perfect attendance records."

"Well, children here like to go to school," he said. "There's more for them to do at school than at home. Besides, homes are small and not much room to play. And parents make them go to school except when the children are bad sick."

As he talked, I noticed five children had entered the room, among them Harriet Tevuk. They stood sheepishly near the doorway with their report cards in their hands. Toby turned and spoke to them in Eskimo. Harriet answered in Eskimo, then looked at me. I looked at Toby, who looked out the window with a half-grin, then back at me and said, "Some of the children don't want to be promoted."

"Why?" I asked, realizing I had promoted everyone except two sixth-graders who had asked to stay in the same grade next year. Also, I was thinking I could perhaps entice some students to go to high school at the BIA boarding school at Mount Edgecumbe near Sitka.

"Well," he grinned, "they say they might get through school too quick if they are promoted."

I turned to the students and said to them, "But if you get through school at Wales, you can then go to high school at Mount Edgecumbe and the Bureau of Indian Affairs will pay for everything."

"We know that," Harriet protested, "but that school is too far away. We would have to stay away too long."

I asked Toby. "How about that? Doesn't anyone ever leave Wales to go on to high school?"

"Only few times. Some children went to Nome, I think, but that's only when their parents move there. But they don't much like it in Nome, and then they move back to Wales," he said. "We one time had two students go to boarding school at Mount Edgecumbe, but they got homesick and came back in about a month. Mt. Edgecumbe is more than a thousand miles away and everything is different down there. Anyway the parents want them to be here."

I looked at Harriet. She handed me her report card and smiled as she said, "I want to stay in seventh grade next year. Some others also want to stay one more year in same grade. Maybe Toby would help you decide it."

Taken aback as I was, I wondered who was the teacher around here anyway. I took back those five report cards, then turned and asked Toby, "Will you help me decide who to promote and who to keep in same grade?"

"Yes, I can help," he replied. We then went into the office and changed the promotions of those five students and seven others. Achievement and IQ had nothing to do with the decisions.

When we finished deciding the promotions and retentions, I said, "I received a memo from Juneau instructing me to attend a workshop in Sitka from June 9 through June 23. It is for all the BIA principals in Alaska. I've got to leave next Saturday."

He said, "But if you are away at that time, you will miss the great migration of bull walrus through the Bering Strait."

"Do they go through the strait the same time every year?" I asked.

"Yes," he said. "Sometimes they go through early in June, sometimes later, but mostly around the same time you will be away."

I was disappointed that I might miss seeing the migration of herds of bull walrus, but I looked forward to attending the workshop and to meeting some of the teachers with whom I had talked on the radio. Several of the men teachers and I had made a compact to let our hair grow long and to wait till we were in Sitka to get a professional haircut for a change. Most haircuts the men got in the various native villages were similar to a haircut received from using a bowl as a guide. Virginia had been cutting mine with scissors and pleaded with me to let her trim it again, but I declined her offer and left for Sitka with hair that covered my ears.

After the afternoon sessions on our second day in Sitka, I walked with half a dozen other men to find the town barbershop. We found two barbershops in town, but only one was open for business. The barbers were waiting-- at least we thought they were barbers. We later discovered that all the real barbers had gone to the Lower Forty-Eight on vacation. Some local boys, learning that BIA teachers were in town for a two-week workshop and that the men were in need of haircuts, borrowed the keys to the shops to make a few extra bucks of their own. Soon the barber shop floor was covered with hair, as each of us got a haircut with patches of dark and gaps of white.

The workshop was a worthwhile experience. We had sessions with instructors dealing in topics of all areas of school and village life. I was most impressed with the sessions I had with Dr. Skarland, a native of Norway who was teaching at the University of Alaska. He was said to be the world's foremost authority on arctic survival. He said, "In the arctic you must learn from the Eskimos, who have mastered the art of survival there. They wear the same clothing as the animals—fur. And they tan their fur with urine which keeps you warmer than fur tanned with tannic acid."

He also said, "White people are the nastiest people living in the arctic, especially those who are from urban areas and have never experienced doing without free-flowing tap water, flush toilets and regular garbage pickup."

His statement reminded me of the husband and wife who were in Wales during the winter just passed. They were from an affluent neighborhood near Los Angeles and lived in a small white house on the beach a half mile from the school and halfway between the village and the Army base. They were on assignment to maintain and operate U.S Navy weather and climatic data gathering equipment.

The couple was thirty-some, sociable and loved to drink beer. It seems they had brought a large supply of beer when they came, in spite of the ordinance of the Wales village council against the importation of alcoholic beverages. Some council members were also concerned that this activity might be a bad influence on some of the young people. Then a few army boys made friends with the couple and began bringing beer from the base to their house for parties, which were held only on weekends at first. Soon the partying increased in frequency, and loud laughter was heard coming from that area of the beach two or three times a week.

Although the partying had no effect on village life or activities, everyone knew what was going on. Beer cans were seen strewn in front of the house and were visible to passersby on dog sleds until drifting snow covered them over.

Toward spring I was invited to go there and "have a beer." I accepted the invitation since I hadn't had a beer in a long time. I heard loud laughter as I arrived. This indicated the party was already in progress. When I stepped inside the door, I was handed a beer and glad-handed by five or six smiling, laughing boys in army fatigues, with Lower Fortyeight accents that ranged from southwest to northeast. I was pounced upon to talk about Eskimos and life in the village, which I did through two beers. Then I went to the restroom, where I saw the honey bucket was full and running over. Someone had placed a large towel in front of the door, perhaps so you could wipe your feet if you exited the bathroom or to prevent seepage from getting into the hallway carpet.

I decided not to use their restroom. I went back into the living room and thanked the people for the beers. "Oh, you're not leaving now, are you?" someone said. "Won't you have another beer?"

"No, thank you. I had better not. I've got to teach school tomorrow." I feigned a laugh.

When I returned to Wales from the workshop at Sitka, I saw the pack ice in the distance to the north and noticed all the shore ice and snow on the beach was gone. There were whitecaps in the strait and breakers beside the beach where we landed. Soon after arriving, I was met by the youthful, energetic and conscientious naval official in charge of the weather outpost, Dr. Gene Bloom, who was there from San Diego. He said he found the naval facilities a mess. He said he hired a crew to clean it up and fired the caretakers. He said, "Wilford, I never saw such a mess in my life. I don't think they took one bag of garbage to the village dump all winter and beer cans were two feet deep in front of the house."

"They had a beer party, Gene," I said.

"You're right, and it must've lasted all winter long."

But I was glad to be home, and Virginia and Tommy looked healthy and happy. Virginia said, "You missed lots of action while you were gone. You should've been here when the shore ice went out. It was a sight to see when it left. There was four or five square miles of it, all going out at once. The ice took away all the village garbage dump and the oil drums."

Later that evening, while Virginia was catching me up on all the village news, I was lying on the couch and noticed a bullet hole in the ceiling. "What made that bullet hole in the ceiling, or was it there all along?" I asked.

She said, "Honey, you won't believe this, but one night I thought I heard a noise in the schoolroom. I decided to get out the twenty-two Hornet. I put a shell in the chamber and pushed the bolt in, and the gun went off. It really scared me when it did. I don't know what happened, and I still don't know what was the noise in the schoolroom."

I thought that if there had been a prowler in the building, they'd probably never be back. "Did the bullet go on through the upstairs and out the roof?"

"I looked, but I didn't see where it went," she said. "I went upstairs to see if the bullet went on through and out the roof, but found no sign of a bullet hole."

While I was in Sitka, the Air Force Distant Early Warning (DEW) line site on top of Cape Mountain was put in service and the Army detachment had abandoned their base up the beach. Toby informed me the Army had left all their Quonset huts, as well as some supplies and equipment. Among the equipment abandoned was a Caterpillar tractor and about a mile of two-inch galvanized piping with connectors. I decided the pipe could immediately be put into village use the same way we brought water down from our mountain spring in North Carolina. So I suggested to Toby, "Let's use the Cat to haul the pipes to the village. We can connect the pipes together to make a water line from the creek on the mountain to a central location in the village where the people can collect their water in buckets the rest of the summer. They won't have to carry or haul it so far."

Toby grinned, "Well, we could do it, but the water would just freeze up starting about first of October. Anyway, I think it will be all right to try it. The people could get water for maybe three months."

"Can you run the Cat?"

"Yes, Army boy show us how before he left."

The waterline to the middle of the village was completed in less than a day. For the next three months, water was handy for everyone in the village. However, it was a grave disappointment when, on September 18th, the line froze solid and had to be disconnected. (Today, a million-gallon tank is filled each summer from the creek on the mountain to supply the school. The village people still melt ice and snow in winter.)

While I was at the teacher's meeting in Sitka, the hunters had been busy replenishing their caches with meat. They had launched their skin boats into the strait every day that was favorable to hunt, sometimes on Sunday. But Joshua Ahwinona, the Eskimo Covenant Mission preacher, had been preaching against hunting on Sunday. He said to me, "Some Wales men have been hunting on Sunday. I tell them they should not be hunting on Sunday. I am Eskimo also and I have to have meat too, but I never hunt on Sunday. I am from White Mountain, south of Nome, and Eskimo people there never hunt on Sunday."

I told Dwight what Joshua had said to me about not hunting on Sunday.

He said, "Yes, he's been preaching against hunting on Sunday. He preaches against it every time now. He is from White Mountain, and weather here is much different than White Mountain. We have to hunt when the weather is good. Sometimes the weather is good for hunting in Wales *only* when it is Sunday."

The weather was nice on Sunday afternoon, July 8, when a knock came on my door. It was Dwight. "We are going out in skin boat," he said. "If you want, you can get ready and come along. We think we see walrus way out."

"Didn't you get enough meat when the bull walrus went through the strait?" I asked.

"We didn't get enough," he answered. "The weather was bad, and when it was good, the ice pack was against the shore ice. So we might not have enough meat to feed the dogs."

Soon five of us were in Dwight's skin boat, heading into the strait. I mentioned to Dwight, "This is Sunday. Did you go to church this morning?"

"Yes," he said. "And Ahwinona preach again this morning not to hunt on Sunday, but we saw with telescope a walrus way out there." He pointed toward East Cape in Siberia.

When we were about eighteen miles out and about ten miles north of the Diomedes, Pete Sereadlook, who was standing up front in the boat with binoculars, pointed and said something in Eskimo.

I asked Dwight, "What did he say?"

"He say he see walrus."

Soon I saw this lone bull with monstrous tusks on the edge of an ice floe about thirty feet in diameter. There was considerable discussion by the men, and I asked, "What are you talking about?"

Dwight cut the motor off, then let the boat drift slowly toward the walrus, which seemed to be unaware of our presence. Was it asleep? Dwight spoke quietly and slowly, first in Eskimo, apparently assessing the situation, then in English to me, "Well, we see the walrus is on the edge of the ice. It might fall in the water if we shoot it. It's a big walrus and I don't think there's enough of us to pull it back up on the ice if it falls in the water. We might not have enough gas to go back home if we try to drag it in the water. We've drifted pretty far north and we have to go home against the current."

The walrus began weaving. Perhaps it was disturbed by our presence and might, at the slightest provocation, slide into the water. The boat was almost still as the men quietly discussed the situation. They lifted their guns and pointed them toward the walrus. Only Dwight was speaking. The walrus continued to weave back and forth, first over the ice, then over the water. At the next instant, it leaned back over the ice and all four high-powered guns fired. The walrus fell straight down with only its tail in the water. The men conversed in Eskimo, seemingly pleased with what they had done and perhaps discussing how to move the two-ton bull toward the center of the floe and

begin the butchering.

I helped pull the boat on top of the floe. Dwight got a
block and tackle from the boat and anchored one end toward the middle of the floe, then he tied the other end to the
tusks. Everyone pulled as we moved the walrus away from
the edge, then rolled it onto its back.

The first cut was made down the belly through the
two-inch hide, from the neck to the flipper. They then
separated the hide on each side until it was lying blubber
side up underneath the carcass. Dwight looked up from his
work and pointed, with blood dripping from his knife,
toward the south. "You can tell from looking at the
Diomede Islands that we are across the International Date
Line," he said. "We are now in Monday. This is not Sunday.
We are not hunting on Sunday. I will tell Ahwinona about
it." Everyone laughed.

I stepped back to take a picture and Dwight warned,
"Don't get too close to the edge. The ice near the edge is
thin by melting from warm water underneath. It might
break off." I agreed.

Later in July, I was in the office when Toby came in and
said, "There's a boat out there from Nome. It's one man. He
say he's going out to Fairway Rock to take pictures. Maybe
you should talk to him. It is too dangerous to go to Fairway

Rock in small boat." Fairway Rock, a remnant neck of an ancient volcano eighteen miles due west of Wales on the American side of the International Date Line, serves as a rookery for tens of thousands of birds. The Wales natives go there once each spring to gather eggs, as weather and sea current conditions permit. This year, the trip was made the last week of June, after which Toby came smiling to our apartment and handed Virginia a huge egg. He said, "Here is good egg. You and Wilford will like."

"But what is it?" she asked when she took it, "an ostrich egg?"

"No, I think white men call it 'murre' or something like that. We call it '*mig-uk*'. The bird only lays one egg a year."

The next morning, Virginia broke the egg into a large frying pan. We ate fresh scrambled egg, not eggs, which tasted like hen eggs, a food we hadn't had in nearly a year.

I walked with Toby to the beach, where five or six men, including Roland Angnaboogok, had gathered around a young white man. He was taking some pictures as I walked up. We greeted and shook hands. I noticed his new twelve-foot fiberglass boat, his Johnson sixty-five horsepower motor, and perhaps thousands of dollars worth of camera equipment. "You sure do have some nice equipment with you," I commented. "The natives here tell me you're going out to Fairway Rock."

"Yes," he responded. "I'm going out to take pictures of the birds on the rookery out there."

"The natives say you should not go. They only go out there in skin boats and when they think conditions are favorable."

"This is a strong boat and motor," he said. "It won't take me long to do it and get back before the weather changes."

"But you don't know what it is really like out there," I pleaded. "About five miles out, you will hit the strong current, and it's flowing like a fast river,"

Roland walked over to me and said in a solemn, low tone, "He shouldn't try it."

I repeated to the young man, "*All* the natives here say you shouldn't go out there."

"I'm going to start out," the young man replied, "and if it gets too rough, I'll just come back, but I don't think I'll have any trouble at all." He was determined to go. We couldn't stop him.

He left, and we stood on the beach and watched him go fast out of sight. We never saw the young man again. About a week later, Winton Weyapuk brought in two pieces of the boat, which he said he found washed ashore on the beach fifteen miles north of the village. I had two radio calls inquiring about the man. A plane came and took the pieces of the boat. As far as I know, the man was never found.

About the middle of July, one of the children opened the door to my office and shouted, "Lots of people out there! They are from Diomede." I opened the door and saw four skin boats had arrived on the beach. About forty or fifty people were walking ashore. They were Little Diomede villagers on their way to Nome, a trip they take each summer to fish for salmon and to sell fur clothing and ivory carvings that they make during the winter. They stop at Wales and stay overnight with friends or relatives before proceeding the next day toward Nome. The villagers were accompanied by BIA teachers from Chicago, who spent the night with us. We stayed up late into the night, swapping stories of happenings of the previous winter. We enjoyed comparing notes of school operations and differences among the children of the two villages. We had numerous experiences in common.

Throughout the late afternoon and early evening, the beach in front of the school was alive with excited Wales and Little Diomede children playing together. The Diomede teacher and I walked outside to watch and listen. Communication was almost entirely in Eskimo. Only the accent of the children from the two villages seemed to differ.

There was one word the Wales children used quite frequently while they played that seemed to puzzle the children from Little Diomede. It was *ee'-see-ah ick-ee* or just *ee'-see-ah*. I mentioned that the Wales schoolchildren had been using this word all year and asked him if he had ever heard that word before. He said he hadn't.

Earlier I had asked Toby, "What is meant by *ee'-see-ah*?" I hear the children saying that word, or *ee'-see-ah ick-ee* all the time."

Toby said, "I been hearing that word too. I don't know

what it means. Maybe some new word. No grownups are saying it."

I deduced from the context in which *ee'-see-ah* was being used, that it meant in English "you're silly," and that, ee'-see-ah ick-ee meant something like "that's very silly," or "that's a silly mistake." I asked Toby if he thought this might be the meaning.

With a broad smile he said, "I think so. Maybe it is."

Later that summer, when the Little Diomede villagers and teachers again stopped to spend the night on their way back to the Island, I noticed the Diomede children also were saying *ee'-see-ah ick-ee* at times while they played.

The following morning, early, Toby and I walked on the beach to the edge of the surf to bid the Little Diomede Islanders and the teachers "goodbye" and watch them depart Wales in four skin boats to go back across the strait to their island home. Three motors were attached to each skin boat. They headed due west till they hit the current, then turned their boats southwest. But I noticed their boats were not moving southwest, they were moving west. "They're really fighting the current out there," I commented to Toby.

"Yes," he said, "but the Little Diomeders know about the current."

"Do they ever have trouble making this crossing?" I asked. "It looks a little foggy right now out there toward the Island."

"Only sometimes do they turn back."

"Do you think they can make it today?" I asked.

"Yes," he replied. "There's some fog, but they have compasses."

Soon the boats were out of sight. I went back into the school to begin preparing the mountain of monthly reports required by the various governmental departments in Nome, Anchorage, Juneau and Washington, and to place carbon copies in the school files, a burden that I finished late that afternoon. After dinner I felt greatly relieved that the monthly secretarial task was done, so I started for a walk to the village store.

As I stepped outside the door, I witnessed the most shocking sight of my life. The Diomede teacher's wife, drenched from head to toe, was walking toward me in heavy clothing, her hair in strings on the side of her face and across her shoulders! Her eyes looked as though she had witnessed death first hand. My first thought was, had she swum the Bering Strait? "My God, what happened?" I said. "And where are the others?"

She was aquiver and her lips were blue. Her voice was shaking and weak and she could hardly speak. "We've been out there all day--fourteen hours! We reached the island but..."

"Where are all the others?" I interrupted.

"Everyone is all right. We're just wet and cold," she responded, trembling, while pointing up the beach into a gray fog. I looked up the beach to where a large crowd was gathering around skin boats with their bows part-way onto the beach. "The men were afraid to land the boats. It was just foggy and rough. We kept taking on water. They were afraid to land. They said, 'it looks like Russian island instead of our island.' " She coughed. "They discussed the situation a long time. We just kept bouncing in the boats. It was awful! They pulled skin covers over the boats and tied them to keep out most of the water. Everything got wet."

I saw women and children going toward houses and said, "Let's get inside and warm up, and get on some dry clothes. Virginia will have some dry clothes for you, and I have some for your husband. Where is he?"

"He's helping the Eskimos carry some things to the store where they're going to dry them out overnight. He will be along shortly."

After our visitors were dried out and Virginia had fed them, we enjoyed another evening of discussion, since the day's harrowing adventure had presented another topic for that. The next morning, all the boats again departed for Little Diomede Island. This time they made it.

Before the end of the summer of 1956, the Bering Strait was to claim three more lives. A radio call came from Nome, "Have you seen, or has anyone reported to you seeing, a tug and barge with three men passing through the Bering Strait?"

"Negative."

"What's your weather been like out there?"

"Wind about twenty-five knots, waves about six feet, whitecaps, fog. It's been this way for several days. Over." Five days later, Roland and Winton retrieved two of the bodies from the beach and reported seeing the wreckage onshore near the twenty-mile inlet--just one more testament to sometimes awesome conditions of weather in the Bering Strait near Cape Prince of Wales, Alaska.

The Cemetery

Above the village, on the northwest slope of the mountain, about one hundred yards from the school, is located one of the two village cemeteries. It is the older of the two and is no longer used for burial by Wales people.

The cemetery on the mountain is decorated with wildflowers, tundra grass and scattered boulders of age-old volcanic ejecta, draped with pods of gray lichen. The ground, except for four or five inches during the summer, remains frozen to great depths the year around, so bodies were never buried underground in years past. They were placed on top of the ground, either wrapped in skins or in boxes made of driftwood poles or sawed lumber. In most cases, the outer coverings and the lids of the boxes have long since been altered by the elements or blown away by the wind. No headstones. No names. The bare skeletons mark the graves and tell their stories.

Several times during my stay at Wales, I walked among the scene and had a feeling of going back in time. Here lies a skeleton with teeth worn flat from a lifetime of crimping soles of mukluks. That's a female. There's a male with a rusted musket and weathered harpoon by his side.

The cemetery used today by the Eskimos of Wales is among the sand dunes one mile north of the village. The village began using the sand dunes for burial under the direction of the U.S. magistrate in Nome after the devastating 1918 flu. The sand of the dunes thaws quicker in spring and to a greater depth than the soil under the vegetation farther inland. Also the dunes are more easily excavated to a depth adequate to place a body in a grave.

The people of Wales have encountered one problem,

however, with burying people in the sand dunes. It results when the wind shifts the sand during the thaws of summer. Although the dunes may move only a few inches each year, in time the movement may amount to feet. Such was the case during the middle of September, my second year in Wales.

Dwight Tevuk came into the schoolroom where I was teaching and said, "I've got to leave the post office. If anyone comes, tell them I'll be back tomorrow. We've got to go rebury my grandmother in the sand dunes. The wind is almost blow the sand off."

"Sure," I said. "Just leave the door open to the hallway. I'll tell Toby where you've gone."

The next morning, I stepped to the post office window in the hallway and asked Dwight, "Did you get your grandmother reburied?"

"Yes, she was getting almost uncovered, but we managed to bury her better."

"How long ago was it when she died?"

"It was something around 1920," he answered somberly. "You know, when I saw her yesterday, still she was frozen. We moved the cover off her face and I remembered her. She looked exactly the same as before when she died."

Two Bits

Two Bits was a cuddly Eskimo husky pup and the only pet dog in the village. He belonged to the Ahwinonas, whose house was just thirty feet from the front door of the school. They allowed "Two Bits" to run loose around the house and village, even though it was strictly against a village ordinance to allow any dog to run loose. Two Bits played with the schoolchildren at recess as if he were one of them, and the children enjoyed playing and running with Two Bits. No one in the village dared try, in this case, to enforce the village ordinance. The Ahwinonas even allowed Two Bits to be inside their house some of the time.

He raced and wrestled with some of the children, while all the other village dogs could only bark and howl, as they were kept chained to iron posts outside their masters' homes except when it came time to pull a sled. Each family had up to fifteen dogs tied outside their houses, much like we would park cars in a driveway.

In walking through the village, one dared not walk through an area where dogs were chained. You would walk around them at a safe distance. If you got too close, the dogs would bark, bare their teeth, then lunge toward you till the end of their chains brought them back to earth.

One day Toby said to me, "That dog, Two Bits, will be no good some day. Wales people never make pets of dogs. Dogs are for work. Not playing. Maybe Eskimos at White Mountain where Ahwinona is from, make pets of dogs, but *we* do not! One time it was tried. One man had a pet dog, then when it got grown up and hooked in dog team, it was no good. It wouldn't pull."

During the fall of our second year in Wales, I noticed

Ahwinona beginning to train Two Bits, now grown, to pull a sled. He never allowed Two Bits to be loose again and kept him tied near the other dogs, where he would pull against his chains and wag his tail and bark at the schoolchildren as if he longed to join them at play.

One day I asked Ahwinona, "How's Two Bits coming along? Is he learning to pull?"

He said, "I dunno. Maybe later he might learn to pull. I'm trying to teach him." He laughed and shook his head.

A few weeks later I asked him if he would take me to the Air Force base at Tin City by dogsled. The base was below the Air Force Distant Early Warning site, ten miles east of Wales and a thousand feet up the side of Cape Mountain. A contingent of eighty men manned the base. Although the Air Force boys were never allowed to visit the village, the CO welcomed village people to occasionally go there and make purchases from the base exchange (BX).

Ahwinona said, "Yes, we'll go. I might buy something also. Anyway I need to give Two Bits more workout." He laughed.

The Saturday morning rose crisp and clear. I stood out back of the church, a safe distance from where his dogs were chained, to watch Ahwinona ready his dogs for the trip around the cape to Tin City. He pushed his twelve-foot homemade wooden sled from inside the rear entrance of the parsonage, then stomped a two-foot steel anchor into the hard snow. He laid out a strong, twenty-eight-foot nylon line with traces, which he attached to the front of the sled. He untangled and spread out the traces where each dog was to be positioned. The dogs began jumping and barking and rattling their chains since they knew they were going to be allowed to run. He first unchained the lead dog, which knew exactly where to go. She led Ahwinona in a trot to the head of the line where she knew she would be harnessed. She then sat on her haunches to watch him unchain the ten other eager dogs, one by one, then lead them to their positions. Two Bits was hooked on the left side, second dog from the back of the line beside an older female. Ahwinona turned to me and laughed as he said, "I usually hook a male beside a female. Never a male beside a male. They would just fight."

When all dogs were hitched and impatiently clawing at snow, Ahwinona said, "Now we are ready to go. You sit in the sled." I sat down, while he stood on the back of the runners with his hands on the handlebars. The dogs jumped and barked and pulled at their traces. "Hold on," he said. "We are ready to go. I am now going to lift the anchor. Mush!"

At the word "Mush," he lifted the anchor. The dogs accelerated, while I held tight to the side rails and took a fast carnival ride, Eskimo style! The fresh dogs left Wales in a dash, going south on the shore ice at the base of the cliffs, then around the point of the cape, then gradually settled into a steady trot.

Ahwinona yelled at Two Bits as I first noticed he wasn't pulling at all. He was jogging along with a limp line, looking left then right. He seemed to enjoy the trip and the scenery while all the lines of the other dogs were taut. Ahwinona again yelled at Two Bits who looked back at us then tightened his line, but only briefly. He yelled again, "Two Bits!" but with the same result.

Soon, Ahwinona began stepping off the sled to run and catch Two Bits and swat him with a rope or his hand. This, too, seemed to help, but only for a short while. Then Two Bits would quit pulling again.

Occasionally the dog running beside Two Bits looked at him as if to say, "Come on, Two Bits. Do your part. You're making it hard on the rest of us." Instead of pulling, Two Bits just let the other dogs pull him *and* the sled. It seemed that he wished he could ride rather than pull. Ahwinona was obviously getting frustrated.

When we arrived at Tin City, Ahwinona drove the sled anchor firmly into the hard, wind-packed snow and walked to the lead dog to rub crusted ice from between the toes of her two front paws. We stayed at the base for about an hour during, which time the dogs could lie down and rest.

The trip back toward the village was no better. I could see that every mile we went, the more aggravated Ahwinona became with Two Bits. Finally, about halfway back to Wales, he said, "Whoa!" which all the dogs understood, even Two Bits. They looked back at us as if to say, *"Ka-ya-nah!"* He walked to Two Bits and unhooked him. He led him by the collar twenty steps away from the sled and took out his pistol and dispatched him with one shot. I was thoroughly shocked and saddened, but said nothing.

Ahwinona put his gun back in its holster, then walked back to the sled. He stood on the runners and said, "Mush!" All ten of the remaining dogs obeyed his command, and we were off again, with a vacant space on the left side, second slot from the rear. I risked a glance in Ahwinona's direction. He was grim-faced and looking straight ahead into the teeth of a cold wind with blowing snow, but I thought I detected a tear as he said, "Two Bits no good."

Babies Born

The BIA hired only husband-and-wife teams to teach in the small remote Eskimo villages in Alaska, because they found that young married couples were the ones least likely to get homesick, especially if they had children of their own. In fact, the long winters in isolation only seemed to increase the numbers of children they had. In this respect, Virginia and I were no exception. When we arrived at Wales we had a son, Tommy, age two, and had decided that he should have a brother or sister. In May the following year we calculated that our second baby would be born sometime in January.

During Virginia's pregnancy we often discussed whether she should go to Nome and wait there for the doctor to deliver the baby or stay in the village and let the midwives do it. We had already observed the proficiency of the midwives in delivering three babies and weren't the slightest apprehensive about letting them deliver ours as well.

Through radio conversations with other teachers in the villages around the Seward Peninsula, we learned that occasionally a teacher's wife had her delivery done by a midwife, but, when possible, most teachers preferred to go to Nome and wait.

The doctor at the little ten-bed hospital in Nome, Dr. Langston, was twice voted "Doctor of the Year" for all of Alaska. He was highly respected throughout the Seward Peninsula and nearby islands. So Virginia and I decided Nome was an option. We were also aware that the midwives were available at any time. The doctor, however, had advised Virginia to come to Nome if she could get there. Such advice was frequently given over the radio to teachers all over the Seward Peninsula. Thus, everyone in much of

Alaska knew when a BIA teacher's wife was expectant.

During November, the teacher at Elim talked frequently with the teacher at the neighboring village of Golovin, which is between Elim and Nome. The Elim teacher had formerly taught at Golovin and wanted a certain sixteen-year-old Eskimo schoolgirl at Golovin to come to Elim to baby-sit with his small children while his pregnant wife went to Nome to have her next baby. The baby sitter had relatives in Elim with whom she could stay at night.

This conversation continued for several days until the arrangements were finalized. The baby-sitter came to Elim on the bush flight carrying the weekly mail, and the teacher's wife climbed aboard the return flight to Nome to wait for her delivery by Dr. Langston.

That night, when I turned my radio on, the teacher's wife was talking on the BIA radio in Nome to her husband in Elim. She was doing "fine" in the Polaris Hotel. The baby-sitter did "fine" with her children while he taught school that day. All seemed well. The next morning, however, when I again had my radio on, my attention was caught by loud, animated conversation between the teacher at Elim and the teacher at Golovin. It went something like this:

Golovin teacher: "What? Did you say Teresa (the baby-sitter) had a baby? I didn't even know she was pregnant!"

Elim teacher: "I didn't know it either. She got off the plane and baby-sat all day with our kids and I had no idea! She had on her parka and I couldn't tell."

Golovin teacher: "Well, she kept her parka on here at school all day every day, too, and I never suspected she was pregnant. Most children keep their parkas on anyway. You can hardly make them take them off."

Elim teacher: "All the adults keep theirs on all day. It's a custom here."

Golovin teacher, slightly lowering his voice: "How's Teresa?"

Elim teacher: "She's fine. The baby's fine. I was just over to see her. She wanted to come to baby-sit but another woman is going to come and stay with the kids today."

The next day, Teresa baby-sat with the Elim teacher's children as well as her own baby, which she continued to do for the next three weeks while his wife waited in Nome for her baby to be born.

On the fifteenth of January, the daylight hours were short. We had received no mail since the sixth of December. The weather had been stormy, with one blizzard after another, either blowing strong with wet snow from the south or in flurries or showers with cold winds from the north. All the while, Virginia was looking more pregnant than ever. We knew she was due anytime. I don't know who was more anxious, she or I.

Each day during school hours, I left the radio receiver turned on with the volume tuned high in case a call came from the BIA office or from our mailman, Bob Jacobs, the Alaska Airlines bush pilot who might ask for a Wales weather report. The radio transmitter and receiver were located on a desk in the office between the schoolroom and our quarters.

While I was helping a student at his seat with a math problem, the student seemed inattentive to my instruction. Instead he looked up at me smiling and said, "Bob Jacobs is calling for you."

"Are you sure?" I asked. I had not heard a call.

"Yes, he's *been* calling."

I went to the radio and pushed the button on top of the mike, "Alaska-Nome, this is Two-Four Wales. Were you calling? Over."

"Two-Four Wales, this is Alaska-Nome. Do you read me? Over." It *was* Bob calling.

"Alaska-Nome, Two-Four Wales back. I read you loud and clear. Over." I thought that he might be bringing our mail today. I also thought of Virginia.

"How's your weather up there, Will?"

"Stand by." I said, then stepped outside the office door to look briefly at the flag and observe the overcast. I hurried back to the radio. "Alaska-Nome, Two-Four Wales. The wind is south about ten. The ceiling is about 300 feet overcast. The visibility is almost unlimited. Over."

"Well, I'm loading the plane now and am going to head up your way. Over."

On going back into the schoolroom, I noticed the children had become talkative and excited, their normal reaction each time "the mail plane is coming." I walked into the school kitchen, where Virginia and three older girls were preparing the school lunch.

I said to Virginia, "The mail plane is coming. Do you want to go in to Nome or just let the midwives deliver the baby? This may be the last plane we get for some time. What do you think?"

"I'll just let the midwives do it," she said as she stirred something in a pot on the stove. The other girls looked at me, then at Virginia, and turned back to stacking small bowls on a table and wrapping spoons in paper towels. As I stepped back inside the classroom, I noticed increased activity and excitement in the hallway beside the post office. The main school entrance door banged constantly. Village people were mailing last-minute letters and packages, and I assumed everyone in the village knew by now that the mail plane was on its way.

Fifteen minutes later, Virginia walked into the schoolroom. She pulled off her apron and handed it to me in front of the children and said, "I've decided. I believe I will go in on this plane to Nome to have it. I'll go get ready." She walked quickly through the office to our quarters.

Soon the plane buzzed the school, then circled to land. Virginia came into the schoolroom with her travel bag in hand; she was ready to go. I turned the children out for recess and walked with her to the plane. Her conversation consisted of last-minute instructions on what to cook, and how to cook, and how to take care of Tommy, but I paid no attention to any of these instructions. She said, "Don't worry about me."

"And don't you worry about us," I replied. Food and stuff was the last thing on my mind. To me, this was a serious interruption of our daily routine. I hoped it would be short-lived.

Soon the plane was off for Nome. Each night for two weeks, Virginia went to the BIA office so we could talk by radio to each other. She usually asked, "How are you doing? How's Tommy?"

"We're fine. Nora Ahwinona has been keeping Tommy during the day. She likes to keep him. She brings him home in the afternoons talking in Eskimo and smelling like blubber. She said he really likes to eat dried whitefish."

Each time we talked, Virginia seemed happy to hear what I said. On her fifteenth day in Nome she said, "Dr. Langston said it won't be long now. He said he may induce labor anyway. He said he does that all the time."

The next afternoon, I got a call from Dr. Langston. He said, "You are the proud father of a seven-pound baby girl. Virginia and baby are both fine. They should be going back to Wales soon."

"Thank you for the call, doctor," I said, then put down the mike. I wiped tears of joy from both eyes and went back into the classroom.

For the next four days, I talked to Virginia each night. She was doing fine. The baby was fine. She sounded excited and happy each time. She said, "The baby is real cute, and I've got lots of things to tell you when I get back to Wales."

Two days later she did get back. I walked to meet the plane, along with Toby and several other people, including five or six giggling teenage schoolgirls, who, I assumed, were anxious to see and hold the little white baby. The temperature was twenty-five below. A stiff breeze was from the north but the sky was clear. Toby opened the door of the plane, and there was a happy, smiling mother standing in the doorway with a bundle wrapped in a rabbit fur blanket in one arm and an overnight bag in the other. Toby took the bag and she handed me the bundle. She said, "You've got it upside down!" I turned it over. I wanted to take a peek but was afraid to in the wind, with the temperature at twenty-five below.

We walked hurriedly back to the school. Inside our quarters, Tommy and I got our first look at Paula. Virginia was excited to see Tommy. She kissed him and said, "You really look good, Tommy. Gosh, how you've grown!"

We exchanged stories for the next fifteen or twenty minutes, then she said, "You will not believe this! You won't believe what I'm going to tell you. You know when I left here to go to Nome, the plane landed at the airstrip at Tin City to leave off some mail for the Air Force boys. Bob didn't know that the wind from that last storm had ripped all the snow off their runway. He was already starting to land with the skis on the runway when he saw it was white sand instead of snow. The plane was just about down before he noticed it. We landed fast and hard! I was afraid I would have the baby right there.

"The Air Force boys were real nice, though. They took me up to the base while snow was hauled in and spread out so we could take off again. I stayed at the base about an hour, then they came and took me back to the plane, and we took off for Nome."

Eight weeks after Paula was born and all the ladies and girls of the village had dropped by to see her, Toby

walked into the classroom and said, "The midwives came for the baby box. I got it for them. It is Martha. She thinks she is ready."

When school was turned out, Toby came into the office with one of the midwives. They each had a grave and worried look on their faces. They were talking in Eskimo. Then Toby faced me and said, "Martha's having some kind of trouble." He turned back to the midwife. They conversed some more, then he said, "The midwives don't know what is happening. They never saw anything like this before. We think maybe you should talk to the doctor."

I made immediate contact with the doctor and described the situation as the midwife told it to Toby in Eskimo and as he in turn told it to me.

The doctor asked, "How's your weather out there?"

"The weather is good here. We have a slight breeze from the north, and the ceiling and visibility are unlimited."

"It's good here too," he said. "I'll charter a plane now to go out to Wales and pick her up. Have her ready to go."

Toby heard the message and said, "I'll go get her ready," then hurriedly left.

In a little over an hour, Bob Jacobs picked up Martha and departed for Nome. Two hours later, Bob called from Nome and said, "Tell Toby his wife has a set of twin girls. The doctor said to tell him they are about three pounds each, and that the mother and babies are doing fine. You wouldn't believe the excitement that took place here in Nome. You know, Will, one of them came out in my pick-up truck while I was driving her to the hospital. We had a time! I thought I had seen everything until that happened. Over."

I went to get my parka to go tell Toby, but I met him as I started to go through the office door. He was excited. He said, "I heard it. I heard on my radio what Bob said. That's good!"

"What will be their names, Toby?" I asked.

"I dunno. Maybe Martha will name them. She always does." He grinned.

The twins were premature; they weighed only two and a half pounds each. Martha and the twins returned to Wales three weeks later. I went to Toby's house to see them. They looked so tiny. I asked Martha, "What are their names?"

She smiled and pointed to each and said, "This is Christine, and this is Matrona."

After the twins had been home for two weeks, Toby came to me in the schoolroom one afternoon with a worried look on his face. He said, "The twins, they are getting very sick. They also, both of them, have some kind of ear trouble."

"I'll go down to take a look as soon as school is out, then call the doctor." I went to his house after school and took their temperatures, which were ninety-one and ninety-two. I noticed their ears were badly infected and swollen. I radioed this information to the BIA doctor at Kotzebue, who said, "Start them on 150 units of penicillin twice a day and keep them wrapped in something warm. Tell the parents to keep them up high in the room, where it is warmer. This should help to elevate their temperatures back to normal. On shooting the penicillin, you don't have much buttocks there to shoot into, but keep on till you get it all in."

I went to the house the next three days to shoot the penicillin but the twins didn't seem to be getting any better. I reported their conditions to the doctor who said, "Increase the dosage of penicillin to 300 units twice a day." I did as he prescribed.

Again, three days later I told the doctor the babies had still made no improvement. He said, "Increase the dosage to 600 units."

"Did you say *six-hundred units*?" I asked. I was dumbfounded. "That's an adult dosage. Over!"

He answered calmly. "Yes, start them on 600 units of penicillin twice a day and keep me informed how they're doing."

I did what he said to do. I spent about a minute each time injecting the dosage to each baby. To my amazement, the twins began to make progress slowly. Then, in six days the twins appeared to be doing well and we stopped giving the penicillin.

Thirty-two years later, I revisited Wales. I got to see Toby, Martha and some others. Toby said, " I want to introduce you to two of my daughters. This is Christine, and this is Matrona." He pointed to each of them. "I have been telling them about you."

Each woman, healthy, with cheeks full and black hair long, smiled and looked straight at me with dark, piercing eyes. Christine had a baby of her own in the pouch of her parka.

Where To Next?

The end of April brought a questionnaire from the BIA office in Juneau. We were given three choices: stay at Wales, transfer to another BIA school, or resign. Virginia suggested, "If we can, let's go to another village where it's not so cold and windy, so our children can be outside more."

I asked for a transfer to another Indian Service village in Alaska and was offered Point Lay, another very windy village on the coast, three hundred miles north of Wales. We declined the offer. Then I applied for a teaching position in the public schools at Fairbanks and was offered a job teaching

Among those who saw us off when we left Wales in 1957 were, from left to right, Jonah Tokienna, Dwight Tevuk, Glenn Sereudlook, Toby Anungazuk (waving), May Tevuk, Katie Tokienna, Fay Ongtovasruk, Ruth Koweluk and Gertrude Kowluk.

sixth grade. I accepted and was asked to stop by Fairbanks to sign a contract on our way "Outside" for vacation.

We were welcomed at the Fairbanks airport by friendly, five-foot-nine, slender and slightly balding schools superintendent, Dr. Cornelius Ryan. He was proud of his school system and happy to have me join it. He gave me a quick tour of the sparkling new Nordale Elementary School on the north end of town, where I was to teach. As we left the building and walked toward the parking lot, he produced from his coat pocket a contract, which I signed over the hood of his car.

Upon returning to the airport, I still had nearly an hour to wait in the terminal lounge for our flight to leave. As I sat on a couch waiting for our flight to be called, I was suddenly struck by the sight of green grass outside and new leaves on a small aspen. The leaves on the tree were not moving. A woman walked by outside and her dress hung straight down. The wind was not blowing. The world was stopped. This was weird! I then recalled the first response Alfred Mazonna made to me when he came back to Wales after his trip to Anchorage. He had said, "*No wind!*" I now realized, for the first time, why he said it. After spending two years in the winds of Wales, I understood what "*no wind*" is like.

While in the air on the first leg of our flight home to North Carolina, Virginia asked me, "Have you looked at yourself in the mirror?"

"No, why?"

"You should go back to the rest room and look at yourself."

"What's wrong with me?"

"Your suntan is only on the front of your face. It's really brown, but the top of your head, the back of your face, your ears and your neck are pale white. I guess it's the way you have been wearing your parka with your hood up." She laughed. "People at home will think it's funny."

I went to the rest room and noticed the contrast between the brown of the front of my face and the stark white of my ears, neck and the top of my forehead. Later in North Carolina, a few people gave my brown and jaundiced facial appearance a double look. One man asked, "Have you had some kind of burn or disease?"

I tried explaining that I had gotten a suntan on my face from the glare of ice and snow and from windburn, during the spring hunting trips in skinboats with the Eskimos. He didn't seem to believe me. "I don't see how you could get a suntan where it is so cold," he said.

Virginia said a woman also asked her, "Is Wilford well?"

During the summer I ran headlong into culture shock. Think about it! I had lived the past two years in a little village on the Bering Strait where everyone walked when they went from one house to another or to the village store or to go to church. I got to know all 128 people who lived there and could recognize some by their manner of walk, even if they were a half mile away. I learned to know them by their gait, their swagger, how they lifted their feet, moved their shoulders. And when I met them as I walked through the village, whether to deliver a message I had received by radio or to shoot penicillin into a baby's buttocks, they smiled and I smiled back.

Now I was back home in North Carolina for the summer, where I knew everyone who lived along the eight miles of rural road on Ellijay Creek. But here I recognized no one I met since they were riding inside their cars. I sometimes expressed my cynicism of this way of life, only to receive sideways looks as if to say, "What's happened to Wilford? Is he in his right mind?"

Nevertheless, I survived the summer by driving fifteen miles daily to the little university across the mountain, where I got my master's degree in education. I mailed a copy of my credits to the school system in Fairbanks so I could get extra pay for teaching.

When we arrived back in Fairbanks and were settled into a furnished apartment, I drove to the school where I was to teach. The school secretary said, "Dr. Ryan wants to see you right away. He's at his office on the second floor of Main School on Cushman Street."

"What does he want to see me about?"

"I don't know. He just said for me to tell you to come by his office when you got here."

Main School was a large, white, three-storied, stucco structure that consumed about half the block. The rest was playground. A sign at the front entrance directed me to the

Education Department at the top of the stairs on the second floor. After a few minutes of small talk with Dr. Ryan in his office, he said, "I notice you have received a Master's Degree this summer. I called your home in North Carolina about a week ago but they said you had already left. The assistant principal's job here in Main School is open and I would like for you to take it. The school has thirty-eight teachers in grades seven, eight and nine, plus four sections in the kindergarten through 3rd grade for students who live near the school."

The job meant a substantial increase in salary, and I quickly accepted the position. Later, I learned I was the *third* assistant principal in Main School in as many years.

My job as assistant principal amounted to scheduling classes for the twenty-four teachers in the junior high section, monitoring the loading and unloading of buses, dealing with disruptive students sent to me by teachers, flooding the skating rink with water after school, filling requisitions for the teachers from the school's dusty supply-room, and a myriad of other boring administrative duties. This included attendance at meetings of the school board whose members were all male and competed to see who could be the most macho. The main item of business discussed was: "Which bar in town do we meet in next, and whose turn is it to buy the drinks?"

During this time, Virginia's sister Hazel and her husband Dennis moved to Anchorage. Hazel was teaching first grade at North Star Elementary School. Dennis had not taught for the past two years, opting instead for flight school and a job as a pilot in the Air Force. Now he was serving full-time in the Alaska Air National Guard, flight training fighter pilots who patrolled western Alaska to intercept any Russian intrusion into U. S. airspace. One Friday in the middle of November, Dennis flew his F-86 into Fairbanks on a "navigational proficiency flight," then caught a cab to our apartment. He spent the night with us in our apartment, sleeping on the roll-out couch with Tommy. The next morning he said, "I slept good except when Tommy kicked during the night."

Virginia and I made plans to get together with Hazel and Dennis in Anchorage for Thanksgiving; however, our plans were suddenly changed on the night of the 23rd. That night, when I went to join Virginia in bed, I left the television set tuned to a Fairbanks station so I could continue listening to an interesting program in progress.

"You didn't turn off the television," Virginia complained.

"It won't hurt anything," I said, but realized this was the first time I had ever gone to bed while leaving the TV on. I fell asleep with the TV running, but I awakened to hear the news at 3:00 a.m. that Dennis was one of four fatalities in a plane crash near Juneau.

I nudged Virginia and said, "I just heard on the television that Dennis was killed!" She was shocked, but skeptical that it really had happened.

The phone rang at ten minutes to six and I answered by saying, "I heard it on the news at three this morning."

It was Hazel, and she was distraught. I told her that we'd get ready to come to Anchorage right away. She insisted it wasn't necessary for us to come, that she had plenty of friends offering assistance to her and her three small children. Nevertheless, we decided we should get ready to go.

Virginia began dressing Tommy and Paula and packing two handbags while I shaved, got dressed and went to warm up the car. The outside temperature was thirty-one below zero. It had seldom been above zero during the past six weeks. I started the car, then unplugged it from the electrical charger and head-bolt heater and checked to make sure the tire chains were still in the trunk. I drove to the corner service station to gas up. While there, I checked the air in the tires and bought a can of de-icer, which I placed in the glove compartment. When I returned to the apartment, Virginia and the children were eating cereal. She said, "We're about ready to go. Eat a bite of cereal." After we finished eating, she put the dishes in the sink while I called the school to tell them what had happened and that we were going to Anchorage.

We departed for Anchorage at 8:00 a.m., with thick deposits of ice on the interior of most of the car's windows, the result of daily driving and weeks of outside parking in frigid Fairbanks temperatures. Warm moisture from the air had formed ice on the inside of every window that did not have frost shields.

We neared Anchorage at 2:00 p.m. I was surprised to see no snow on the ground and noticed the outside temperature was quite warm. Suddenly, Virginia screamed as I hit a bump in the road that jarred loose buckets of ice onto the children, the car seats and the floorboard. I stopped the car and we spent the next ten minutes throwing out ice.

Our visit in Anchorage was indeed sad, as we helped Hazel make plans to move with her three children back to North Carolina. A memorial service on Elmendorf Air Force Base was scheduled in three days, and funeral services in North Carolina in ten. Although Virginia and I wanted to be present at all the services, Hazel insisted that we not subject our children to the disruption. She said we should go on back to Fairbanks and get on with our lives. We left Anchorage late on the afternoon of the 25th.

Our return trip to Fairbanks was all in darkness, but despite the fresh snow that had fallen, the road was well plowed and we encountered practically no traffic. At a point 150 miles from Fairbanks, I noticed something strange about the snowbank I had just passed on the right side of the road. I stopped the car and began backing.

Virginia muttered, "*What* are you doing?"

"I think there may be something below the road. Maybe a car down there." I stopped the car and stepped outside, and saw that car tracks, indeed, led through the snowbank. I walked to the edge and saw a car on its side about fifty feet down a steep embankment. Its headlights shone dimly in the deep snow.

A man's voice yelled, "Yes, we're here. Just the two of us. We're all right." Then a man in his thirties climbed out the upper side door and reached inside to lift out his small daughter, whom he struggled to carry in two-foot-deep snow up the embankment to the road.

"How can we help?" I asked.

"Would you just take us to the nearest facility where we can be warm and get help?" he asked with a slight shiver. I noticed that neither of them was dressed for exposure to this cold for any extended period of time. He said he didn't know why he wrecked but that he may have fallen asleep. He said they were heading for Anchorage and had been wrecked for about two hours. I left them at the nearest roadhouse, about twenty miles up the road.

In Fairbanks, I developed a close friendship with Al Baumeister who was born and raised in Fairbanks and now taught ninth grade history in the room next to my office. He came in often to chat with me about various school and worldly problems. Being from the mountains of North Carolina, where the Scotch-Irish tradition held that the first Christmas present given to a boy was a pocket knife, I always carried one, even in Fairbanks while serving as vice principal, for use in sharpening pencils, opening packages or trimming fingernails, even though Fairbanks school rules did not allow students to carry "weapons." One day in February, a smiling Al stepped into my office and proudly produced from his pocket a brand new pocket knife, which he said was the first one he ever owned.

My most enjoyable experience in Fairbanks was with Al after ice breakup on the Chena River. His wife dropped us off about ten miles upriver. Al used a stick to break a twelve foot wide chunk of ice from the riverbank, which we used for a raft as we fished for Dolly Varden trout all the way back to town.

But enjoyable experiences were rare in this town. For me, it was too crowded, too boring, too much of a concrete jungle and too "Lower Forty-eight". I could hardly wait for school to end so I could head for the wide open spaces. At the end of the last day of school, I said good-by to some of my colleagues, then walked to the superintendent's office to resign and list my forwarding address where the secretary could mail my last check. I wrote, "Cullasaja, NC."

The following morning, Paula, Tommy, Virginia and I were in our car heading down the Alaska Highway.

I applied for another BIA school in Alaska. No luck. I then applied, and was accepted, to teach ninth-grade general science in my hometown in North Carolina, where I told stories of my experiences at Cape Prince of Wales on the Bering Strait.

Exactly forty years later I received a telephone call from a student I had in one of those classes. She now holds a doctorate in education, had served as superintendent of two different county school systems and four years as assistant school superintendent of the State of North Carolina. She, like me, is one who thrives on thrills of adventure.

She said, "Remember me? This is Betty Wallace. I used to be Betty Cloer."

"Yes, I remember."

"Well Wilford, this is going to surprise you, but I'm going to be principal at your old school at Wales."

"Wow! Where are you calling from?"

"I'm calling from Golovin. It's a little village southeast of Nome. I've been principal here for the last two years. And before that I was working at Point Barrow. Wilford, I just love it up here. And your stories, years ago, in the ninth-grade science class are probably the main reason I am here."

While teaching ninth-grade science in North Carolina, I again applied for another Indian Service school in Alaska. Again, I had no luck, but was accepted to teach eighth-grade in Anchorage. We drove up the Alaska Highway with an additional member of our family, our three-week-old son, Carroll.

While in Anchorage, you might say I was continually longing for adventure someplace in the outback such as Wales or the Bering Strait. I remembered the excitement and pride Katie Tokienna's father must have felt after walking across the strait and wondered why no white man has tried it. I also remembered Toby saying the ice in the strait is less concentrated now than before. He had said, "It's only in February now that the ice is sometimes thick enough in the strait that a person might walk across." So I believed if that feat were to be repeated, it must be done soon. I wrote to Intourist in Moscow asking for permission to walk across on the ice and go ashore at East Cape in Siberia.

"But they won't give permission for you to do that," said Virginia.

"You'll never know till you ask. They've recently opened up their country to American tourists to enter through Europe. Why not the Bering Strait also?"

"But why do you want to walk across the strait?"

"Because it's there. Same reason people climb a mountain. Suppose I become the first white man to walk across?"

"What will you do if they give you permission?"

"Then I'll start looking for sponsors, magazines, suppliers."

"What if you start walking and run into open water?"

"If that happens, I'll rig a sail on a floe."

"But if you do that you won't be walking. You'll be sailing."

The answer came by mail from Moscow: permission denied!

I continued to apply for a BIA school. No luck. That summer, while we were home in North Carolina on vacation, I applied for a teaching position in the high-paying Rockville, Maryland, school system on the outskirts of Washington, DC. Late that summer I drove to Maryland for an interview to teach sixth grade. I was accepted, then signed the contract and was given a tour of the school. On my return home, a telegram from the BIA office in Juneau was waiting. It offered me a position at another tiny Eskimo village, Scammon Bay, on the Yukon-Kuskokwim Delta. I couldn't get to Western Union fast enough to wire acceptance! I mailed letters of resignation to the Anchorage and Rockville school systems.

To Scammon Bay

Scammon Bay is a Yup'ik village on the coast of the Bering Sea, 550 miles north of the Aleutian Islands and 140 miles northwest of Bethel. When I went there as a Bureau of Indian Affairs teacher in 1960, the people referred to themselves as Eskimo and as speaking the Eskimo language. A BIA brochure said the school was established in 1954 and that the population of the village was 140, with forty-two children in grades one through eight.

We flew by turbo-prop from Anchorage to Bethel, where we were to spend the night and proceed to the village by bush plane the following day. We stayed overnight in the ten-room Bethel Roadhouse and ate family-style with other guests at a large table. The food was in large bowls and the handles of the serving spoons were bent into a crook so they wouldn't slip into the food.

The next morning, we met the bush pilot at his four-seat float plane on the bank of the Kuskokwim River. He was a dark-haired white man, slight of build, about thirty years of age, wearing dark, horn-rimmed sunglasses. I handed him the tickets for our flight. He introduced himself as Gary. Then he looked at my feet and said, "When we arrive at Scammon Bay, we will be landing on the river and you'll be stepping off the float of the plane and walking through wet mud to the top of the bank. You should change from those street shoes to rubber boots, if you have any."

I dug into one of the three navy sea bags which held most of our belongings and retrieved a new pair of hip boots, which I slipped on. I passed Virginia her ten-inch red rubber boots, then handed our bags to Gary. He placed them behind the seats. Virginia climbed aboard with Carroll. I handed Paula to Gary, who set her inside. Tommy crawled into the plane without assistance. I sat down in the seat beside Gary. He looked to see that everyone was buckled in their seats, then began revving his motor for take-off down river into a sharp breeze.

The river was choppy, and the plane hit a few bumps on the noisy, vibrating take-off, but soon quieted to a purr as it leveled off, heading northwest. We then flew about 300 feet over slum-looking houses on the outskirts of town. Ten minutes after leaving Bethel, I pointed to a cluster of fifteen or twenty rustic buildings we were passing on our left. Gary said, "That's Kasigluk. It's the last village we'll see before we get to Scammon Bay. That white building with the red roof is the school. All the BIA school buildings are painted that way."

We flew over numerous lakes with scattered pairs of large white birds. Some were in the water and others were standing on the tundra. Gary said, "Those white birds are swans. They come north in the summer to raise their young. This is nesting grounds for millions of birds. There's brown geese and ducks down there, too. You can't see them, but the tundra is covered up with them."

After thirty minutes of flying, we passed three low craters, each of which looked to be several hundred feet across. Gary said, "Those are ancient volcanoes. All the mountains beside Scammon Bay were formed by volcanic action long ago."

Soon we flew through a low pass near the east end of the Askinuk Mountains and came in sight of the Bering Sea on the horizon to our west. We dropped quickly over a flat plain, then came into view of Kun River meandering between hundreds of lakes. Gary nudged me, pointed to the left and said, "There's the village. That's Scammon Bay."

The village was nestled against the side of the mountain near a tall remnant dike of igneous rock above the mouth of the river. At the upper end of the village was a small stream with waterfalls cascading beside a large, white, frame building with a red roof. This, I thought, was the one-room schoolhouse and our home for the next two years. Two other wooden buildings at opposite ends of the village were painted and had steeples. About twenty smaller structures I assumed were homes of the village

people. All, except the two structures with steeples, were unpainted but also appeared to be of wood. The sight would have appeared bleak and desolate to us if we hadn't already experienced two years at the remote, isolated village of Wales on the Bering Strait. We didn't regret or think twice about our choice to come here, even though we knew our relations with the outside world would be limited to infrequent contact by radio and mail by bush plane.

We approached a lake at the north end of the village, below the school and between the hill and the river. I wondered if that might be where we were going to land but recalled that Gary had said we would be landing on the river. He banked the plane toward the west and flew low over the north side of the river as clouds of geese rose into the air from the tundra beneath us. Ahead, I saw the mouth of the river where it emptied into the bay. Gary made a one-eighty and landed upriver into the wind on low waves. He taxied to the edge of the river at the mouth of the little stream, where a group of four or five men and several children were standing at the top of the riverbank, smiling. Some of the children had large sores on their faces. What's that? I wondered.

A husky man with hip boots stepped into mud five inches deep and hooked a rope around a cleat on the right float. He held it while a wiry man, about five-nine, who wore glasses and had coal black hair sticking about an inch over his ears underneath a baseball cap, climbed onto the float and opened the door from the outside. I stepped to the door. He smiled broadly, showing pearly-white teeth, and spoke rapidly. "I'm Lars Hunter, the school janitor. We will carry your stuff up to the school." His clear and distinctive English surprised me since I had been told that the school had been established in Scammon Bay for only six years. Was Lars an Eskimo from some other village?

"Hi! I'm the new teacher," I said, as we shook hands. I glanced on the bank at two other men, who nodded their heads and smiled. Yes, I thought, Eskimo-land is a friendly place and we are greeted warmly!

Lars lifted Tommy off the float, then handed him to another man standing in the mud, who stood him on top of the bank. This process was repeated with Paula, Carroll and, finally, our baggage. I stepped into the mud, then turned to brace Virginia as she stepped off the float, first with her right foot, then with her left. As she started to take her first step, her right foot slipped out of her boot, now mired six inches deep in the dark gray mud. She stopped and leaned against me while holding her stocking foot above the mud. I said, "Careful now! Step your foot back-wards into your boot and bring your boot out with your foot." She did as I suggested and retrieved her boot while some of the men laughed. We slogged through the sticky mud to the top of the bank, where tundra grass waved lightly in a chilly breeze from the northeast.

Lars pointed to two men and said, "These are Tom Tunutmuk and John Amukon. They will help carry your baggage." The men smiled and each picked up a bag. I carried Carroll, while Virginia led Paula. Tommy walked behind, as we began the 100-yard walk toward the school on a well trodden trail alongside the small stream. Shortly, the path turned up the gently sloping hill, where we came alongside a pair of wooden rails, two feet apart, that ex-tended straight through the village to the school. Lars commented, "This is the village railroad tracks. We have a winch at the school and we use it when the BIA ship, *North Star*, comes with the supplies. We pull everything on a cart up the hill from the river to the store and to the school."

We walked past low, unpainted houses, some made of plywood, others of driftwood logs. The logs on some structures were horizontal, on others vertical. Above the galvanized metal roof of every house was a windmill, whirling and whining in the breeze.

Halfway to the school, our entourage passed two young women wearing decorative fur parkas. They were standing on the low porch of a building, under a rustic sign which read, "Amukon's Store." They nodded and smiled as we walked by. A ten-or twelve-year-old boy, also smiling, but with an ulcerated sore on his chin the size of a Coca Cola bottle cap, came alongside Lars and spoke to him in Eskimo. Lars answered in Eskimo.

I wondered whether the sores on the children's faces were caused by injuries or some sort of disease. I wondered, too, how these children could smile with such facial disorder or disease. The next day, I described the condition by radio to the doctor at Bethel. He said, "The children have impetigo, a disease of the skin which mainly affects only children and is spread by scratching." He told us what to do. Virginia and I, as well as a young Eskimo woman, Eula Johnson, the village health aide, were to spend the next two months scrubbing off sores with soap and applying antibiotics and Band-Aids. Eula, thirty-some, bilingual and willing to consult the BIA doctor at Bethel by radio concerning village health problems, was welcome news to me.

On arrival at the school, we walked up a flight of steps to a small porch. The sound of the stream as it cascaded over large volcanic boulders by our apartment was like rain on a metal roof. We went inside, where the men set our baggage down in the living room. I turned to Tom and John and said "Thank you." Both men smiled as they said, "*Ee-ee*," then left.

Lars gave us a tour of the building, which was considerably smaller and newer than the school at Wales. Our quarters, with two bedrooms on the main floor and a company room with two cots upstairs, looked inviting and cozy. The building had flush toilets and hot and cold tap water. Electricity was supplied from a five-kilowatt Witte diesel electric generator in a building above the school. The schoolroom was twenty-four by forty-five feet, with a cloak room near the entrance, and a kitchen, storage room and restroom off a narrow hallway.

I stepped outside the front entrance to the school onto a porch. Below me in the schoolyard, eight or ten teenage boys were playing soccer with, of all things, a human skull! I saw the village cemetery about a hundred yards to the east around the side of the hill, then made my first directive to the children at Scammon Bay: "Take that skull back out to the cemetery!"

A boy of about fourteen asked, "Do you have a ball?"

I said, "Yes, I think so," then stepped back inside the schoolroom to look for one. The boy came to the door and pointed behind me to the corner. He said, "In beeg box, over there."

I turned and went to a two-foot by three-foot wooden box in the back corner of the room, where I found a soccer ball, which I threw out to the children. Each raced to be first to get it.

One boy smiled and said, "Thank-a-you." I noticed another child was running with the skull to the cemetery.

Scammon Bay was the only school in an Eskimo village in Alaska to have tap water and flush toilets. Lars said water was piped into the building from the stream that coursed by the building year-round, even though it froze over and was covered by deep snow in winter. I knew I was going to enjoy the luxury of free-flowing water all year, a luxury we did not have at Wales.

The water supply came from a concrete catch basin built across the stream fifty yards above the school. The basin had a thirty-foot drop in elevation, so water could flow into the school by gravity. A two-inch pipeline extended underground to the building, through the basement and back to the edge of the stream, sixty feet down the hill below the school. The end of the pipe had no cut-off valve, so the water gushed continuously onto the bank then flowed back into the stream. The idea was that running water would not freeze. A valve installed on the line in the basement of the school was used to shut off the water flowing toward the stream for a short while, forcing water to flow up through a "T" in the line and fill a thousand-gallon water storage tank

in a room off the hallway. From there, a water pump supplied pressure for the rest-rooms and the kitchens in the
school and living quarters. When the storage tank was filled,
the valve in the basement was again opened so the water in
the pipe could resume flowing to the edge of the stream.
People who lived in nearby homes came to the end of this
pipeline with buckets to get their water.

Lars said, "The only problem with this system is, when
it gets real cold it freezes up. No more water all winter."

"What?" I asked in near shock. "Did you say our water
will freeze up? How can it freeze as long as the water is
kept flowing through the pipe? I've never known fast-flowing water to freeze."

"But it gets real cold here. It's different from other
places," he said. "When the weather is real cold, the end of
the pipe where the water flows out starts building up a
cone of ice around the end, and the end of the pipe will
soon close up and the water can't flow. This happens
around November or December, when the whole pipeline
will freeze and can't be thawed till next spring. This is the
way it happens every year since the school was built."

"You mean we will have to go back to melting snow or
ice?" I asked. The thought of being without a continuous
supply of running water, which required us to carry snow
or ice to melt, was putting a damper on the enthusiasm I
had about Scammon Bay. There were five of us now in our
family, and we all liked to stand in a shower or soak in a
tub. Virginia let Paula and Carroll play in the bathtub with
little toy ducks and boats and splatter water all over the
floor. The thought that, sometime around November or
December, the luxury of having plenty of running water
would not be available set me in a mild depression.

That night in bed, I kept thinking that soon our water
pipe would freeze and stay frozen the rest of the winter, and
we would have to carry water as we did at Wales. There had
to be a better way! I repeated over and over in my mind how
Lars described the freeze-up of the water line. I remembered
how splattering water near waterfalls in North Carolina can
cause thick ice to form in winter. Although I had never seen
it happen before, I imagined how splattering water would
indeed cause an ice buildup which could eventually enclose

the end of the pipe, especially when the weather was extremely cold and windy. There just had to be a way to keep the water running. Then the idea suddenly came to me. I knew how it could be done. It was so simple!

The next morning, when Lars arrived at the school, I said, "I know how we can keep the water flowing all winter and you won't have to carry it to the tank."

"But it can't be done," he said. "It gets too cold here. The cone will freeze at the end of the pipe and the pipe will freeze up. Then I will carry in the snow to put in the tank like always. I will do it. That's my job."

"No, listen," I said. "What we need to do is extend the end of the pipe over those rocks and into the creek so that the end is under the water, out of the air, where it can't freeze."

His face brightened, then he laughed and said, "It will work! Why didn't somebody think of that before? I know it will work. It will work. I'll go do it."

"Do you have enough pipe and tools to do it?"

"I have everything I need in the basement. I'll go do it now."

"Do you need any help?"

"No, I can do it myself."

Two hours later, Lars came into the schoolroom with a broad smile and announced, "It's all finished. I put the end of the pipe under the water." We had running water during the two years we were at Scammon Bay, and Lars didn't carry a single load of ice, water or snow into the building.

During the thirty-nine years since that day in 1960, the population of Scammon Bay has tripled to 434. Today, the village has piped water and a sewer system connecting most of the homes, as well as a large school and gymnasium. I believe the rapid growth of the population is due mainly to the availability of good water from the fast-flowing stream.

One hour before the first day of school, Lars came running into my quarters and said, "Patrick has been shot!"

"Patrick Amukon?"

"Yes. On the hand with his shotgun. He's in the radio room now. You can call for a plane."

I went into the radio room, which also held the cabinets of first-aid supplies, where the seventeen-year-old, eighth-grade student with a fresh haircut was in total shock and pain. I retrieved some large sterile compresses and gauze from the medicine cabinet, then pulled away the bloody rag around the wound to see that three fingers and half the palm of his right hand were completely blown away. I re-bandaged his hand tightly, then untied a rag around his arm and gave him two Phenobarbital tablets with a glass of water. I called Bethel for a plane to pick him up to take him to the hospital.

I asked Lars, "What happened?"

He said, "Well, I found out the boys were excited about school going to start today, and they went out to hunt early in the morning while the young Canada geese are flying. The geese fly early in the mornings when, I guess, they're getting their wings ready to fly away south. Patrick's gun was jamming and he would hit it on the ground so it would shoot, but this time he had his hand at the end of the barrel when he did it, and all three shots came out from his automatic shotgun."

The plane landed on the river at nine, and the depressed village watched Patrick climb aboard and depart for Bethel Hospital. The dispirited first day of school began at ten.

Margarretta at her Scammon Bay driftwood log home, 1960.

Land for Free

Three weeks after school started, I received a two-and-a-half page memo from the Department of the Interior, Bureau of Indian Affairs, Washington, DC. It said the natives of Scammon Bay did not own real estate property, not even the land on which their houses stood, and instructed me to explain the provision passed by Congress whereby the village people could own land free of charge.

I asked Lars to call a meeting of all the heads of households and anyone else who might want to attend. The meeting was on a Friday evening. About twenty-five men showed up; no women or children came.

I paraphrased the memo line by line and gave examples. Lars interpreted. I finished my presentation in about fifteen minutes.

In brief, the memo stated that for Scammon Bay natives to own land, all that was required of them was to drive stakes in the ground to show where they wanted their land to be located. The government would then survey the tract free of charge. Each family would be allowed to own up to 640 acres.

I told them they could select land by the bay, sea, river, lakes, the mountains or the flats--wherever they liked. They would be given a paper called a "deed" showing the land was theirs, at no cost to them whatsoever.

The men began talking and talking, all in Eskimo. The only word I understood was a frequent *ee-ee*, yes. It seemed to me that the meeting was harmonious, that they felt fortunate to be granted the United States government's offer of free real estate.

While they talked, I sat there thinking that if many

heads of households were to accept the offer of free land, government surveyors would soon be coming and planes might start flying in and out of Scammon Bay daily. Their conversation showed no sign of ending soon, so I stepped into the office, thinking my absence might speed things up. I could still hear them talking. After twenty minutes, I returned into the schoolroom, but the talking continued so I left again.

After another twenty minutes, I again walked into the schoolroom and took a seat beside Lars. This time the talking stopped. Everyone sat quietly. The men looked at me and at Lars. Lars didn't speak. He was looking down.

I decided to break the stalemate. "What did they say, Lars?"

He hesitated, then looked at the wall with a sly grin, then back at the floor, and began speaking. "Well, they don't much like it," he said. "They say maybe if somebody put up fence around their land, then dog teams couldn't go that way. They say if somebody owns land beside river, maybe others can't put boat in river. They say if somebody owns a lake or stream, others might not be allowed to catch fish or set traps. They say maybe they be required to build house only on their land and the houses might be far apart, then if somebody needs help, others may be too far away to help them. They say it is different here from the States. They don't believe you should own land. They believe the land should be for everyone."

I was completely stunned by his statement. I thought, "Well, good speech, Lars," but forced a smile and said, "Thank you." I then turned to the others and said, *"Ka-ya-nah."*

Some men looked at me and smiled as they nodded their heads up and down. Some said, "Thank you." Others said, *"Ka-ya-nah."* They got up and went out the door laughing and talking in Eskimo.

Movie Time

Later that fall, I thought of the Saturday night Eskimo dances at Wales in the winter months and asked Lars, "Do Scammon Bay people have dances?"

He said, "We don't have dances, just games. People like to come to school to play games. I think they also like for you to order movies to show on the school projectors. The people will pay admission to see it."

I browsed through a movie catalogue and saw that we could rent *Bambi*. I thought perhaps *Bambi* might be a movie that most of the people would enjoy seeing.

I asked Lars, "Have they ever seen the movie *Bambi*?

"They haven't seen it," he said.

"OK, I'll order it then."

I put the order on the next mail flight that left the village. The movie came in three weeks. It created considerable excitement among the schoolchildren when they saw Lars put the two large, metal containers of film on my schoolroom desk. After school, I discussed with Lars how much we should charge for admission to cover the rent and postage. We scheduled the showing for the following night at 7:00.

The following night, as people began arriving, Lars and Teresa Sundown, a seventeen-year-old eighth-grader, took up money for admission. At fifteen minutes till seven, people quit coming and the room was crowded. Every chair was filled. People were sitting on desks around the edge of the room. Some sat on bookcases. Two or three were standing, and the floor up front was packed with children. Two or three young women had babies in the pouches of their parkas behind their heads.

Lars said, "We maybe should start the movie. Maybe no more going to come."

I motioned for Lars to turn out the lights, and he flipped the switch. The room was in dead silence. I started the film rolling. Everyone paid attention. Two minutes into the film, two men got up and walked out without saying a word. I wondered where they were going. Within another minute, a half dozen more got up and left. Then others filed out quietly, including three seventh-and eighth-grade boys. Why are they leaving?

I was appalled. I walked to the side of the room where Lars stood grinning, and asked, "Why are the people leaving?"

"Well," he said. "They don't like the talking animals. They don't like the little animals acting like people. They believe the animals are more for food and clothing."

"Should we give them back their money?"

"No, they don't want the money." He giggled.

Others left and two mothers came to the front, smiled at me, then led their children out. Only ten children and four young men and women stayed for the whole show.

I was still in shock the next morning when I asked Lars, "What kind of movies do the people like?"

"Mostly it's westerns and cowboy movies they like. Maybe you can order one."

"I will," I said, and ordered western movies from that day forward.

Cultural Clash

At the end of each school day, when the children were gone home, Lars came into the schoolroom to clean, and usually he shared with me any news of consequence that occurred in the village during the day. One afternoon in late spring he said, "Some visitors have come to the village. They are down at Amukon's store. It's some men and boys from village twenty, or maybe thirty, miles north of Scammon Bay."

"You mean there's another village that close?" I had listened to radio conversations of teachers and bush pilots throughout the Yukon-Kuskokwim Delta and thought I was familiar with all the villages in the area.

"Yes, it's a new village. Only been there few years. They came by dog team and brought furs to trade with John Amukon."

I was curious to learn what these people were like. I thought they might have some interesting stories to tell, then asked, "Do you think it would be all right if I went down to talk to them?"

"Yes, I think it will be all right if you go talk to them. But you will need interpreter because they speak no English."

On entering the store I first noticed large bundles of mink and muskrat furs in the middle of the floor. John Amukon, the owner, was sitting behind a small table on the left side of the room. When my eyes became adjusted to the dim light, I saw three men and four school-age boys sitting on benches and kegs along the other side of the room. Each was dressed in a fur parka, pants and mukluks. Their

ruffs were lowered to their shoulders and their hair pro-
truded from underneath baseball caps and completely hid
their ears. Each one eyed me stoically. I smiled and said
"Hi." Except for a slight grin and show of pearly teeth from
an older gentleman with greying hair and bushy eyebrows,
my gesture was met with cold stares. I turned to Amukon,
who was smiling, and asked, "Can you interpret for me?"

He shook his head and said, "I think not."

At that point I began to feel like an intruder and suspected he might be in the process of negotiating prices with
the visitors, so I decided to leave. As I left for the door, I
smiled and held up the palm of my hand toward the visitors
with fingers pointing up, but their only response was to
watch me go.

When I arrived back at the school, Lars paused in
mopping the floor. He leaned on the handle then looked at
me and asked, "Did you talk with the visitors?"

"No," I answered. "They didn't seem to want to talk and
John wouldn't interpret. I wonder why?"

Lars chuckled, then said, "Well, I think maybe they
were afraid of you."

"Afraid of *me*? Why should they be afraid of me?"

"They were probably thinking you might be going to try
to make their children go to school or something."

"I wouldn't do that. I couldn't. No way would I even try
to do that."

"Yes, but one time, I think it was the same time the
government built the school here at Scammon Bay, they
also built a school at their village, but as soon as the school
was built, the whole village moved away to another place
and built their village where it is now. At that time a BIA
man—he was a white man—went to their new village and
tried to talk to them and make them go back to their old
village where the new school was built. But the people, they
wouldn't go back. Then I think the BIA man got mad about
it or something." Lars giggled.

"But *why* did they move the village away from the new
school building?" I asked.

"They moved to the new place because it is better for
hunting and trapping."

I thought, what if I had struck up a conversation with

the men? What if I had suggested to the men that they put these boys in school? Would their response have been essentially the same as the old man's response in 1893 to the U.S. Marshal when he came to Wales after the three boys were put to death for murdering the schoolteacher, Harrison R. Thornton: "*We already teach them?*"

That spring, school had been going on at Scammon Bay for six years, almost seven, during which the children learned reading, writing and arithmetic, and took tests. Ah, yes, tests! Every year while I was in school, I also took tests. And every year since I've taught school, I've *given* tests, so this year was no different. Near the end of school in the spring I gave a standardized achievement test. One question: *The sun rises in the A) south, B) west, C) east, D) north.* The answer is C) east. But at this latitude, at this time of year, the sun circled the school to shine in every window during the day. The sun rose well above the horizon at noon, then sank below a gorgeous sunset in the northwest near midnight to rise a short couple of hours later in the *north.* So the children at Scammon Bay wrote *D) North,* and I counted their answers correct.

Dog Sled Travels

Each family in Scammon Bay owned a team of sled dogs, which they kept chained to stakes apart from each other to prevent fighting and at a safe distance from the four village walking paths to keep them from attacking people. Lars gave us the same advice Toby had given us when we were at Wales: "Walk only on the village trails. Be careful when the snow is drifting and you can't see the trail because sometimes the dogs just curl up and get covered over with snow. You should watch where you walk so you don't step on one. The dogs will attack anyone except the people who feed them."

The presence of these canines was most noticeable our first stormy night in the village. When we went to bed I was

conscious of the howling east wind that was shaking the building and the doleful sound of a hundred howling dogs, which amounted to a bloodcurdling scream.

I sensed that Virginia was somewhat frightened and tried to cheer her up by saying, "Listen to the dogs. They're singing a cappella."

"Don't be funny," she quipped. "The sound is lonesome, and scary."

The following morning when the storm had somewhat abated, I said to Lars, "The dogs were sure howling last night. I was slow in getting to sleep."

"I noticed the howling, too," he said. "The dogs howl mostly at night when it gets real windy. Wolves also howl in windy times. These dogs are like wolves. I think the whistling of the wind around buildings and rock cliffs hurt their ears."

The first snowfall that quickened the village came on the fifth of October. That morning before school, Lars stomped loose snow off his army boots as he came through the front door smiling. Large flakes were coming down and the ground was gaining a whiteness that was to last for the next nine months.

"Isn't this a little early for the first snowfall?" I asked.

"No," he said, while wiping moisture from his black horned-rimmed glasses with a piece of paper towel, "It is time for the first snow and freeze-up to start. First snow usually comes around first week of October. Sometimes later, sometimes earlier, but mostly it starts the first week of October."

During that day in school, the children were especially charged with excitement. They frequently looked out the window at swirling snowflakes, then made comments in Eskimo to their seat mates. At recess, the din of shouting children competed with the barking of dogs, as the children chased one another while throwing the new-fallen snow.

After school, while Lars was sweeping the floor and picking up pencils that had rolled off desks, I said, "The children were more talkative and excited in school today."

"Yes, they always get that way when the first snow comes. They play more, same as the animals. All the animals get excited and play when first snow comes. I think children are like the animals." He laughed. "The dogs in the village have been just barking all day. I think they want to start pulling sleds. I saw John Amukon already went out with his dogs a while ago. I think Sundown is getting ready to go out too, and maybe few others."

Later, I went for a walk in the two-inch snow through the south end of the village. I crossed the little stream and began following dog and sled tracks leading toward the head of the bay at the mouth of the river. After following the trail a few hundred yards, I noticed the tracks were purple. What was this? I turned to look at the tracks where I had stepped. They too were purple. I kicked aside some purple snow and uncovered squashed berries on the crowberry vine, a ground-hugging evergreen that has pink blossoms in springtime but now was filled with black, blueberry-like berries.

That night after dinner, I was sitting in the office listening to some Bethel-area teachers chatting on the radio and waiting for my chance to get in a word or two, when Virginia came to the door. She said, "I wish you would come in here and look out there below the house in the porch light. The children and I have been watching a little animal running back and forth and jumping and turning in the snow. It looks like a weasel. There it is now!"

I stepped into the living room for a view through the picture window, as a small, slender, brownish animal darted from underneath our front porch steps then turned and ran back toward the basement of the school. "That's an ermine," I said. "It's not yet changed to its winter coat of white. It likes to play in the snow. Lars said that *all* animals like to play when the first snow falls." Immediately it ran from the basement of the school, turned a flip in the air, jumped as if catching snowflakes, then darted into a hole underneath the Catholic church, only to quickly emerge again and continue an hour-long show of running, jumping, twisting, turning and rolling in the snow.

While we watched, Tommy said, "Maybe it's putting on the show just for us."

The following morning, when Lars arrived at the school, I told him about the antics of the frolicsome weasel. I also mentioned the purple sled dog tracks I observed the previous afternoon.

"Yes," he said. "The women and girls have been picking those berries. They've been picking lots of berries but the snow has stopped them picking now." He laughed. "The berries stay frozen in deep freeze all winter. When spring comes and the berries are uncovered, sometimes they can pick some more."

But dogsled travel was of more interest to Lars than picking berries. He said, "I started getting my dogs ready yesterday. You should go with me on my dogsled. Teachers before always like to go on dogsled. I go out every weekend when weather is good for hunting or fishing. Some men have traps out, but I can't set traps because of working here at the school. I like to go fishing upriver through the ice and sometimes ptarmigan hunting. I think you and Virginia will like fresh fish and ptarmigan."

"I would love to go," I said. I needed more recreation and decided I should stop wasting weekends writing the following week's five boring lesson plans for each of nine grades. Thereafter, my lesson plans were seldom written and were instantly concocted at the beginning of classes, which I rationalized were more spontaneous, exciting and interesting to the children. My weekends were also free to help Lars bring home food for his family and his dogs, while I put fresh meat on our table as well.

During sled dog trips, I usually sat in the sled while Lars held the handlebars and stood on the back of the runners so he could step on the brake when necessary. We sometimes exchanged positions, and when the dogs approached a steep hill, we both stepped off to run alongside.

Dog sled travel on the tundra is in stark contrast to traveling on roadways by car or trails through a forest. It's more like traveling by ship at sea, in which one may go in any direction up to 360 degrees. Here you are traveling in complete wilderness with nothing around you except the sight of whiteness and the swishing sound of sled runners over smooth snow. No exhaust fumes or rattle and clanging of pistons inside of cylinders.

One Saturday as Lars and I were traveling by dog team a half mile north from the village, I was sitting in the sled

when I saw another team on the horizon coming directly toward us. I pointed and said, "I see another dog team coming."

"Yes, I see it," he said. "I think it is Andrew Ulak."

Lars spoke to the dogs, "Gee." His lead dog responded by guiding the team to the right a few degrees but gradually returned to trotting in the direction of Ulak's team. Lars repeated sharply, "*Gee*," and again the dogs turned to the right, only to again swerve to running in the direction of Ulak's team.

I sensed Lars did not want our dogs to approach the other team in the same pathway. I asked, "What do you do when you meet another team?"

"Each team goes to his right," he quickly responded, then repeated, "*Gee*" louder than before. But the dogs paid him no heed. Instead they increased pace and headed straight toward the other team, now less than two hundred yards from us, and whose musher was also unsuccessful in steering his dogs to *his* right. Lars yelled again, "*Gee! Gee!*" But his dogs continued straight at Ulak's team, which was now coming directly at us. I asked, "What will they do when they meet?"

"They *fight*," he said then screamed, "*Gee! Gee! Gee!*" He jumped on his brake, a two-pronged set of iron points between the back of the runners that he pushed deep into the snow. That failed to slow the powerful legs of his eleven dogs. They were hell-bent to meet Ulak's team of thirteen, bearing down hard on us with bristling fur and menacing white teeth. That's when I concluded the sled was no place for me! I rolled off as Lars, riding his brake, passed by like a water-skier and spewed snow from a foot-deep furrow.

The teams met in a cloud of snow dust that was seen all the way back in the village. Twenty-four dogs met in mortal combat, snarling, slashing, gnashing and shaking any canine ear, leg, tail or body within range—no matter which team it belonged to.

I stood clear as Lars and Ulak retrieved long chains which they swung at any—and as many—dogs, as fast as they could. Any dog stopped fighting that was struck by a chain, but then only momentarily. Chain-lashing of several minutes was required to stop all the dogs from fighting. But just when I thought all fighting was stopped, two dogs that were not yet cowed erupted in a duel. Lars struck them once and that fight was stopped as well.

The men were breathing fast when they laid their chains on their sleds. They discussed in Eskimo the predicament and assessed the damage. They appeared not to place blame on each other. I noticed spots of blood on the snow as well as the fur, faces, legs and backs of every dog. Ropes and harnesses were tattered and tangled. I wondered if we would now have to walk home. I stood aside as Lars and Ulak spent the next twenty minutes fashioning harnesses from pieces of ropes, slapping dogs that growled, and returning each dog to its position.

When our tired and limping team was going again, I asked, "Do dogs get into fights like that often?"

"No, hardly ever. That's only second fight I saw." I suddenly realized I failed to record a picture.

"Do all mushers carry chains in their sleds?"

"Yes, we have village law to carry chains," he replied. "Only way to stop dog teams from fighting is with chains."

After school one day in late March, Lars said, "You should visit a real Eskimo igloo like the one where I was born."

"Where?" I asked.

"About twenty miles from here. We go two miles past

Cape Romanzof. It's about halfway toward Hooper Bay. An old woman and old man live there all their lives in Eskimo sod house. I know them well."

One Saturday, we left to go there by Lars' team of nine dogs. The temperature was twenty degrees above zero, with a slight north wind. We left on the ice of the bay, going west along the base of the Askinuk Mountains to our left, which rose abruptly two thousand feet and were topped by menacing ledges of overhanging snow. Suddenly, at about the nine-mile point, we came upon a bank of deep snow that blocked our way and extended fifty yards onto the ice. Lars directed the dogs to turn to the right and go around the snowbank. He said, "That was an avalanche come down."

"I'm sure glad we weren't here when it happened," I said.

"Yes, avalanches come off the mountain every year. We don't come this way later in spring when snow gets soft on top of mountain, because even a little vibration like dog's feet or sled going over bumps can cause avalanche to come down. But if that ever happens when you are around, if it comes toward you, don't try to run from it. The snow will knock you down and run you over and bury you. Scammon Bay Eskimos know from long ago not to run from avalanche. They say you should run toward avalanche and get on top if you can. Two Scammon Bay men were saved one time by running on top of avalanche."

As we approached the cape, the wind was to our backs and had blown off all the snow. The ice was slick like glass, and reminded me of slippery conditions of the shore ice after a period of strong south winds at Cape Prince of Wales. The tail wind here made for easy pulling and presented no problem until a strong gust blew our sled into the rear dogs. Two or three were momentarily knocked down, but quickly scrambled to their feet. I was relieved to see no dog was injured and wondered why Lars hadn't stepped on his brake to slow the sled.

On arriving at the sod house, the snow was level to the roof except ten feet in front of the entrance, where a row of blocks of hard snow were stacked on each side five feet high and three feet apart. I followed Lars as he walked between the snow blocks and pushed aside a reindeer hide hanging over the entrance, then stooped low to enter a dark, narrow passageway eight feet long, lined on the sides and the roof with poles of driftwood. I took off my sunglasses. Some guns, harpoons, ice shovels and long, straight ice picks were hanging on the walls. We walked past a pan of frozen meat, then approached another skin hanging over a doorway. Lars didn't knock. Nowhere to knock. He pushed aside the skin as he spoke in Eskimo. A woman's sharp voice answered from inside.

Lars greeted an old man and old woman. She was sitting on the floor, he on the edge of a bunk with a rumpled pile of blankets. Both were wrinkle-faced and gray-haired, smiling broadly. They were wearing skin parkas with wolverine-ruffed hoods lowered to their shoulders. The man looked my way, smiling, then said something in Eskimo.

I said "Hi!"

Lars interceded, "He said 'Hi'. He said he was glad you came."

I nodded and said, "*Ee-ee.*"

The old man laughed, then began conversing with Lars. Lars and I remained standing and the old couple sat.

While they talked, I noticed the small room was lined with driftwood logs, chinked with tundra grass and moss. A dim light came through a three-foot square, translucent skin of seal stomach, near the center of the ceiling. At the back of the room, a pot of meat simmered on a small woodstove. The smell was inviting. Was it seal, duck, ptarmigan? Several pieces of short driftwood sticks were stacked against the wall.

After three or four minutes, Lars turned to me and said, "They just like to hear news about Scammon Bay." He talked and laughed with the couple for another ten minutes. They seemed most happy that we came. When we left and were walking back to the dog team, Lars said, "They asked for us to come back. They like for visitors to come see them. They even asked for us to stay and spend the night." He laughed.

I said, "They seem happy and content to be living here all by themselves. I didn't even see a radio."

"It's true. This is the same as house my parents had till I was five. We had a skin window in the roof like the one you saw in there. Once two white men came to our house and were taking pictures. One of them walked around outside and fell through the skin into our house and everybody laughed." He giggled.

Lars soon had the dogs underway again on the glazed ice, heading home. We were now facing a headwind that seemed stronger than before--and became stronger still the closer we came to the cape. The dogs' feet began to slip, but this seemed not to deter them the slightest. They knew the direction home. When we neared the point of the cape, the lead dog went down in a strong gust. It slid into the other dogs, who also went down in domino-like fashion, then slid in a disordered wad against the sled. The sled, with us and dogs, began sliding on the ice as off a long steep roof. When would we stop? After two hundred yards of sliding, we slowed, then the sled and dogs stopped. Lars laughed and turned the dogs into the wind, again pulling toward the cape.

Our second attempt to get past the cape was no easier than the first. But the dogs seemed to know the problem. They pulled low and steady, with their fur fanning in the wind and their feet spread with claws clutching ice. Their rear leg muscles bulged. I thought, "Another hundred yards and we will be past the point of the cape where the wind will not be so strong."

But this was not to be. Just as I thought we were going to make it past the cape, a stronger gust hit us hard. The left front paw of the lead dog slipped, then she went down and slid into the other dogs. The other dogs also fell and slid into the sled. Oh, no! Here we go again! We went sliding, this time faster than before. The sled went sideways across bumps and cracks in the ice. We passed the dogs. Then the dogs passed us, as they clawed ice to get back on their feet but continued to fall. Then the sled again spun around and was ahead of the dogs. When would we stop sliding?

"Can you try stepping on the brake?" I shouted.

"Better not," Lars said calmly. "It might go in one of these cracks in the ice and break the sled."

When the sliding finally slowed, Lars touched the brake lightly and scratched thin grooves in the ice. As the sled gradually came to a stop, we found ourselves farther back than before, and the dogs were a tangled mass. Lars, slipping and sliding in the wind, stepped off the sled to realign the team. One dog was on the wrong side. He threw it across its teammate.

The thought entered my mind that we might not make it around the cape, that we might have to accept the invitation of the old couple and wait in their sod house for a calmer day. There was no way we could go inland over the sheer cliffs of the mountains. I suggested, "Maybe it's better on the ice further out from the cape, where the wind may not be as strong."

"No, let's try it again here. It's just these gusts of wind." He seemed not nearly as concerned as I.

This time we made it--barely. We made it past the cape, where the wind was not so strong. I felt relieved as I looked up at Lars and smiled. He also smiled as he glanced at me, then motioned for me to look at a point high on the cliffs above. He said, "Bald eagles there."

The eagles were sitting on a rocky pinnacle about a thousand feet above us. Had they been watching the action below? And what were they thinking?

I made friends by radio with Tom and Paula Maloy, the teachers at neighboring Chevak, twenty-five miles to the south. We talked to each other almost daily. Tom visited us briefly via the mail plane once. He said, "I wish you would come and visit us by dogsled and bring your daughter, Paula, and spend the night with us sometime. She and our son, Theron, will enjoy playing together. They're both the same age--four."

I mentioned to Lars the possibility of taking such a trip to Chevak.

"We'll go," he quickly replied. "I have some very good friends there to stay with."

We left for Chevak on a beautiful clear Saturday in March. The temperature was twenty-eight degrees below zero, with a slight breeze from the north. We went east and turned uphill to go through Igiayarok pass, then turned south onto completely flat tundra for the rest of the way.

We were appropriately dressed for the cold. Paula was sitting in an eiderdown sleeping bag up front in the sled. I sat behind her. Lars stood on the back of the runners. Eleven dogs were pulling.

Lars had borrowed John Amukon's dogs for the trip. He said, "Amukon's dogs are good for long trip."

"Is that a *good* lead dog?" I asked.

"That lead dog is the best lead dog in the village," he answered. "You can go anywhere with him. All you have to do is point and he knows where you want to go."

I was reassured, since I saw no sign of a trail. Apparently no dog team had been this way for days. There was nothing in sight ahead of us, except hard, wind-packed snow on the flat landscape and a purple, bluish horizon. The dogs moved onward at a steady gait as snow drifted between their legs.

When we neared the halfway point of the trip, Paula said to me, "I need to go to the bathroom."

"Wait till we get there."

After another mile or two, Paula again said, "Daddy, I need to go to the bathroom."

"There is no bathroom here, Paula." I thought it was just too cold.

She responded with a half-laugh and half-whimper, "But I've got to go."

I asked Lars, "What do you think? Do you think she can go?"

He smiled as he said, "I don't know. She'll get cold."

We continued on, but she began whimpering again and said, "But, Daddy, I've *got* to go to the bathroom. I can't wait!"

I turned to Lars and said, "Let's stop the dogs," He said something in Eskimo to the dogs then stepped on the brake. The dogs stopped and looked back. Paula crawled from the sleeping bag and stepped off the sled.

I pointed to a spot ten feet away and said, "Over there."

She walked to the spot I indicated, which was no different from any other spot on this monotonously flat, frozen plain, and pulled down her two pairs of pants and long underwear. Fifteen seconds later she started crying and said, "I can't."

"Get back into the sled," I ordered. "You'll just have to go in your pants. Mrs. Maloy will have some clothes for you."

She cried as she climbed back into the sleeping bag, where she soon became quiet for the remaining ten miles of the trip. On arrival at Chevak, Lars pulled the sled beside the teacher's quarters. Mrs. Maloy was there to greet us. I said, "I think we have a wet girl here."

"*What?*" she almost screamed. "You should *never*, but never, let a kid wet herself in such cold weather!" She scolded me some more. I tried to no avail to explain what it was really like out there.

Other than disagreeing about Paula's problem and discomfort, we had a most enjoyable visit, seeing the village, catching up on area gossip and discussing school problems we had in common.

The next day, we were up early with plans for that morning. Mrs. Maloy served a delicious breakfast of fresh eggs, bacon and cereal, which we were enjoying as a knock came on the door. It was Lars with a look of urgency on his face. He said, "We had better start back. A big storm is coming." He pointed toward the northwest, where I saw a low black cloud had developed all the way across the entire horizon.

Soon we were on our way. Paula was wearing some of Theron's pants; her own clothes were not yet dry. I saw the black cloud on the horizon continue to widen. A couple of miles out, we hit snowflakes, then harder snow. Snow was coming down fast and the wind was blowing, making it difficult to see the lead dog. Suddenly, I couldn't see the lead dog, no matter how hard I strained to look. Next, I could only make out the two dogs in the rear. But we moved along at a steady pace.

Although I had heard it said that lead dogs know their way whatever the condition, I still had my doubts. Here we were, in zero visibility, attempting to go from pin-point A to pin-point B twenty-five miles apart, without a compass and with no road or tracks or trail or landmark to follow, and we could see only a few feet in front of us.

I thought, "What if something happens? What if the dogs get lost? What if we miss the village and keep on going, hundreds of miles onto the frozen Bering Sea? Eskimos had said that people have disappeared out there before."

I still could not see the lead dog! I looked back and saw only two feet of the trail we were making. My concern for our safety was mounting, so I looked up at Lars and asked,

"Does that lead dog know where he is going?"

He grinned as he said, "He knows."

I checked Paula. She was asleep.

The blizzard never let up the whole way. After we came through the pass and were nearing the village, the dogs picked up the pace. They sensed their chore was coming to an end and that they soon would be fed. Lars said, "Hold on, the dogs will now get faster."

At Amukon's house, my legs were stiff as I stepped off the sled, then lifted Paula onto her feet. We dusted snow off our clothing, then walked up the hill to the warmth of our living quarters. Home at last!

Whiteout

I was sitting at my desk after school one day, when Lars came in with a broom to clean up. He said, "There's a big whiteout over the other side of the river."

I walked to the door, where I could see that the north quadrant from the earth to the zenith was white, then commented, "That sure is white."

"Yes, we been watching it. It came up out there fast. Sometimes whiteouts form fast and you can't avoid them. If planes are flying, sometimes they go into them, and sometimes they crash. It's happened before. If pilots get in whiteout, they can't tell up or down or anything. Whiteouts happen mostly when it's cold and the air is still, even when the sky is clear."

The air was clear and chilly, but not windy, that day in February, when I was returning with veteran bush pilot, Gary, from a dental appointment in Bethel. We were about fifty miles from Bethel when Gary pointed in the direction we were heading and said, "You see there where the earth and sky are meeting? That's a whiteout." I looked but saw nothing but white from sky to earth. There was no horizon. He banked westward and said, "We don't go near that. Whiteouts sometimes expand in a hurry. We will go around."

Then I recalled the time at Wales when I was riding north of the village along the beach with Roland Angnaboogok in his dogsled, while he checked his traps for white fox. Roland stood on the back of the sled runners while I sat in the sled. We were about five miles out when, suddenly, everything around us became ghostly white.

To my left and to my right was total whiteness. The dogs were trotting at a steady gait as if on a cloud, and my head seemed to start whirling. I wondered if we were going uphill or down. With my eyes open, I saw nothing but us, the dogs, the sled and white. It was ghostly, eerie white and I experienced vertigo as my head pitched forward. I raised up. I looked at Angnaboogok, who was facing straight ahead. He smiled and spoke softly, "Whiteout."

I turned to look forward and saw, for the first time in the past five minutes, another distinguishable object. It appeared to be a pole as large as an electric power pole but without wires, standing upright in the snow about a hundred yards distant. Was this pole there to serve as a landmark for passing ships? No. Suddenly I noticed the pole coming toward us fast. My head swirled and I blinked my eyes as the "pole" passed by us fast on the right. Only then did I recognize it for what it really was: a stem of dry tundra grass about ten inches tall and one-eighth inch in diameter sticking out of the snow.

Just before noon on December 21, I was in the schoolroom when I recognized Tom Maloy's voice on the radio calling, "Four-Nine Scammon Bay, Four-Nine Scammon Bay, this is Two-Two Chevak. Do you read me, Will? Over."

I walked into the office, picked up the mike and answered, "Two-Two Chevak, Four-Nine Scammon Bay. I read you loud and clear, Tom. Over."

"Four-Nine, this is Two-Two Chevak. Leroy Behuvslov, the Alaska Fish and Wildlife Service man, is here. He wants to fly to Scammon Bay to check the villagers for bounties on hair seals. How's your weather out there? Over."

"Two-Two Chevak, Four-Nine Scammon Bay. Right now, the ceiling and visibility are unlimited and the wind is almost calm. Over."

"Four-Nine, Two-Two. Thanks, Will. Leroy says he will be leaving for Scammon Bay shortly. Two-Two Chevak clear."

"Roger, Tom. Four-Nine clear."

About an hour later I heard a plane fly over the school. I presumed it was Leroy. I assumed that he might be in the village for several hours to check hair seal bounties and would likely be spending the night with us, since the hours of daylight flying time in late December are very short.

After school, while Lars was sweeping the schoolroom

floor, I asked, "Why do they have a bounty on hair seals?"

He said, "Well, the government thinks there will be more salmon if they kill off more of the hair seals. They think the hair seals are eating all of the salmon."

"What do *you* think about it? *Are* they eating all of the salmon?"

He laughed. "I don't think the seals will ever eat all the salmon. There's too many salmon for seals to get all of them. Anyway, the men like to get some extra pay for the seals they kill."

"How much bounty money do they get for each seal they kill?"

"It is six dollars they get for every one killed," he answered.

"What part of the seal do the Fish and Wildlife use for identification?"

"It's the part of the scalp next to the eyes."

"I wonder how long the Fish and Wildlife Service man will be in the village checking the bounties?" I asked, thinking that he might be staying overnight with us and Virginia might need to do a little extra cooking.

"The Fish and Wildlife Service man did not come to Scammon Bay."

"He didn't come to the village?" I was puzzled. "Tom Maloy at Chevak said he was on the way here to check hair seal bounty. He was supposed to have left Chevak around noon and I heard a plane."

"Yes, but it was not the Fish and Wildlife man. It was Gary's plane," he said. "He brought a woman back from the hospital, then went back to Bethel."

"Gary's plane, you say? I never heard him leave. Then what happened to the Fish and Wildlife Service man?" I went to the radio either to find where Leroy had gone or to report him missing.

I first called Chevak. Tom said, "He left here about ten minutes after we talked to you earlier. He headed toward the pass in the mountains west of Scammon Bay." I began a radio search of the missing plane, while talking the next hour and a half to radio operators in villages within a 200-mile radius of Scammon Bay. Leroy was nowhere to be found. Darkness had now set in and a storm was brewing.

Search planes would be out looking as soon as daylight and weather permitted. I asked Lars to ask the men of the village to be on the lookout for a downed plane when traveling from the village by dog team.

The next morning the weather was bad, and Lars said, "Several men are going out today to look for the plane. Also I think some men will be going by dog team from Chevak and some from Hopper Bay." Weather conditions the next three days made air search impossible.

After dinner on Christmas Eve, I walked into the living room and sat down on the couch to listen to the news over an Anchorage radio station. Virginia had other ideas, however. "We should do something special for Christmas. There's nothing we can do about the missing pilot. Why don't you get out the tape recorder and we'll tape a message to send home. Our parents would love to hear the children talk."

I agreed. I got a reel-to-reel recorder from the schoolroom, then placed it near the middle of the living room floor. I plugged the cord into a wall socket and snapped on a new reel. I said, "OK. Everybody, come in here," but was interrupted with a series of loud knocks on the front door. What would somebody be wanting now? I got up from my seat and opened the door. There stood the most grossly disheveled white man I had ever seen in my entire life. He had three days growth of beard, and his hollow eyes looked through me to the wall behind. I said, "You are ..." and repeated, "You are ...?" Then he showed me some teeth, as he quivered and said, "Yes, I am!"

"You are Leroy Behuvslov! Come in this house! Man, have we been wondering about *you*!"

"You don't know how glad I am to see the inside of a house again."

"You must be totally famished. I know you are starved. My wife will get something for you to eat."

"Thank you, but all I want right now is a glass of water and to enjoy the warmth of a house for a change. I'm in no hurry to eat."

Virginia quickly went to the kitchen and poured a glass of water, which she brought to him and asked, "But what would you like to eat?"

"Oh, anything. But nothing right now. All I want right

now is to calm down and enjoy," he said, then took a sip of water.

"Lots of people have been wondering about you," I said. "I want to hear what happened. I have this tape recorder here. We were just now getting ready to record a Christmas message for home. But while my wife gets something for you to eat, would you tell what happened? Just talk right into the recorder."

"I'll be glad to," he said, then took another sip of water. I switched on the recorder as he began to tell his harrowing story. I have the complete story on tape, in his words, but I have paraphrased it here.

Leroy had left Chevak, headed for Scammon Bay shortly after he had called me to ask about the weather. As he neared Scammon Bay, however, he encountered a white-out, making it impossible to tell where the ground was from the horizon. He made a 180-degree turn and flew back a mile or two, then made another 180-degree turn and flew back closer to the foothills, to see if the storm would lift. It didn't, so he decided to head back to Chevak.

That's when he hit the second whiteout. Now he couldn't tell where the pass was. He couldn't tell where anything was. He decided to set the plane down on the ice and sit out the weather.

He made several passes, then landed on what appeared to be very solid, very smooth ice. As soon as he stopped the plane, though, the ice began to groan and crack. Half a minute later, the plane had sunk to within a foot of the wings.

Thinking quickly, Leroy tossed out his suitcase and tent, then crawled out of the plane onto the ice, falling through several times before he reached solid ice. He never had time to send out a "Mayday" to let anyone know he was in trouble.

He set up his tent, donned a set of Eddie Bauer down underwear and mittens from his suitcase, as well as his down parka, and sat out the night, cold, wet and alone.

Next morning, he noticed that the plane seemed to be raising out of the ice and discovered that when the tide went out the plane was left sitting on the mud. The ice was only about three inches thick. He tried to move the plane, but it was too heavy. Then he moved everything out of the plane onto the ice. Whiteouts continued to obscure his surroundings.

The following morning, he awoke to find himself afloat on the ice, about 800 yards from the shore. He moved closer to the airplane, in case the ice broke up, reasoning that he could ride the wings if he needed to. The ice was moving fairly fast, and the land kept moving farther away.

A compass and map gave him a pretty good idea of where he was: in the main bay of Scammon Bay, heading west. Suddenly, the tide changed, and a pack of ice, about two feet thick, began to move toward him.

"When it hit this ice, it just pulverized it. It kept moving right directly toward the airplane, and I mean it was moving fast. I ... figured in ten minutes that I would either be in the bottom of the Scammon Bay or I would have to crawl on something, and I knew the airplane was going to go under."

He grabbed some food, an emergency kit, a firepot, a couple of briefcases he needed to keep, and his suitcase and threw them onto his dismantled tent. He intended to drag it to the shore, but the ice was thin and slushy, so he transferred everything in 100-yard shifts.

"So I kept hustling just as fast as I could and, of course, by that time my tongue is out a foot and I'm real tired, and I kept throwing off stuff all along the way -- one big constant trail of my emergency gear and everything else strung from the airplane to the shore....

"I had just moved the last load upon the banks, and I hadn't been on the shore five minutes, when I turned around and could hear a great crack and a groan, and five seconds later there was fifty yards of water between the piece of ice I was on and the shore, and ten minutes later the ice was out of sight."

He made a fire and melted snow water to drink, then sat out the long, cold night.

The next morning Leroy decided that the continuing bad weather made rescue anytime soon unlikely, so he might as well try to walk to Scammon Bay. He took everything he could carry on his back, plus a native mask that was made in Chevak, and a flashlight, and started out.

He climbed up the side of a hill and walked along it for about a mile and a half, until he came to where the pack ice had crammed against the shore. Then he walked along the pack ice. He saw the plane that flew from Scammon Bay to Chevak and tried to signal with a flare, but the pilot didn't see him.

He kept walking and finally came to some dogsled tracks. After about four and a half hours, he sat down to rest, when he heard a "yip" behind him. There was a native with a dog team.

The man, Daniel Tunutmuk, gave Leroy a ride the rest of the way to Scammon Bay. In return, Leroy gave him an ax.

"I can say that probably without a good pup tent and without some good down winter clothing, including mittens, and just some plain old guts, I doubt if I would be sitting here telling anyone this story."

When he finished, I walked to the radio and reported to Bethel air search and rescue that Leroy had just walked into our schoolhouse at Scammon Bay.

Virginia came to the living room door and said, "I have some soup and sandwiches on the table. Would you come in and eat?"

"Thank you," Leroy said. "But if you don't mind, if I can, I'd rather clean up first."

I showed him to the shower, then went to get some of my clothes for him to wear.

The East Wind Blows

The most powerful winds at Scammon Bay are from the east. They roar off the mountain, with gusts sometimes reaching hurricane force, reminding me of the winds at Cape Prince of Wales on the Bering Strait.

One night in February, a mighty east wind placed the village under a siege that lasted till dawn. The children walked to school that morning in a gentle breeze. The air was clear as they made fresh trails over new snowbanks. At morning recess, Gemma Rose Hunter, a bright, round-faced first-grader, rushed into the schoolroom with a tea-cup full of crowberries. She was ecstatic, and her brown eyes shone like new money as she held the berries up for me to see. She said, "See berries. Wind blow snow off them. We pick them up there." She pointed up the hill.

A few days later, the wind was again strong from the east. Only this time school was in session. In such cases, I seldom let the children go outside at recess to play, because the door swung open toward the east and the pressure of the wind against the door was a hazard that might get a small child hurt.

That afternoon, as grades kindergarten through three were leaving for the day, a student came to me and said, "Mr. Corbin, we can't open door. It's real windy out."

I went to the door and found all the children huddled in the cloakroom looking at me. Some had their parkas on and were expecting me to help them leave the building. Three giggling second-graders repeated in singsong unison, "We can't open the door. We can't open the door."

I admired their sense of humor and use of English but gave them a stern look. They laughed. I pushed hard with my right shoulder to open the door, while gushes of powdery snow swirled throughout the cloakroom. I then braced my feet and leaned hard against it, while five or six children who had donned their parkas and mittens could leave. When they were out, I let the door slam shut, then waited for another group to gather to leave.

When the second group was ready to exit, I pushed the door open with my right shoulder close to the edge for greater leverage. I was unaware that my ring finger on my right hand was past the edge. I again let the pressure of the wind close it, and that's when it happened! I felt the door nip my finger and saw that half of the last digit was gone! Some children also saw my wounded finger and ran, talking in Eskimo, to get Lars, who was in the pump room. I pressed the stub against my shirt above my belt to stop the bleeding, then headed toward the medicine cabinet. I met the children returning with Lars, his face ashen. He asked, "What happened?"

"I cut off my finger on the door," I said and showed the stub to him as the blood dripped. He said, "I will go look for it. Maybe they can sew it back on if we find it." He quickly turned and rushed toward the door. The children followed.

While keeping the stub of my finger pressed against my shirt, I followed behind them, in hopes the finger could be found. Ten or twelve children were waiting quietly in the cloakroom. Lars spoke to them in Eskimo. They looked around the floor. Several spoke to Lars, then he turned to me and said, "The finger is not inside. Maybe it blew outside. I'll go look outside for it. If we find it, you could go to Bethel and get it sewed back on. I will let the children out. You go get bandaged."

Ten minutes later he returned to me in the first aid room and said, "We couldn't find it. Maybe it blew away."

I held school for the next three days with a bandaged finger, waiting for the weather to clear. Then I took a bush flight into the little hospital at Bethel, where a team of three doctors worked four hours trimming, repairing and grafting skin to what was left of the finger.

Two weeks after I returned to the village, I stepped outside the schoolroom door as a strong wind was again blowing from the east. Snow was falling fast and drifting by the door, directly toward the area where John Amukon's dogs were tied. It was then when I wondered if one of those dogs might have gotten a taste of a finger. On going back inside, several students smiled as they watched me carefully close the door. They knew I had learned a lesson.

The storm raged throughout that night, then abated to a gale by morning as red-cheeked students arrived inside the school door, where they stomped loose snow from their mukluks, then hung their parkas on hooks in the cloakroom.

Checking the roll, I found Laura and Anthony Ulak, sister and brother, who had never missed a day in the past two years, were both absent. I said to Lars, "I notice that Laura and Anthony are not at school today."

He laughed and said, "Yes, a big drift is covered over their house and they can't get out. They have to wait for some others to dig their house out from outside. They can't dig themselves out because they would just pile snow inside. I think some men are already started digging now."

At 10:30, Laura and Anthony arrived, smiling, inside the school entryway, then dusted snow from their mukluks and parkas. Some students laughed at them and made comments in Eskimo. I counted Laura and Anthony present for the entire day.

Laura and Anthony's snow-covered house, before villagers began digging it out.

"When their house is covered over, they have to wait for someone to dig them out from the outside."

Paula with Agnes and Dorothy Sundown, picking berries in February.

Father Donahue
Comes to the Village

The Catholic church at Scammon Bay, located about a hundred feet below the school, was of wood frame and clapboard construction. The exterior was painted white. The upper side had one set of windows facing the school, about four-feet-square each and twelve feet apart.

Affable Father Donahue, Irish, greying, six-feet two and slender, came to the village every six weeks and served the mission and some sixty-five parishioners for a week or two at a time. He usually arrived by dogsled or bush plane during school hours and created excitement among the schoolchildren, who anticipated the goodies he would bring. He always brought a bag of hard candy, which he used as a powerful incentive for the children to attend church regularly. The disturbance caused by the father's arrival, if he came during school hours, was so overwhelming that I had difficulty getting the children's attention and might as well dismiss school for the rest of that day, which I sometimes did.

He held morning mass and taught catechism after school to some of the children. Everyone seemed to enjoy his visits to the village, and Virginia and I occasionally invited him to join us for an evening meal. He also invited Tommy and Paula to join his church sessions after school with the Eskimo children. After school one day in late March, while I was in the radio room listening to some BIA communication from the district office at Bethel, Virginia stepped to the door and exclaimed, "I wish you would just look down there at those two silly little girls. They're walking around the church and hitting the side of it with sticks!"

I turned in my chair to look out the window, and saw Gemma Rose Hunter and Flora Amukon, two of my bright, lovable little first-grade students, walking along the upper side of the building, which was exposed to the prevailing east winds and void of deep snow. They were striking the side of the building about every sixth or eighth step they took with what appeared to be thin sticks of driftwood, four feet long. "Would you go out and get them to stop?" I asked.

"I'm not getting involved," Virginia responded, as she turned and walked back into our apartment. Just then, the girls struck the side of the church again and went out of sight around the right corner of the church.

Soon the girls returned, walking in march step along the left side of the building, while they continued to strike the side of it as if in rhythm. I stepped outside the front door onto the porch, where I heard the girls singing a ditty in Eskimo, while they marched in step to the tune. They struck the side of the church each time they came to a certain word in the song which rhymed with "blue," to which they gave special emphasis as they swung their sticks. I was completely flabbergasted and wondered whether this might be some kind of church activity or assignment from Father Donahue. Perhaps they were upset about something or were just playing a game of their own invention.

Nevertheless, I didn't see any harm in what they were doing, until a word in the song they were singing happened to occur when the girls were directly beside the window on the upper side of the building. At this point they paused in their marching and singing to look momentarily at each other, then crashed their sticks through two window panes and began singing again. I yelled "Hey!" They stopped and briefly glanced my way, then darted around the building out of sight to my right.

Father Donahue somehow learned that I knew about the incident and came to the school to visit us that evening. He brought up the subject about the pane breakage and explained, "Gemma Rose and Flora failed to memorize the verses I assigned them and I was holding back giving them some candy. But there's no harm done. I've already made it up to them now."

Is it Legal?

In late spring, when the snow and ice melted, the tundra grass and the lakes came alive with millions, if not billions, of geese, swans, cranes and smaller birds that took up spots to build their nests. Lars commented about this avian invasion one afternoon when school was dismissed. He said, "It won't be long till we can get eggs."

"Get eggs?" I asked. "What kinds of eggs?"

"Well, it's mostly Canada geese eggs we'll get," he responded. "They are the best. You will like them, too. They're much better than chicken eggs. Besides, we get them fresh."

One week later he said, "It's getting closer to time to get eggs. Only few more days now."

Four days later Lars said to me, "Tomorrow we go get eggs. We will take along sacks to put the eggs in. We go up the river in boat about five miles to lakes where there's lots of nests. You need to wear parka and rubber hip boots Another boat will go along. We also going to change the river. Some men have decided to dig the river through." I wondered what he meant by that last statement, but didn't ask.

The next day was Saturday, and the air was clear and brisk. It was a good day for the excursion. When I stepped into Lars' twelve-foot wooden boat, I saw three shovels and some sacks on the floorboards. He cranked the 60-horse-power Johnson motor, then we headed up Kun River, a deep, slow-flowing, meandering river forty yards wide, as our noise flushed geese, cranes, ducks and other birds into the air from their nearby nesting spots on the tundra.

When we arrived seven miles up the river, Lars guided the boat to the bank, where two other men stood beside another boat. He shut off the motor as the boat coasted to the bank; then he said, "Here is where we are going to change the river." I stepped out of the boat and climbed to the top of the five-foot riverbank, where I saw another river the same size as Kun River, just thirty feet away. The other river was flowing south while our river was flowing north. The men pulled both boats on top of the bank.

Lars pointed to the other river and said, "This is same river as the one we came on. It loops around about five miles that way to the south. Now it takes long time to go around and too much gas. Sometimes we portage at this place, but with loaded boat is not easy. We are going to dig a channel across and let the river go through here. Then it will be closer to go up river by boat."

"Is it legal to do this?" I asked.

"We do this one time before at other place," he replied. "I think it is all right to do."

I pitched in to help dig a trench two feet wide to connect the two parts of the river. After we dug through the tough roots of the tundra grass, the digging in the thawed, black volcanic dirt was easy. We piled the dirt on top of the ground on each side of the ditch and only needed to dig two feet deep to reach the water level on the upper part of the river. Soon a trickle of water was flowing through our ditch and began eroding particles of soil from the sides and the bottom.

We stopped shoveling, then stood back to watch the trickle slowly become a small stream, while dirt and grass began caving into the flow and washing downstream. We backed further away as the flow increased in volume and the banks gradually became farther apart. Then suddenly a large section of the bank caved in our direction with a loud plop, as the flow rapidly increased. Lars yelled something in Eskimo which to me meant, "*Run! The river is bursting through!*" We dashed a short distance to safety, then stopped and looked back as great chunks of each bank fell into the roil. The men laughed.

Soon the banks stopped collapsing as four thousand square feet of tundra grass and hundreds of tons of soil were now replaced by a channel of water thirty-five yards wide. Downstream, a coal-black flood rumbled toward the bay. Then I looked across the new channel, where an oxbow lake was undulating gently with waters glistening in the sun -- waters that now had no place to go.

When the river quieted, the boats were lowered into the new channel. Lars and I stepped into his boat, which he guided upstream for two more miles. Then he stood and pointed toward a lake and said, "Here is where we'll stop." He guided the boat to the bank as the other boat passed and continued upstream.

I stepped to the top of the bank as Lars anchored the boat. He waved his hand toward the lake, which was approximately a half mile long by an eighth of a mile across. He said, "This is the lake where we will get eggs. You go this way around the lake and I will go that way. We will meet on the other side. When you see a grassy hummock in the lake, walk out and check it. That's where the geese lay their eggs. They lay their eggs there so the foxes can't get them. The foxes don't go out in the lake. You won't see any geese. They already fly away when they heard the boat. Just look on the little grassy hummocks in the lake and if you see pile of feathers, that will be a nest. The feathers will be warm. Just separate them and get some eggs."

I asked. "Is it all right to leave one egg? We used to leave one egg in hen nests back home. Then the hens would lay more eggs."

"I dunno. I think it will be all right to leave one egg. You can leave one, then put the feathers back over it. Maybe they *will* lay more."

I walked around the lake to the left, while Lars went to the right. Soon I spotted a grassy hummock about twenty yards from the edge. I stepped into the lake, where the water came up to my knees. I waded toward the hummock and noticed the bottom of the lake was smooth, frozen and of uniform depth.

When I approached the hummock, I saw feathers on top, which I parted and counted nine eggs slightly larger than hen eggs. They were still warm. I put eight in my sack, then pushed the feathers back over the one I left. I walked to the bank and continued around the lake gathering eggs from nests on every grassy hummock I inspected. Shortly, my sack was heavy with eggs, so I passed other hummocks, then walked on to meet Lars.

When we met, he said, "I have enough eggs. Did you get many?"

I showed him my sack and asked, "Is it legal to do this?"

"I dunno," he laughed. "But this is only way we have to get eggs. We can't have chickens here. What would we feed them?"

Tundra Flowers

On our return trip down the river Lars announced that, as soon as school was out, the village people were leaving for summer camp to pick berries and catch and dry salmon. "I'm taking leave from school work and also taking my family to camp. Your family will be about the only ones left in the village. And maybe only a few old people," he said, smiling.

Sure enough, when school was out, the population dropped suddenly to less than ten, older people who did not go and whose job, I observed, was to feed the dogs in the village. To us that remained, the village resembled a ghost town and we felt deserted.

One week after school was out, a radio call came from the BIA office in Bethel, "Four-Nine Scammon Bay. Four-Nine Scammon Bay. Do you read? Over."

I stepped to the radio and picked up the mike. "Seven-Four Bethel. I read you loud and clear. Over."

"Roger, Four-Nine. Seven-Four Bethel back. Will, a scientist from Sweden is here. He's a botanist, associated with the Arctic Institute of North America and says he wants to collect the plants in the Scammon Bay area. He says, to his knowledge, the flora there is unknown and no botanical collections have been made. He wants to be out there about two weeks and wonders if he can stay with you while he does his collecting. Over."

Virginia was listening. She said, "Tell him to come on."

"Seven-Four Bethel, Four-Nine Scammon Bay. Yes, we have nothing much going on here in the village now, so tell him to come on. Over."

There was a pause, then, "Roger, Will. He says he will

be going out as soon as the weather permits."

Two days later, I met the plane on the river. A tall, slender, fair-skinned, stoop-shouldered man in his late sixties stepped from the plane to the top of the bank with a smile and said, "Hi! I'm Eric Hulten. I'm from Riks Museum in Stockholm."

"Hi!" I said. "I'm Wilford Corbin, the teacher here. I'll help carry your baggage to the school." He had a suitcase, two camera bags and a large amount of plant-drying materials, which were bulky but not heavy.

For the first few days, the old man left the school alone, carrying a large, empty sack and a camera. He took no sandwiches and said he could find drinking water along the way. When he returned each afternoon, his sack was full of plants. I pitched in to help place the plants between layers of newspaper, inkblotter pads and corrugated

cardboard, then press and tie them in bundles and hang them above the stoves to dry overnight.

While we worked, I occasionally asked the name of a plant and he gave me both its Latin and common names. He said, "*You* should learn the names of all the plants. That wouldn't be hard to do, because there's only about 150. Then you could teach them to your students."

"Good idea!" I responded. "Studying plants that grow here might be of more interest to the children than reading about Dick and Jane or 'see Spot run.' Besides, Spot never pulls a sled."

He laughed. "That's true. Why don't you go out with me and make a collection to label and show to your students?

You could dry them in my equipment when I dry mine."

During the next ten days, I took botany lessons under the world's foremost authority on arctic flora, after whom we later named our third son. We took excursions on the northern slopes of Askinuk Mountains and on the surrounding tundra flats both to the east and west of the village.

At the end of each day's work, Eric cleaned up and put on a dinner jacket and tie. We enjoyed his stories of collecting trips throughout the tundra regions of Alaska, Canada and Siberia. He said, "We once collected a previously undiscovered plant on the North Slope of Alaska. We found only four specimens, but we needed six for museum collections. Several plant collectors made trips back to the area to look for the plants--I went back once--but no more plants of this species were ever found. We may have collected the last of this plant that grows on the earth."

He also told of his experiences as a young botanist in 1917 during the Bolshevik Revolution. He said, "When I was collecting plants on the Kamchatka Peninsula in eastern Russia, the Communists were taking over their country, and I made a few extra bucks smuggling ammo and messages. I would go through military checkpoints and the guards never checked my bag once. They thought I was just another weird scientist carrying a sack full of weeds." He laughed and said, "For my smuggling work, I was later an honored guest of Joseph Stalin at a banquet in the Kremlin in Moscow." He showed us a picture of himself sitting beside Stalin.

In September, when Lars returned to the village, I showed him the plant collection and said, "As soon as school starts, I plan to take the children on field trips and let them make collections of their own."

"They will like that," he responded. "It will be good for them to learn the names--what *you* call the plants. They only know the Eskimo names of some of them."

Lars stapled my plant collection on the left wall of the hallway, then covered it with a thick grade of clear plastic and hung plywood doors on hinges to keep the plants in darkness, except when viewing. When he finished the project he said, "Now the children can see the plants and learn the names."

I soon learned, however, that only the girls were interested. During one outing on the side of the hill above the school, I noticed the boys were more interested in finding the caches of seeds the lemmings had stored for the winter. One boy came running to show me something in his collection bag. "Look, see what I have," he said.

I looked in his bag and saw nothing but seeds. "What's that?" I asked.

"It is seeds that the mice have gathered. We found it out there under those rocks." He pointed.

"What are you going to do with seeds?" I asked.

"I take them to my home. We boil them. Makes good—what *you* call—cereal."

"OK," I said, "but how about collecting some plants to dry?" I was becoming frustrated with the boys' lack of interest in botany.

"No! That is girl work. Let the girls do it," he responded, then ran with his bag to rejoin his group of boys, who were peering into another pile of rocks. I never pressed the issue to compel the boys to gather plants. I assumed that this activity was placed in the same category as berry picking, or as Lars said, "It's the women's job."

Geese Roundup

In late September, each time the mail plane came in low over the tundra to land on the river, the horizon became blackened with Canada geese, which rose into the air with a honking noise so loud that it drowned out the roar of the plane. Lars said, "Maybe they fly up from the ground to protect the young geese that cannot fly." He then said, "The village is going to have geese roundup tomorrow."

"Geese roundup! What's that?" I asked.

"Geese roundup is for getting young geese. Soon the young geese will get their feathers and fly. We mostly get them before they fly away. The whole village will go across the river and make big circle. We walk toward the center and wave our arms and drive the young geese toward the center, and when we get them all together, we hit them with sticks. We get lots of geese that way, maybe enough to last till geese round-up next year. Young geese are the best kind to eat."

"Is it legal to do this?" I asked, recalling the migratory game bird treaty the U.S. has with Canada and Mexico. "The hunting season doesn't open till much later."

"We know this," he said, "but when the hunting season gets open, the birds have all fly away to the south. We get the geese when it is best time to get them--before they are gone."

The next morning, I stood on the school porch and watched the geese roundup across the river. It began with about a hundred men, women and children, each with stick in hand, in a circle two hundred yards in diameter. They walked toward the center while waving their sticks and driving goslings. When geese and people were concentrated near the center, a melee of thrashing and slashing began. After ten or fifteen minutes, the slaughter stopped, then the harvest was loaded into boats and brought across the river to the village. Lars brought us two, which Virginia baked. I rank baked Canada goose gosling right up there with the best food I have ever tasted.

Mud

All summer long, the banks of Kun River and its tributaries are covered by fine volcanic mud, no vegetation. It is wet, sticky and six to eight inches deep between high and low tide levels and extends from the water's edge to the tundra grass on top of the bank. This mud has the color and consistency of wet concrete and will grasp any boot not firmly attached to a foot. To exit a boat or float plane in the river, you slog with difficulty about ten feet through this mud to the top of the bank. It's a common annoyance, to which the Eskimos at Scammon Bay have long since learned to cope. They walk through it every time they step into their kayaks or boats to go into the bay or upriver to hunt, fish or pick berries. For them, it's a way of life. They contend with mud matter-of-factly.

One calm, clear summer day, six men and I were each wearing hip-boots as we went by boat around Cape Romanzof to the Air Force DEW Line site to shop at their BX. While there, we were invited for cake and coffee in the mess hall, where we sat and talked with the commanding officer and some of the boys. The CO said, "It is good for the boys to meet the natives. They enjoy talking to them." We visited there for over an hour.

When we stepped outside to leave, I noticed a construction crew had just poured a large slab of fresh concrete that spread to within eight feet of the door. The commanding officer said, "They're starting to build an addition to our motor pool." The concrete had a smooth, wet surface. It was eight inches thick and resembled the volcanic mud along the banks of Kun River. We walked around it; that is, all of us except Andrew Aguchak, whose first concern was to observe the weather, an old Eskimo custom when exiting a building.

He stepped into the "mud," then plodded five or six steps with difficulty, while looking over the roof of the building to see if the weather was still holding. A construction crewman was aghast. Lars said something to Andrew in Eskimo as the other Eskimos laughed. Andrew looked down, then, in total shock and embarrassment, ran high-stepping from the concrete.

I asked the CO, "Should we help smooth it back up?"

He chuckled and said, "Don't worry about it. The men will fix it back."

Lost Baggage

The end of our second year in Scammon Bay was fast approaching. Tommy, Paula and Carroll were two years older than when we came. Although they enjoyed Scammon Bay and playing with the Eskimo children, Virginia and I had mixed emotions about whether we should leave Scammon Bay. I had grown to love the quiet and peaceful village and the adventures I was experiencing. Nevertheless, we decided the children should grow up in the complex modern world of the white man, which we felt offered greater opportunities for their future. We resolved that some day, when our children were grown, we would be back. I applied to teach in an Indian Service school near my hometown at Cherokee, North Carolina, and was accepted.

We began making plans to leave. We knew that we would be leaving during the spring thaw, while huge snow-drifts in the village would be turning to slush, yet the temperature would still be chilly enough to wear parkas.

Since Tom Maloy, the teacher at Chevak, had taken his family to New Mexico on vacation the previous summer, I asked him how we could best manage our departure.

He said, "You'll be leaving when the snow is melting and turning to slush so you'll need to wear parkas and rubber boots, but the terminal at Anchorage has small rooms which your family can rent. You can even take a shower there, then change into stateside clothes for your flight to Seattle. Your schedule will have a two-hour delay. This should give you enough time to get your baggage, shower and change clothes."

When we were packing our belongings and getting ready to leave, Lars suggested, "You should take two black-fish with you. They make good pets."

"Make pets out of blackfish?"

"Yes, they have lungs and gills. They breathe air and water. You can put them in water in a mayonnaise jar and take them to North Carolina with you."

"But the jar will be sealed and they couldn't survive the trip!"

"They will be all right. They can stop breathing but still be alive."

"You sure? Where can I get them?"

"At Sundown's. He has oil barrel full. It's down by his house. It's what he feeds his dogs."

"Would he care if I took two?"

"He won't care."

Sundown's house was fifty yards below the school. He spoke no English, so I waited till I saw him feeding his dogs, then walked down and said, "Hi!"

He smiled broadly and said, "Ee-ee."

I held up two fingers and pointed first to the barrel then to my chest. He laughed while pointing to the barrel, indicating he understood what I wanted.

The barrel was two-thirds full of black, smooth-skinned lungfish with lobed fins. None were moving. They looked lifeless. Each was four to five inches in length. They felt flabby as I put two in a paper bag. I carried them to the house and put them in a gallon jar of fresh water, where they became active at once and happily dashed from side to side and up and down. I screwed the lid tightly, then turned the jar over to check for leakage. Seeing none, I wrapped the jar in a blanket, then placed it in the middle of a large canvas sea bag with sheets and pillows.

Our plane arrived and landed on the lake below the school. People stepped outside their houses to tell us "good-bye" as we walked along the muddy trail through slush to meet the plane. Lars and two other men and I carried all of our baggage--three navy sea bags and two large suitcases. Virginia carried her purse and led Carroll, who was now three. Tommy, age nine, and Paula, five, walked. The bush pilot stashed our baggage, then we were off to Bethel.

After landing at Bethel, the pilot drove us in his pickup truck through the muddy streets to the station house. He helped us carry our baggage inside, where the station manager informed us and three other passengers in the waiting room, "The turbo-prop plane is on its way from Anchorage and will be here in thirty minutes." He then turned to me and said, "We'll have to check your baggage. It'll have to be carried in the baggage compartment. There's no room for your baggage in the passenger section."

Virginia pointed to a brown suitcase and asked, "Can we carry that suitcase with us?"

"No, it's too big," he said, then began placing all our baggage on a cart ready for loading. Virginia was allowed to carry only her purse.

Fifty minutes passed. No plane. Another passenger looked at his watch and exclaimed, "The plane is late." The station manager came in and announced, "The plane will be slightly delayed. We just found out it had a flat tire in Dillingham. But they said they'll be coming as soon as they get it fixed. You'll still have plenty of time to make your connections."

Virginia turned to me and asked, "But will we have enough time in Anchorage to get our baggage and change clothes?"

"I hope so," I said.

We waited and waited as time passed. One passenger was pacing back and forth, and I worried that we might miss our connection from Anchorage to Seattle. Virginia said, "Get those children back in here. They're out there playing in the mud." I did.

Another hour passed, and the station manager announced, "The plane is arriving."

I looked at my watch and said, "The plane is two hours late! I hope we'll have enough time to change clothes in Anchorage. We can't go on dressed like this."

Virginia asked, "How will we manage if we can't change clothes in Anchorage?"

"Maybe they will let us change our flight schedule and get a hotel room overnight then go on tomorrow."

"That will be OK if we can do it," she responded.

As we approached Anchorage, the pilot announced, "Everyone who is catching the flight to Seattle will have to get straight on. Your plane is waiting."

I said to Virginia, "Since we won't have time to change clothes now, let's check at the desk to see if we can get our baggage and wait till tomorrow to go on to Seattle."

After we landed, we hurried inside the terminal and I said to the airlines desk clerk, "We are going to Seattle and just came in from Bethel and ..."

"Get on your plane," he interrupted. "It's leaving in five minutes."

"Is our baggage transferred to it?" I quickly asked.

"Your baggage is already on. Get yourselves on," he responded. We boarded the plane with our boots still muddy and our parkas under our arms. Other passengers stared as I walked to my seat.

We placed our parkas in the rack above our seats and settled in for the overnight flight to Seattle. A stewardess walked by, and I stopped her to explain why we were dirty and dressed as we were. She smiled and said, "I understand. It happens all the time up here." She brought pillows for the children.

When we were thirty minutes into the flight, Virginia asked, "What are we going to do if there's no place in Seattle for us to change clothes? We can't go on like this."

"How about when we arrive in Seattle tomorrow morning, we just get our baggage and change in a restroom. I'll get my razor out and shave there. We will have a two-hour delay. That should give us plenty of time."

When we arrived in Seattle it was broad daylight. I walked to the desk and told the clerk who we were and that we had just come down from the arctic. I said, "We would like to retrieve our baggage so we can change clothes before we go on to Chicago." She smiled sympathetically and said, "Anchorage told us that your baggage didn't get on the flight. It's still in Anchorage. They said they would put it on tomorrow's flight. Do you want to wait here till tomorrow?"

"Are you sure they'll get our baggage on tomorrow's flight?" I asked, thinking, "What if our baggage doesn't make that flight either?"

"Your baggage will be here tomorrow," she answered.

Virginia said, "Let's just go on. They can ship our baggage to North Carolina."

I turned to the clerk, "We'll just go on. Is there a store here where I can buy a razor?"

"This is Sunday," she responded. "There's nothing

open in the terminal, and I don't think any stores in town will be open till this afternoon."

Tired, disappointed, disheveled and depressed, we boarded our flight to O'Hare, in Chicago, and walked toward our seats as other passengers stared. I didn't explain the reason for our appearance to anyone except the man who sat beside me. He said he understood and mentioned a similar experience he once had on a flight from the Bahamas. After thirty minutes of further discussion and tale-swapping, he said, "I'm from Chicago. I've been on a hunting trip out of Fairbanks. We had a guide and I got a bear." Then he lowered his voice and said, "You don't live but once. I also killed a bald eagle up there and I'm taking his claws and tail feathers to give to my son."

We arrived at O'Hare on Sunday afternoon at one o'clock and took seats in a lounge to await our flight to Knoxville. The terminal was immaculate and the floors glistened. People dressed in their "Sunday best" walked by where we sat. They glanced our way as they passed but quickly looked away when my eyes caught theirs. Tommy's muskrat parka was lying on the floor and Carroll's dirty boots were on his seat. Although I felt terrible and we were beat and very tired, I had no thought to explain our predicament to anyone.

What happened next I'll never forget: Three men, dressed in dark suits, with ties and shined shoes, walked briskly by and I overheard one of them say, "Southern trash!"

To me, that was the last straw. I got up from my seat, caught up with them and stood in front. They stopped and faced me with expressions of near horror. I said, "I heard what one of you just said. Let me tell you something ..." I explained where we had come from, and how our baggage had been misplaced and what we had been through. When I finished, they each smiled and apologized. One man asked, "Where are you folks going?"

I said, "North Carolina." They then walked over and spoke a few minutes to Virginia and the children.

Ten minutes after the men left, a reporter and a photographer came to our seats. The reporter said, "We heard you just arrived from the Arctic. Could I talk to you and ask some questions?"

"Sure, go ahead. Shoot." I thought this would be a

good way to pass the remaining time while we waited for our flight to be called. The photographer took pictures. The reporter asked questions for nearly an hour and wrote notes of everything I said. People looked our way and smiled as they walked by. Several gathered close enough to listen to what was said.

When the reporter stopped asking questions, I asked, "Do you really think your paper will publish this story?"

"Absolutely," he responded. "This is the kind of human interest story this paper likes."

"Will you send me a copy after it comes out?" I asked.

"Sure, be glad to. What is your address?"

"Cullasaja, North Carolina."

He wrote my name and address on the top margin of his pad, but I never heard whether his story was published or not.

The time of waiting quickly passed and soon we were off to North Carolina. Our baggage arrived the following Friday. I was certain the fish would be dead and decomposing. When I opened the bag and unwrapped the jar, I found both fish lifeless, lying on their sides. I emptied them into the kitchen sink and let the water drain down. The fish turned aright and wiggled on their fins. I plugged the sink drain and opened the cold water faucet. Miraculously, the fish began swimming. They were alive! I put them in a two-gallon tank.

During the summer we became acquainted with the fish. They ate just about anything we fed them from the kitchen table. They could live in or out of the water. The children gave them names and put them on the floor to demonstrate to visitors. Sometimes the fish leaped from the tank by themselves and were usually found in corners or behind furniture. When out of the water for any length of time, they stopped moving and their skin shriveled. But their form was quickly restored and they swam lively each time they were returned to the water. We lost one when it was stepped on. The other jumped into a dishpan of soapy suds when I was changing the water and I mourned the end of the last of two lively pet fish.

Later that summer, when I was driving to the Cherokee

Indian Reservation, where I was going to teach, I stopped at the
local Cullasaja Elementary School to enroll Tommy. I said to
the secretary, "I'm teaching at Cherokee but I have a son who
will be starting school here in the fourth grade." I handed her a
sheet of paper with Tommy's full name and date of birth.

"Where's his school records?" she asked.

"There's no school records. We weren't allowed to keep
records of him in the Bureau of Indian Affairs school," I said.
She said nothing and didn't smile. Instead, she looked me in
the eye. As my eyes caught hers, she glanced over my head
to the ceiling as if to say, "Why the hell did they ever let *him*
start teaching?"

I turned without further word to walk out of the school
and be on my way to Cherokee, forty miles across the
Cowee Mountain. While I was driving, my thoughts returned to the Alaska Native Service policy concerning
school-age children of teachers. During orientation in
Juneau, the head of the education department had said,
"You are not legally allowed to enroll your children in the
Indian Service school. Some teachers do home-schooling
for their children. Some teachers let their children sit in the
school with the native children, but if you decide to do that,
just don't keep any records."

We tried home-schooling with Tommy after school
hours in Scammon Bay when Virginia and I were off work.
But this was usually the time when the Eskimo children
were outside sledding, playing soccer or swinging on
swings, and Tommy wanted to join them. They sometimes
invited him to visit in their homes for snacks of smoked or
dried salmon or seal meat. They enjoyed the companion-
ship of the blond-haired white boy and he enjoyed the
attention they gave to him as well.

During school hours, we allowed Tommy to be in
school with the other children and sit with the second- and
third-grade students. There, he performed the same tasks
assigned by their upper-grade tutors, who spoke entirely in
Eskimo or broken English--languages which Tommy
quickly learned.

Virginia and I sometimes laughed when Tommy spoke
to us in broken English interspersed with an occasional
Eskimo word. He seemed proud that he understood words

that we didn't, but Virginia was concerned about the education he was missing. "What effect is this going to have on his future?" she asked.

"I don't know," I answered. "I only remember at the university studying about an experiment in which children were deprived of schooling during their elementary years but caught up academically later in high school."

I saw Tommy's fourth-grade teacher soon after the start of school. She said, "Tommy is terribly behind, but I've never seen a child try so hard." At the end of school that year, she said, "Tommy made more improvement this year than any student I have ever taught."

Each of his sixth- and seventh-grade teachers said, "Tommy really likes school and he learns fast." In high school and college he usually made the honor roll and never--as far as I could tell--experienced school burnout.

Revisit

In 1989, Virginia's brother Harry said to me, "I would like to go with you to Wales, Alaska and meet some of the Eskimo people you've been telling me about for the last thirty years. Would you be my guide? We'll go to Nome for a few days and catch a day when the weather is good, then go on out to Wales." Harry was also a retired teacher, who had miraculously escaped death in WWII when over 900 of his navy shipmates were killed on the aircraft carrier *U.S.S. Franklin* by Japanese suicide bombers.

I accepted his request with enthusiasm. Later that month, we parked our car at the Atlanta airport, where we departed for Denver on the first leg of our flight.

While we were waiting in the airport lounge at Denver for our flight to Anchorage to be called, an announcement came over the public address system.

Harry said, "Did you hear that?"

"Hear what?" I asked.

"That announcement," he answered. "The announcer said some *USA Today* people are on this flight and want to sit with anyone who has lived in Alaska. You should get with them."

Harry knew I never tired of talking about my Alaska experiences, and I suspected he preferred I would sit with someone else. I walked to a group of about eight young people standing in the middle of the lobby with handbags and briefcases and asked a sandy-haired young man wearing glasses, "Are you *USA Today*?"

"Yes," he said, looking me straight in the eye.

I said, "I taught school in Eskimo villages back in the '50s and '60s."

A black-haired young man standing nearby had apparently overheard our conversation. He interrupted and said, "He can sit with me." Then turning to me, he smiled and said, "We are doing some features on Alaska. Would you talk to me on the way up?"

I agreed and, frankly, talked and talked as the young man asked questions, took notes and smiled the entire flight, which seemed the shortest I had ever taken. We spent the night in Anchorage and left for Nome the next morning.

My return visit to the two-story Polaris Hotel in Nome was thirty-two years almost to the day since Virginia, Tommy, Paula and I spent the night there on our way home from Wales for summer vacation in North Carolina. As Harry and I checked into the Polaris, I noticed the hotel was not as clean and neatly kept as when I last saw it and when it was the only hotel in Nome. I wished we had made reservations in the Nugget Inn, a newer hotel across the street next to the seawall. It was now the hotel used by tourists and most non-native visitors.

When we set our bags on the beds in our upstairs room, I said to Harry, "Let's go for a walk. I have a list of names of former Wales people who are now living in Nome, whom Toby said I should look up."

Wearing baseball caps and light jackets, we left the hotel and walked east on the seaward side of Front Street, which now was paved. I looked for a telephone booth or someone who might know of the whereabouts of former Wales people now living in Nome. We walked past the Nugget Inn, where a bus was loading with tourists from Taiwan on their way to pan some gold on the beach and to see an Eskimo dance and blanket toss. We passed a bar with loud country music and Eskimos sitting on stools and at tables. We walked past the large combination hardware, clothing and grocery store formerly known as Northern Commercial Company, but which now was larger and had a new name. Five or six vehicles were parked out front with their motors idling, which I assumed was from habit after the long cold winter, during which if one shuts the motor off for any length of time, one may not get it restarted.

After walking past two more bars and several craft stores, Harry tapped me on the shoulder and pointed up the street behind us. I turned and saw he was referring to an Eskimo woman with her parka askew on her shoulder, staggering in our direction in the middle of the street about forty yards from where we stood. Suddenly she fell on her side. Harry asked, "Can we help her?"

"I dunno. I think she's drunk," I responded as she struggled to stand up, while a pickup truck drove around her going east. She got back on her feet, then wobbled to the other side of the street and went out of sight between some small shacks.

After walking a short distance further down the street, we approached two elderly Eskimo women sitting on the seawall with their parka hoods lowered to their shoulders and who appeared to be quite alert. I said, "I think I'll ask these women if they might know some Wales people and where they live." I walked over to where they were sitting and said "Hi!"

They each smiled and said "Hi!"

I noticed one of them had a front tooth either missing or broken. I took out my list of names of Wales people and said, "I would like to locate some Wales people you might know."

The one with the missing front tooth smiled and said, "Maybe I can help."

I asked her about Dorothy Tevuk, Emily Tokienna, Nora Ahwinona, Alfred Mazonna, Willie Angnaboogok and Harriet Tevuk. I was surprised that she knew the address of each one, except for Alfred, who she said was now dead, but that his family lived in the last house on the east end of the street next to the beach. She pointed in that direction, then volunteered, "I can also tell you their telephone numbers and you can call them."

"OK," I said, and wrote the numbers as she gave them to me. Then came the surprise shocker of my life: She smiled and said, "*You* were my teacher!"

Completely dumbfounded and taken aback, I said, "Now, you will just have to tell me *who* you are."

"I am Ella Weyapuk," she said.

Immediately, I recalled and recognized the bright fifth-grader with the beautiful smile. I also recognized that time had taken a toll but that she had lost none of her friendly Eskimo pleasantness, intellect and charm.

Our sleep in the Polaris that night was disrupted by

bright sunlight coming through our room window, by loud partying downstairs in the lounge, and by someone outside at the back of the hotel between the hours of two and four intermittently calling in monotone for "Sam." It was "Sam," and few minutes later, "Sam" again. When morning came, I noticed the sky was clear and a northerly breeze was off-shore as we walked across the street to the Nugget Inn for breakfast. The proprietor there was sympathetic to our plight at the Polaris and invited us to move to a room in his inn for the remainder of our stay in Nome. He said the room would be ready by early afternoon.

After breakfast, I called the airport to see if a flight might be going to Wales "today." I was told that the weather was good and a bush plane would be leaving for the village around nine-thirty. We arrived at the airport at nine and were met in the waiting room by an attendant, who asked me, "Are you Corbin?"

"Yes," I answered.

"Walter Weyapuk wants to talk to you."

"Walter Weyapuk? He was a former student of mine at Wales." I said.

"Yes, he said you were his teacher. He's the postmaster in Wales now and he gives us the weather. He's on the phone in there." He pointed to a room off the lobby.

I stepped through the door and picked up the phone. "Hi," I said. "Is this Walter?"

"How are you, Mr. Corbin?"

"Fine. It's good to hear you, Walter."

"You too. Toby said you were coming to Wales today. He said he would meet you when the plane lands."

Our flight to Wales was uneventful, except when we approached the fog-shrouded cape. Fog rolled fast around Cape Mountain and indicated a strong wind on the south side, so the pilot chose to fly above the fog and cross the tip of the peninsula to approach the village from the north. He circled over the water, then dropped through a hole in the fog as the village came into view underneath a 200-foot overcast. I first noticed the large new school and monstrous laundromat. Otherwise the village was a familiar sight.

The wind sloshed water onto the bank of a nearby lake as we landed one mile north of the village on a widened and lengthened landing strip at the same location as the iron matting landing strip had been thirty-two years before. The plane turned at the north end of the runway, then taxied to the south end, where an older van was waiting.

When the plane stopped its engines, a three-wheeler approached with an elderly man and woman wearing pull-over parkas with full wolf ruffs waving in the wind. The woman sat behind the man with her arms around his waist. When they came closer, I recognized them and said to Harry, "Hey, there's Toby and Martha!"

I stepped off the plane and embraced them both. Toby smiled and said, "You look same. You haven't changed."

"You too, Toby. You look the same as before."

"Maybe, but getting old is not good for my health." He laughed.

I said, "It is sure good to see you again."

He said, "The plane can only be here one hour. While plane waits, you need to go see village. You ride in the van. I will follow on my three-wheeler."

In the village, Toby gave us a quick tour. I noticed TV satellite dishes beside every house. He pointed proudly to the electric generator house, the village laundromat and the large new school building. He laughed as he said, "Beside the laundromat is a million-gallon water tank. It is filled each summer with water from the creek on the mountain. Janitors no more carry water."

"Did you say janitors? More than one janitor?"

"Yes, we have more than one now." He laughed.

"Where do the village people get their water now?" I asked.

"Well, we get our water from the washeteria in the summer. But in winter we mostly get our water same as before, from snow or ice. And people still use honey buckets." He laughed. "Also, the school has five teachers and four teacher's aides. It now goes all the way through high school. But the village is not much bigger than when you were here."

Except for the large new structures, I noticed little change in village housing in the past thirty-two years. I turned, facing south, and saw the old school building, now eighty-six years old and in need of paint. I asked, "Is the old building still in use?"

"Yes, but now it's only used for storage."

Then I noticed snowmobiles parked outside the houses and said, "I don't see any dogs, Toby. Where are the dogs?"

"No more dogs in the village. The village has not one dog." Then he said, "While you are here you should go see Katie Tokienna and Jonah. You remember Jonah. They want to see you. Katie is now the oldest person in the village, and feels important."

"Where do they live?"

"Right there," he said, pointing. "They live there long time, same as before."

I then recognized the house was the same house where the Tokiennas lived thirty-two years before. Inside, I found Katie, the eighty-six-year-old daughter of a Siberian father and Alaskan mother, now proud that her seniority empowered her to be the village advisor on all activities, both social and economic. Her sixty-year-old son, Jonah, spoke bitterly of the adverse effects of white man's oil money on the traditional Eskimo way of life, and of alcoholism in Nome in particular. Then hc said, "My sister, Florence; she wants to see you."

"Florence? Where is she?" I asked, recalling the fat-cheeked, conscientious third-grader who made 100s on every spelling test she took during my two years at Wales.

"She's in the back room," he said as he pointed to a blanket draped over a doorway. "She's dying of cancer. She's married to Walter Weyapuk and has two boys, but Walter is the postmaster and can't take care of her, so she's staying here with us now."

I walked to the doorway and pushed the blanket aside, then stepped into a dark room with the only light coming through a thick curtain over a two-foot square window. The light from the window shone dimly on her wan face as she lay underneath a thick layer of blankets. Her left arm, in the sleeve of a red and black crocheted woolen sweater, was lying outside the covers by her side. Her facial features gave no resemblance of the Florence I remembered, but I detected a faint smile, then said, "Hi!"

She responded weakly, "Hi!"

"It's good to see you, Florence."

"It's good to see you, too." Her voice was weak.

I groped for words to respond, then said, "I understand you and Walter have two boys. I know you are proud of them."

She smiled faintly as she said, "Thanks for coming."

I squeezed her hand lightly and noticed a slight reciprocation, then turned and left the room, wanting to cry. Outside, Harry was waiting with Toby. They were joined by three old men sitting on a bench in front of the house next door. They were wearing traditional skin parkas with white cloth covers. They were each smiling broadly, but I did not recognize them until Toby said, "These are Clarence Ongtowasruk, Frank Oxereok and Glen Sereadlook. You remember them."

I said, "Hi!"

They each nodded and smiled and said "*Ee-ee.*" Frank said something else in Eskimo and laughed. I smiled back at them, thinking he may have been referring to the time he and I went for a "ride" on the ice floe.

Toby said that all the other people I would know were now either dead, gone to summer camp or moved away from the village.

On arriving back at Nome, I sat in the back seat of the taxi as it carried us back to the hotel. Harry sat next to the driver who asked, "Are you men visiting here in Nome?"

Harry said, "Yes, we came in yesterday."

The driver said, "There's a teacher visiting here now that taught school thirty-two years ago out on the Bering Strait."

"Is that right?" Harry said, then looked back at me with a smile and winked and said, "This town is surely starved for news if word is spread here that fast."

The driver looked briefly at Harry but said nothing.

For the next three days we rented an old pickup truck and drove the three new unpaved roads leading out of Nome that had been carved wide and straight in recent years with free-flowing oil money.

On our first day out of town we drove north toward Pilgrim Hot Springs and encountered no traffic. After five miles, we stopped to walk on the tundra and found it covered with a mattress-like carpet of flowering plants, but found ourselves swatting mosquitoes so we hurriedly got back inside the truck and went back to town.

The next day, we returned with insect repellent, which we dabbed on our faces and necks. This helped. Again we stopped to walk and saw the *empertrum nigrum*, or crow-berry vine, with its tiny white blossoms intertwined among the moss, which in six weeks would produce black berries one-half centimeter in diameter – the same kind of berries picked by Martha Anungazuk to make Eskimo ice cream. We saw patches of *rubus chamaemorus*, or salmon berry, with its inch-wide purple flowers pointing skyward on stiff three-inch stems waving gently in the breeze, which by fall will become orange, strawberry-shaped berries and picked by Inuit women, then mixed with seal oil and packed inside sealskin pokes.

Later, we stopped at Grand Central River and stood on the bridge, where we watched salmon swim underneath on their way to spawn in the tributaries upstream. The next day, we drove west on the road toward Teller and saw a herd of reindeer grazing on the side of a hill a quarter of a mile away. Another day we stopped twenty miles southeast of Nome at the first sign of civilization we encountered outside of town. It was a roadhouse with a sign on the door which read, "Come in and help yourself." We stepped inside a room with two small tables and a bar with four stools. Soon the owner came through a door behind the bar and said, "We had a big crowd here last night." After we left, Harry said, "I wonder where that 'big crowd' was served, and where it came from?"

In Nome, I visited each of the Wales people on my list. Dorothy Tevuk was now a secretary at Nome Hospital and introduced me to her grown daughter and six-year-old granddaughter. Emily Tokienna was now married to a white man and living in a neat, comfortable house two streets back from the beach. Nora Ahwinona, now in her late eighties, was living alone and was as jovial and fun-loving as ever. Harry enjoyed hearing her laugh as she related the stories about thumbtacks in my mukluks and how she taught Tommy to eat blubber.

The day before we left Nome, we found Harriet Tevuk and Willie Angnaboogok and his wife at the mouth of Nome River, one mile southeast of town. They and two other families had gill nets set along the beach to catch and dry chum salmon, which were now beginning to run. Harriet was now a little heavier, strong, and full-bodied, but just as energetic and conscientious as the sixteen-year-old tutor I remembered in Wales thirty-two years before.

Willie was also lively and hadn't lost much of his drive since the time in Wales when I took his picture with the polar bear hide after a day-long hunt, before his wife carried the pot of meat to the school for the polar bear feast. He said, "You should take some fresh salmon back to North Carolina with you when you go."

"How is that possible?" I asked. "We are leaving tomorrow."

"You can get a cooler at the store and pack it with ice and the fish will be just fine. I'm going out now to check my net. You can go with me if you like. We'll get some salmon and Harriet can filet them for you."

I quickly agreed to join him as I felt my adrenaline starting to flow.

Harry said, "While you're gone to check the net, I'll drive back to town to get a cooler."

I stepped to the front of Willie's twelve-foot wooden boat, and he shoved it off the sandy beach of crystal clear Nome River. He then drove fifty yards past the mouth to the red and white floats of his four-hundred-foot gill net bobbing in the swells. He shut off the motor, then began lifting the net on the left side and pulling the boat along at the same time. He pulled up no fish till the halfway point, where he extracted one and slammed its head against the gunwale then dropped it inside the boat. Farther out, more fish were caught. I helped extricate them from the mesh toward the end of the net and the floor was covered with wiggling and flopping fish. Willie laughed as one jumped overboard.

When we returned to Nome River, Willie drove the boat ashore, where Harry was waiting with a three-foot Styrofoam cooler and three bags of ice. Harriet was standing there also with an ulu in her hand. "How many fish do you want to take?" she asked.

Willie looked at the cooler, then said, "They can take maybe eighteen."

I thought the prospect of getting home with fresh tasty

Alaska salmon would be a pleasant surprise for Virginia. Harry and I watched as Harriet skillfully and quickly plied her ulu to the three-pound fish, which she converted to beautiful pink slices and pushed them aside on her platform. She raked the heads and entrails off the side into a five-gallon bucket.

"What do you do with those guts and heads?" I asked.

"We take them in boat to that sandbar over there on the other side, where the sea gulls eat them," she said as she pointed with her ulu toward the sandbar forty-five yards directly across the river, where swarms of sea gulls had already gathered.

While Harriet worked, our attention was diverted to her five-year-old granddaughter and another playmate about the same age, who were wearing summer parkas and rubber boots, and playing with a half-grown flounder swimming near the edge.

"The fish are ready," Harriet said as she began packing the pink slices with ice into the cooler. She managed to pack only twelve of the salmon.

"That's enough anyway," Harry said.

We attached the lid with duct tape, then took the cooler to the store's freezer locker to leave it overnight.

The next morning we picked up the cooler and flew to Anchorage, where we boarded a red-eye flight by United to Chicago, then changed to Delta for Atlanta.

After retrieving the cooler in Atlanta and placing it in the trunk of the car in 100-degree heat, we headed north on I-85. When we were about thirty miles up the road, Harry said, "Let's stop and check the fish."

I stopped the car, opened the trunk, cut loose the duct tape and lifted the lid. We were greeted with an unpleasant smell and saw the fish were now blanched in warm water.

"Can we save them?" I asked.

"I don't think so. They're ruined," Harry said, then dumped them in the foot-high grass as passing motorists stared. He threw the cooler back into the trunk.

Utterly dejected and disappointed, we got back in the car and I raced at ten miles above the speed limit to regain my position in the dense traffic, then moved over to the second lane from the left. As I observed the zip, zip, blur of the traffic in the southbound lanes, something flew over the hood of my car from the lane on my left. "What was that?" I asked.

"I dunno," said Harry. "It looked like a hubcap."

I glanced in my rearview mirror and saw that the big truck that had been racing near my right flank was now slowed in the distance, as was all the other traffic following behind us. I said, "Whatever it was must've hit something. The traffic behind us is slowed. Boy, are we back in the soup now." I looked over at Harry. He winced.

We continued on as my mind revisited the time when Virginia and I first arrived at the village of Wales thirty-two years ago. It was a simpler time, a different way of life. I thought of Toby Anungazuk and his description of the Outside, Alfred Mazonna and the "no wind" at Anchorage, Nora Ahwinona and the mukluks she made for me, the walrus hunting with "Old Man" Ongtowasruk, Dwight Tevuk and Roland Angnaboogok, the sled dog trips, Eskimo ice cream, the northern lights, little Victor's eyes and lessons the Eskimos taught me.

The author reading from his manuscript to some of the descendents of his former students. Six out of ten students in this class have the last name Ongtowasruk.

272

*Above, Cape Prince of Wales School, right, in 1998. The church is on the left.
Below, this million-gallon water tank is filled each summer from the stream on
the mountain. Bottom, Christine Anungazuk and baby, Wales, 1989.*

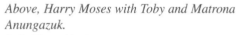

Above, Harry Moses with Toby and Matrona Anungazuk.
Left, Nora Ahwinona.
Below, a former student and former patient in 1998.

Order Form

To order additional copies of *A World Apart; My Life Among the Eskimos of Alaska*, send $19.95 for each book, plus $4 shipping and handling for the first book and $1 for each additional book. Orders should be mailed, faxed or e-mailed to:

Wizard Works
P.O. Box 1125
Homer, AK 99603
(907) 235-8757
wizard@xyz.net

Please send _____ book(s) @ $19.95. $_____
                                    Postage & handling $_____
                                    Total $_____

[   ] Check enclosed
[   ] Credit card (MasterCard, VISA, or Discover)

____ ____ ____ ____

expires:

Ship to:

_____

_____

_____

_____

Signature

For more books about Alaska, send for the *Alaska Small Press Catalog*, available from Wizard Works for $2.00.